WHEN ELEPHANTS WEEP

The Emotional Lives of Animals

. . . man and the higher animals, especially the primates, have some few
instincts in common. All have the same senses, intuitions, and sensations,
similar passions, affections, and emotions, even the more complex ones
such as jealousy, suspicion, emulation, gratitude, and magnanimity; they
practise deceit and are revengeful; they are sometimes susceptible to
ridicule, and even have a sense of humour; they feel wonder and curiosity;
they possess the same faculties of imitation, attention, deliberation, choice,
memory, imagination, the association of ideas, and reason though in very
different degrees.

Charles Darwin, *The Descent of Man and Selection
in Relation to Sex*, 1871

WHEN ELEPHANTS WEEP

The Emotional Lives of Animals

Jeffrey Moussaieff Masson
and Susan McCarthy

WITH DRAWINGS BY BARBARA DOWNS

JONATHAN CAPE
LONDON

First published 1994

1 3 5 7 9 10 8 6 4 2

© Jeffrey Moussaieff Masson and Susan McCarthy 1994

Jeffrey Moussaieff Masson and Susan McCarthy have asserted their right
under the Copyright, Designs and Patents Act 1988
to be identified as the authors of this work

Final 'stanza of 'Passer Mortuus Est' by Edna St. Vincent
Millay. From COLLECTED POEMS, HarperCollins. Copyright 1921,
1948 by Edna St. Vincent Millay. Reprinted by permission
of Elizabeth Barnett, literary executor.

First published in the United Kingdom in 1994 by Jonathan Cape
Random House, 20 Vauxhall Bridge Road, London SW1V 2SA

Random House Australia (Pty) Limited
20 Alfred Street, Milsons Point, Sydney,
New South Wales 2061, Australia

Random House New Zealand Limited
18 Poland Road, Glenfield,
Auckland 10, New Zealand

Random House South Africa (Pty) Limited
PO Box 337, Bergvlei, South Africa

Random House UK Limited Reg. No. 954009

A CIP catalogue record for this book
is available from the British Library

ISBN 0–224–03554–1

Printed in Great Britain by Clays Ltd, St Ives PLC

For the Fu
and Fiona

Other books by
Jeffrey Masson

FREUD: THE ASSAULT ON TRUTH
AGAINST THERAPY
FINAL ANALYSIS
MY FATHER'S GURU

CONTENTS

ACKNOWLEDGEMENTS

While researching this book we talked to many scientists, animal trainers, and others whose expertise was invaluable. In particular we acknowledge the help of George Archibald, Mattie Sue Athan, Kim Bartlett, John Beckman, Marc Bekoff, Tim Benneke, Joseph Berger, Nedim Buyukmihci, Suzanne Chevalier-Skolnikoff, Lisa De Nault, Ralph Dennard, Pat Derby, Ian Dunbar, Mary Lynn Fischer, Maria Fitzgerald, Lois Flynne, Roger Fouts, Nigel Franks, William Frey, Jane Goodall, Wendy Gordon, Nancy Hall, Ralph Helfer, Gerald Jacobs, William Jankowiak, Marti Kheel, Adriaan Kortlandt, Wolf Lepenies, Charles Lindholm, Sarah McCarthy, David Mech, Jim Mullen, Kenneth Norris, Cindy Ott-Bales, Joel Parrott, Irene Pepperberg, Leonard Plotnicov, Karen Reina of Bristol-Myers Squibb, Diana Reiss, Lynn Rogers, Vivian Siegel, Barbara Smuts, Richard Vane-Wright, Ron Whitfield and Gerald S. Wilkinson among others. Any errors we have made and any wild speculations are not to be laid at their doors.

More personal thanks are owed to our friends and family for their support and assistance, especially Daniel Gunther, Joseph Gunther, Kitty Rose McCarthy, Martha Coyote, John McCarthy, Mary Susan Kuhn, Andrew Gunther, Thomas Goldstein and Bernard Taper; and Daidie Donnelley, Fred Goode, Jane Matteson, Eileen Max, Simone Masson and Barbara Sonnenborn.

Catharine MacKinnon inspired our collaboration. Barbara Downs showed extraordinary dedication to the drawings. Elaine Markson was again the perfect agent. Tony Colwell, our tactful editor, believed in this book from the beginning. As for Kitty, only we know what she is owed.

'The Indian elephant is said sometimes to weep.'
Charles Darwin

Searching the Heart of the Other

A NIMALS CRY. At least, they vocalise pain or distress, and perhaps call for help. Most people believe, therefore, that animals can be unhappy and also that they have such feelings as happiness, anger and fear. But there is a tremendous gap between the common sense viewpoint and that of official science on this subject. The ordinary layperson readily believes that his dog, her cat, their parrot or horse, feels. They not only believe it but have constant evidence of it before their eyes. All of us have extraordinary stories of animals we know well. Yet, by dint of rigorous training and great efforts of the mind, most modern scientists – especially those who study the behaviour of animals – have succeeded in becoming almost blind to these matters.

Donald Griffin's book, *The Question of Animal Awareness*, first excited my interest in the emotional lives of animals.[1] Griffin's book, which was attacked in many quarters, discussed the possible intellectual lives of animals and asked whether science

11

was examining issues of their cognition and consciousness fairly. I was provoked to wonder about animals' emotional lives – not how intelligent they were, but how sensitive, how feeling. When I looked for information on this subject, I found virtually nothing. Surprisingly, there is almost no investigation of the emotional lives of animals in modern scientific literature. Why should this be so? One answer is that scientists, animal behaviourists, zoologists and ethologists have been fearful of being accused of anthropomorphism, a form of scientific blasphemy. I had stumbled on a topic even more forbidden to scientific discourse than that of animal intelligence. Not only are the emotions of animals not a respectable field of study, the words of emotion are not to be applied to them.

Why is it controversial to discuss the inner lives of animals, their emotional capacities, their feelings of joy, disappointment, nostalgia and sadness? As Jane Goodall has written recently of her work with chimpanzees, 'When, in the early 1960s, I brazenly used such words as "childhood", "adolescence", "motivation", "excitement" and "mood" I was much criticised. Even worse was my crime of suggesting that chimpanzees had "personalities". I was ascribing human characteristics to nonhuman animals and was thus guilty of that worst of ethological sins – anthropomorphism.'[2]

Among the first people I asked about the emotional lives of animals were researchers working with dolphins, since dolphins show such delight in performing, even in creating new performances of their own, that an elaborate emotional component seems obvious. Thinking that experts who work with and study animals might offer observations in person that they would be reluctant to put into a scientific article, I asked two renowned scholars of dolphin behaviour about their experience with the emotions their dolphins expressed. Both were unwilling to speculate or even to offer observations. One said, 'I don't know what emotion means'. The other referred the matter to his female graduate students, implying that the subject was somehow beneath his scientific (or male?) dignity.

What these scholars said was undermined by what they did. One hugged his prize dolphin in a clearly emotional moment, at least for the researcher. The other could hardly leave at night, so attached had he become to what he called his 'subjects'. The female graduate students had many stories to tell about mutual affection between researchers and dolphins, even some free-living dolphins. It is hard to believe that these scientists would express intense feelings to creatures they genuinely felt were emotionally insensate and could not return them or respond to them in any way.

Psychiatric lexicons contain the term 'alexithymia' for the condition of people who cannot describe or recognise emotions, who are able to define them 'only in terms of somatic sensations or of behavioral reaction rather than relating them to accompanying thoughts'. Such people do not seem to understand what feelings are.[3] It is curious that the study of animal behaviour should demand that its practitioners turn themselves into alexithymics.

In any event, how can anyone know that an animal feels nothing if the question has never been investigated? To conclude without study that it has no feelings or cannot feel is to proceed on an unscientific bias, a prejudice. This is not the only area in which scientists cling to an unscientific dogma. Consider how long psychoanalysts denied the reality of child sexual abuse.

Sometimes humans merely treat animals as badly as they do other humans. Native people do not share the historic contempt for animals and rarely have. Lame Deer, for example, said he was appalled by

> the terrible arrogance of the white man who determines 'I will let this animal live because it makes money'; saying 'This animal must go, it brings no income, the space it occupies can be used in a better way. The only good coyote is a dead coyote.' They are treating coyotes almost as badly as they used to treat Indians.[4]

At Sea World in San Diego, the public relations director told me bluntly that he disapproved of the notion of animal emotions and would not permit Sea World to be associated with my research because it 'smacked of anthropomorphism'. Imagine my surprise on attending the shows, in which the killer whale and the dolphins were trained to wave, shake hands and splash water at the spectators. They had been trained to behave like people, people who were amusing slaves, not dignified creatures deserving of respect. This was not anthropomorphism, it was anthropocentrism in the service of commercial exploitation.

Why do most people consider it obvious that animals they are close to have emotions, while most scientists consider it not only far from obvious but positively wrong, pernicious and unscientific? Part of the explanation is wariness of an area where objective measurement is so difficult, and part of it arises from zeal to belong to and be accepted in an exclusive and powerful club. The rest appears to be stubbornness, ignorance and a lingering need to affirm species dominance. The geoscientist Edward Bullard put it this way:

> There is always a strong inclination for a body of professionals to oppose an unorthodox view. Such a group has a considerable investment in orthodoxy; they have learned to interpret a large body of data in terms of the old view, and they have prepared lectures and perhaps written books with the old background. To think the whole subject through again when one is no longer young is not easy and involves admitting a partially misspent youth . . . Clearly it is more prudent to keep quiet, to be a moderate defender of orthodoxy, or to maintain that all is doubtful, sit on the fence, and wait in statesmanlike ambiguity for more data.[5]

Charles Darwin, in *The Expression of the Emotions in Man and Animals*,[6] had no hesitation in writing of animal emotions. He wrote of their indications in facial expression and body language. Earlier, Darwin had dared to imagine a dog's conscious life: 'But can we feel sure that an old dog with an excellent memory and some power of imagination, as shewn by his dreams, never reflects on his past pleasures in the chase? and this would be a form of self-consciousness.' Even more evocatively, he asked: 'Who can say what cows feel, when they surround and stare intently on a dying or dead companion?'[7] He was also unafraid to speculate about areas that seemed to require further investigation.

The Expression of the Emotions in Man and Animals may have been the high-water mark thus far in the careful study of animal emotions. The scientific indignation aroused shortly thereafter by George Romanes' *Animal Intelligence*, published in 1898, was followed by the ascent of behaviourism. Romanes' work was largely ignored because scientists criticised its reliance on anecdotes from acquaintances and readers. Not only was it anecdotal, it was soft, it was sentimental, it was anthropomorphic, it treated animals as if they were in important respects like people. This was wrong, this was dangerous, this was unscientific, it was said. In reaction to this, science fled as far as possible in the opposite direction.

Comparative psychology, to this day, discusses observable behaviour and physical states of animals, and evolutionary explanations for their existence, but shies away from the mental states that are inextricably involved in that behaviour.[8] To the extent such states are examined, the focus is on cognition and not on emotion. The more recent discipline of ethology, the science of animal behaviour, with its strong focus on distinctions between species, also seeks functional and causal, not emotive, explanations for behaviour. It is concerned with explanations that fall into the evolutionary model and not with emotional possibility. The explanations offered by ethology as causal, like those offered by comparative psychology, centre on its theory of 'ultimate causation' – the animal pairs because this increases reproductive success – as distinguished from 'proximate causation' – the animal pairs because it has fallen in love. Although the two explanations are not necessarily mutually exclusive – and one of the best-known figures of ethology, Konrad Lorenz, spoke confidently of animals falling in love, becoming demoralised or mourning – the field as a whole continued to treat such things as unworthy of scientific attention.[9]

With the advent of laboratory studies of animals, especially in the 1960s, the distance maintained from the world of animal feeling became even greater. This distance supported scientists conducting painful experiments on animals in the belief that animals feel no pain or suffering, or at least on the assumption that the pain they feel is removed enough from the pain it is believed fellow humans feel that one need not take it into account in devising experiments. The professional and financial interest in continuing animal experimentation helps to explain at least some resistance to the notion that animals have a complex emotional life and are capable of experiencing the higher emotions, such as love, compassion, altruism, disappointment and nostalgia. To acknowledge such a possibility implies certain moral obligations. If chimpanzees can experience loneliness and mental anguish, it becomes more wrong to use them for experiments in which they are isolated and anticipate daily pain. At the very least, this poses a matter for serious debate – a debate that has scarcely begun.

An interest in elevating human needs and capacities over those of animals, often reproducing in our views of animals the worst of human failings, has supported the lack of attention to animal emotions and can be traced in diverse settings. In October 1993, one of the first exhibits encountered in the hall of mammals in the National Museum of Natural History at the Smithsonian Institution in Washington DC was entitled 'Some Beneficial Mammals'. Gophers and blue-tailed bats were included. Beneficial to whom, I wondered. The mountain beaver and the woodchuck were in a later section labelled 'Destructive Mammals'. A few exhibits further on there was a small notice headed, 'What's Wrong?' It said, 'The world and our perception of it have changed dramatically since 1960 when these mammal exhibits were installed. Following are misconceptions we intend to eliminate in our new exhibits: Humans are the standard. Humans are treated as more important than other mammals, which are judged as good or bad depending on their interaction with us. Males are the standard. Female animals are portrayed in ways that make them appear deviant or substandard as compared to male animals.' This signals a shift in understanding that is moving us away from the prejudices that have animated much human understanding of the nature and value of animal life (as well as human life). Increasingly, people are coming to see that gophers and bats as well as beavers and woodchucks live meaningful lives quite apart from their impact or lack of impact on human life. They have lives valuable in themselves, without need of valuation or interpretation by us. It is reasonable to ask whether emotion plays a role in these lives.

Some of the most innovative work being done with animals today is directed at language use, self-awareness and other cognitive abilities, so that the wilful blindness of science to the world of animal emotion seems to be on the verge of crumbling. While Griffin did not explore emotion, he points to it as an area that needs investigation. What data there is on animal emotion comes not from laboratory work but from field studies. Some of the most esteemed animal researchers of our day, from Jane Goodall to Frans de Waal, from time to time defy orthodoxy from their position of eminence and insist on using words like 'love' and 'suffering' to describe animals. Yet these aspects of their work are virtually ignored, nor is it safe for less well-established scientists to use such terms.

Times are changing though. Recently Sue Savage-Rumbaugh, a scientist at the Yerkes Primate Center in Atlanta, Georgia, wrote in the preface to a recent book, *Ape Language*:

It is possible, if one looks beyond the slightly differently shaped face, to read the emotions of apes as easily and as accurately as one reads the emotions and feelings of other human beings. There are few feelings that apes do not share with us, except perhaps self-hatred. They certainly experience and express exuberance, joy, guilt, remorse, disdain, disbelief, awe, sadness, wonder, tenderness, loyalty, anger, distrust and love. Someday, perhaps, we will be able to demonstrate the existence of such emotions at a neurological level. Until then, only those who live and interact with apes as closely as they do with members of their own species will be able to understand the immense depth of the behavioral similarities between ape and man.[10]

The interest is certainly budding, but as yet no prominent scientist has undertaken a sustained treatment of animal emotions. It is to be hoped, for the sake of animals as well as humans, that scientists will be persuaded to look more seriously at the feelings of the animals who share the world with us.

Jeffrey Moussaieff Masson
Berlin, March 1994

CHAPTER ONE

In Defence of Emotions

S OMEWHERE in India, a blind river dolphin seeks her companion. Under the dark waters of the Ganges she will sleep
next to him. She has never needed to see. These dolphins find
everything they want and need by listening to echoes. Above
them in the sky, two cranes from the East are flying back from
China to their western breeding territory in Siberia. The cranes are
a mile up in the sky, looking down with their golden eyes. What
is in their hearts, or in the hearts of the dolphins? Wholly apart
from us, their lives of turmoil and satisfaction are not beyond our
imagination. When the dolphin rises out of the muddy waters, or
the cranes stretch their necks in flight, we are filled with a sudden
sense of familiarity, the recognition that we share an emotional
heritage they feel and we feel, no matter how difficult it is to
know just what their feelings are.

After a promising start with Darwin, very few scientists have
acknowledged, researched, or even speculated about animal emo-

19

tions. So persistent are the forces that militate against admitting the possibility of emotions in the lives of animals that the topic seems disreputable, not a respectable field of study, almost taboo. The scholarly literature on animals contains many observations, accounts, anecdotes and stories that suggest interpretation in terms of the emotions the animals may be experiencing or expressing, or call for further research into this possibility. Little to none is forthcoming.

One illustration of animals experiencing strong emotions occurs in *Elephant Bill*, an early British account of working elephants in Burma.[1] A mother elephant with her three-month-old calf was reported trapped in a fast-rising torrent in the Upper Taungdwin River in heavy flood. The calf was screaming with terror. The mother encircled it with her trunk, pulling it upstream. But the heavy waters tore the baby away and swept it downstream. The mother swam after it and was able to catch it fifty yards downstream. She picked it up in her trunk, reared up until she was standing on her hind legs, and placed it on a narrow shelf of rock above the flood level. She fell back into the raging torrent and was washed away. The calf stood shivering and terrified, on a ledge just wide enough to hold its feet. But help was on its way. Her mother had crossed the river, got up the bank, and was making her way back with tremendous speed calling the whole time. When she saw her calf she stopped roaring and began rumbling, a sound not unlike the purr of a giant cat.

Anger, love, terror, the pleasure of relief – accounts like these, systematically developed, could provide evidence for a world of deep emotional experience on the part of animals, but there appears little place for them in scientific literature. One-time incidents are dismissed as 'anecdotes', yet there is no reason to ignore rare events. In some cases it is feasible to try to collect other instances or even to repeat rare events, yet this is seldom done, so scathing do scientists find the charge of 'using anecdotal evidence'. Discussing the ability of symbol-using chimpanzees to improvise unusual and impressive combinations of symbols, Sue Savage-Rumbaugh calls such spontaneous occurrences 'arguably the most important sort of data we have', but notes, 'we have avoided describing these in our published reports'.[2]

Jane Goodall finds the scientific reluctance to accept anecdotal evidence a serious problem, one that colours all of science. 'I've always collected anecdotes, because I think they're terribly important. Most scientists scorn anecdotal evidence . . .'

What is an anecdote? It is a careful description of an unusual event. Goodall tells of a research assistant charged with logging the response of male rhesus monkeys in a laboratory to females, some of whom were being treated with hormones or had had their ovaries removed. 'She told me . . . the most fascinating thing to her was the one old female who she observed in all these different states, ending up with having her ovaries out, and whatever state she was in, she was the most popular. But she was *one* monkey and that was ignored. There must be literally millions of observations like that that have never crept into the literature.'[3]

Observations of this kind provide a rich and suggestive ground for analysis and further investigation, yet there is almost none. While it is possible and customary to describe such events without using any words that connote emotion, such a lean description is not necessarily more accurate.

This book defines emotions as subjective experiences, as what people refer to when they say 'I feel sad', or 'I am happy', or 'I am disappointed', or 'I miss my children'. An emotion is not distinguished from a feeling, a passion, a sentiment, or what scientists call 'affect'. Similarly, a mood simply refers to a feeling that lasts for some protracted time. These words refer to inner states, to something that is felt.

People who work closely with animals, such as animal trainers, take it as a matter of fact that animals have emotions. Any account by those who work with elephants, for example, makes it clear that one ignores an elephant's 'mood' at one's peril. The British philosopher Mary Midgley puts it well:

> Obviously the mahouts may have many beliefs about the elephants which are false because they are 'anthropomorphic' – that is, they misinterpret some outlying aspects of elephant behaviour by relying on a human pattern which is inappropriate. But if they were doing this about the basic everyday feelings – about whether their elephant is pleased, annoyed, frightened, excited, tired, sore, suspicious or angry – they would not only be out of business, they would often simply be dead.[4]

Training will meet with little success if the trainer has no insight

21

into the animals' feelings. Some trainers say they work with certain animals better than others because they understand the feelings of that species or individual better. Circus trainer Gunther Gebel-Williams noted individual differences in the emotions of the tigers with whom he worked: 'Not every tiger . . . can be trained to jump through a ring of fire. When I incorporated that trick into the tiger act I had to find several from among the twenty I was working with at the time who were not afraid of fire. That was no easy task, because most tigers will not go near flames.[5]

The place of empathy such as this in the direct observation of animals is controversial. But wondering what one would feel in the place of an animal can be fruitful if the questions are asked with a full understanding of the peculiarities of the species. In addition, almost all scientists working with animals in the wild make inferences based on empathy, such as, 'If I had just lost my closest companion, I too would not feel like eating for some time'. Thinking about feelings can be a valuable way of thinking about behaviour.

Evidence of emotion in captive animals and pets is often discounted as irrelevant. The argument goes that these animals are in unnatural situations, or that what domesticated animals do is irrelevant to what animals are really like. While it is true that genuinely domesticated animals are different from wild animals, domestic and tame do not mean the same thing. Domestic animals are animals that have been bred to live with humans – they have been changed genetically. Dogs, cats and cows are domestic animals. Elephants are not, since through the generations that people have trained elephants, they have almost invariably caught and tamed wild elephants, rather than *bred* elephants. They have not changed the nature of elephants. This means that observations on tame or captive elephants are more relevant to free-living elephants than would otherwise be the case.

That captive and domestic animals are in an unnatural situation is not a valid objection to taking observations of them seriously, for humans are in just as unnatural a situation. We did not evolve in the world in which we now live, with its deferred rewards and strange demands (sitting in classrooms or punching time clocks). All the same, we do not dismiss our emotions as not existing or authentic to us as human beings because they don't take place in small groups of hunter-gatherers on an African savannah where human life is thought to have begun. We are ourselves domesticated animals. In other words, we can be at a distance from our origins and still claim that our emotions are real and characteristic of our species. The same is true of animals.

To give another example, it is not natural for humans to be in prison. Yet if we are put in prison and feel emotions that we don't usually feel, no one doubts that they are real emotions. An animal in a zoo, or kept as a pet, may feel emotions that it would not otherwise have felt, but these are still real emotions. Neither do we always understand what a natural situation is like. Many laboratory scientists underestimate the amount of contact wild animals have with other kinds of animals. Yet without comparative evidence, accounts of interactions between different species of captive animals are dismissed as being unlike anything that happens in the wild. This is then used to claim that the emotions observed in zoos or by pet-keepers are irrelevant to 'genuine' (and, by implication, unknowable) emotions experienced only by animals living in the wild. George Schaller's comment that 'A loving dog-owner can tell you more about animal awareness than some laboratory behaviorists'[6] is closer to the truth. It is true that there are fewer opportunities to observe at close range the emotions, and even the social relations, in a free-living wolf-pack, or in a pod of wild orcas, but only when this is finally achieved can a comparative study be made between the wild and the tame species. It is fascinating to consider whether wolves and dogs have comparable emotions, or whether the dog's emotions have been influenced by proximity to humans. Captive wolves, who often bond with a particular human, certainly seem similar to dogs in the range and depth of their emotional attachments.

To find out if her observations of captive dwarf mongooses told her anything accurate about mongooses in a natural state, Anne Rasa, author of *Mongoose Watch*, went to Kenya to study them in the bush for several years. She discovered that the behaviour of captive mongoose groups in large enclosures closely followed that of wild ones with two exceptions. The wild mongooses had to spend much more time gathering food, and hence less time playing and socialising. Their lives were also strongly coloured by the actions of other species. Eagles and snakes preyed on them. They spent a significant time mobbing snakes to drive them away. They quarrelled with the larger blacktip mongooses. They usually ignored lizards and ground squirrels, but occasionally tried to play with them. Often they were awakened in the morning by yellow-billed hornbills, who were eager for the mongooses to begin foraging so that the hornbills could follow and snatch up insects they disturbed. In other words, their emotional range was to some extent determined by the opportunities that presented themselves. Curiosity and play, however, were common to both groups.[7]

The point is not that captivity never changes emotions and behaviour, only that both captive and wild animals have feelings, and that the emotions of captive animals are as real as those of wild animals. Female baboons kept together in a cage form a rigid hierarchy unlike anything seen in the species in the wild.[8] In another laboratory, baboons were provided with a slide-viewing apparatus. The male baboons monopolised the device, pressing buttons until they learned to operate it, while the (much smaller) females looked on from a distance. The males were removed when the testing was done, whereupon the females went over and began to view slides without needing any learning period.[9] The situation in which males were able to monopolise an attractive – although unnatural – resource was probably unlike anything occurring in the wild.

Emotions seldom come pure, in isolation from other emotions. In people, anger and fear, fear and love, love and shame, shame and sorrow often converge. If animals have these emotions, they may experience the same mix of emotions. Does a dolphin mother who carries her dead baby around with her for several days feel love and sorrow? Hope Ryden describes a half-grown elk calf guarding the body of another calf killed by coyotes after the elk herd had moved on. For at least two days the calf straddled the body, aggressively chased coyotes away, and from time to time sniffed and nuzzled the face of the dead calf. Eventually (after coyotes had succeeded in partly eating the body) the calf moved on.[10] The calf may have felt grief; it may have felt lonely for the rest of the herd; it may have felt anger at the coyotes. Perhaps it feared the coyotes. Perhaps it felt love for the dead calf. That feelings may be complex does not mean they are not there.

Since the behaviour of animal species differ, their feeling life may differ as well. This is often overlooked when arguing from animal examples. 'Geese mate for life', people declare. 'Robins

24

kick their young out of the nest when they're old enough to be on their own. The dog doesn't stay and help the bitch raise the puppies – that's just the way it is.' Geese mate for life, but grouse do not. The male grouse mates with as many females as he can and leaves them to raise the young on their own. The female Tasmanian native hen often mates with two males and the trio raises the young together.[11] The female phalarope lays eggs in several nests and leaves the males to sit on the eggs. Condors stay with their parents for years. Male and female wolves raise their puppies together. These differences often produce a kind of sociobiology parlour game in which people try to prove points about human behaviour by pointing to an animal species which exhibits the behaviour they want to define as 'natural' for humans. But animal species differ in some ways from each other emotionally as well as, presumably, from human animals. Evidence that elephants feel compassion or sorrow does not mean that hippos feel compassion or that penguins feel sorrow. Perhaps they do, perhaps not.

Animals also differ from one another as individuals. Among elephants, one may be timid and another bold. One may be prone to attacks of rage, another peaceable. One Victorian commented on working elephants at Rangoon, 'There are willing workers and there are skulkers; there are gentle tempers and there are others as dour as a door-nail. Some of them will drag a log two tons in weight without a groan; while others, who are equally powerful but less willing, will make a dreadful fuss over a stick that is, comparatively speaking, nothing.'[12] Of a species he hunted, Theodore Roosevelt wrote: 'Bears differ individually in courage and ferocity precisely as men do . . . One grizzly can scarcely be bullied into resistance; the next may fight to the end, against any odds, without flinching, or even attack unprovoked . . . Even old hunters – who indeed, as a class, are very narrow-minded and opinionated – often generalize just as rashly as beginners.'[13]

Most ordinary people who have direct contact with animals freely concede their belief in the reality of animal emotions. They do so because of the evidence of their senses. A person who hears birds attacking a cat near their nest usually experiences them as angry. We see a squirrel flee from us and think that it is afraid. We see a cat licking its kittens and we feel it loves them. We see a bird throbbing with song and suppose it to be happy. Even those with

25

only indirect experience of animals often recognise what they see to be an emotional state, a feeling, which they correlate to a similar human feeling. And still there is no sustained effort to inquire into animal emotions, to investigate them systematically or in depth.

In spite of the lack of scholarly work on animal emotions, there is today a greater interest in the realities of the lives of animals than ever before. There is increasing awareness of the complexity of animal actions, cognitive, perceptual and behavioural, individual and social, and a correspondingly greater recognition of the humility required to face questions of the range of animal capacities. Humans are no longer as prepared as once they were to pronounce upon what an animal can and cannot be and do. It is becoming clear that we do not know and are only beginning to learn.

While the study of emotion is a respectable field, those who work in it are usually in departments of psychology where they confine their studies to human emotions. The standard reference work, *The Oxford Companion to Animal Behaviour*, advises animal behaviourists that 'One is well advised to study the behaviour, rather than attempting to get at any underlying emotion'.[14] Why? They may be elusive or difficult to measure or otherwise establish, but this does not mean feelings do not exist and are not important.

Human beings are not always aware of what they are feeling. Like animals, they may not be able to put their feelings into words. This does not mean they have no feelings. Sigmund Freud once speculated that a man could be in love with a woman for six years and not know it until many years later. Such a man, with all the good will in the world, could not have verbalised what he did not know. He had the feelings, but he did not know about them. It may sound like a paradox, yet it is beyond question that we can 'have' feelings that we do not know about – paradoxical because when we think of a feeling, we think of something which we are consciously aware of feeling. Perhaps the same people who refuse to recognise (or cannot because it is beneath the threshold of their conscious knowledge) the reality, importance and content of their own emotions, also resist recognising the role of emotions in others, including animals. After all, in Freud's example, the man's life was tragically altered by his ignorance of his own love.

Psychological theorists generally speak of a set of fundamental human emotions that are universal, discrete and which they consider to be innate.[15] These fundamental emotions are like the basic colours and can give rise to many variations. One psychologist compiled a list of 154 emotion names, from abhorrence to worry.[16] Theorists do not agree on which emotions are the basic ones. René Descartes said there were six basic emotions: love, hate, astonishment, desire, joy and sorrow. Immanuel Kant found five: love, hope, modesty, joy and sorrow. William James defined four: love, fear, grief and rage.[17] Behaviourist J.B. Watson postulated three basic emotions, X, Y and Z, roughly equivalent to fear, anger and love.[18] Such modern theorists as Robert Plutchik, Carroll Izard and Silvan Tomkins found either six or eight basic emotions – but not the same ones.[19] In his *Human Emotions*, Izard discusses interest–excitement, joy, surprise, distress–grief, anger–contempt, fear–anxiety, shame–shyness and guilt–conscience–morality.[20] Another list includes interest, joy, surprise, sadness, anger, disgust, contempt, fear, shame/shyness, envy, jealousy and guilt. Notice that love is not given as an emotion on most modern lists. Many scientists prefer to call it a drive or a motivation, if they refer to it at all. No emotion in these commonly used and accepted lists has not been thought by some researchers to be observed among animals.

There are probably other emotions and variations which from time to time everybody, from whatever culture, feels. Compiling a full list can be hazardous, as the Polish linguist Anna Wierzbicka points out when she observes that in some non-Western cultures, for example in Aboriginal Australia, a concept related to 'shame', but by no means identical to it, plays a social role evidently missing in our culture.[21] The word describing this emotion can include within its range the English concepts of 'shame', 'embarrassment', 'shyness' and 'respect'. Does this mean the feeling itself would be unrecognisable to somebody from another culture? That seems unlikely.

Where emotions are concerned, languages around the world seem to make many of the same distinctions and to refer to similar experiences. But can we feel an emotion for which our culture either provides no word or no examples? There are no doubt emotions promoted in one culture and not another, but this does not mean they are not experienced. It may be difficult to define them given the language to which one is born; it may even be difficult to think about them, and especially to convey them to another person. Yet the feeling itself will no doubt exist. Similarly, animals may have emotional experiences it would be almost impossible to put into words, even if they had them, but they would not for that reason cease to be feelings. Nonetheless, humans may well share with animals the vast majority of feelings of which the species is capable. Wierzbicks would probably disagree. She writes of 'a whole series of words referring to emotions (and to bodily results of emotions) akin to both sadness and love in the Australian Aboriginal language Pintupi, which demonstrate a degree of love and concern for one's kin and one's land unparalleled in Western culture'. [22] Though the words may not be there in English, can love and concern for kin, no matter how intense, possibly be confined to one part of the world? It was not so long ago that ethnologists thought that there were some cultures (obviously inferior) where the full range of Western emotions could not be expressed, and thus were probably not experienced. It seemed as pointless to enquire about compassion or aesthetic awe among certain hill tribes as it was to catalogue aesthetic rapture among bears. This prejudice is slowly receding. The capacity to feel such emotions may be universal. Great literature suggests that certain feeling states are universal, or at least that the capacity to experience them crosses cultures, although different cultures and different individuals may describe them differently, or attach differing importance to combinations of feeling. If feelings can cross cultures, it seems likely they can cross species.

What are feelings for? Most non-scientists will find this a strange question. Feelings just are. They justify themselves. Emotions give meaning and depth to life. They need serve no other purpose in order to exist. On the other hand, many evolutionary biologists, in contrast to animal behaviourists, acknowledge some emotions because they see them as serving a survival function. For both animals and humans, fear motivates the avoidance of danger, love is necessary to care for young, anger prepares one to hold ground. But the fact that behaviour functions to serve survival need not mean that that is why it is done. Other scientists have attributed the same behaviour to conditioning, learned responses. Certainly reflexes and fixed action patterns can occur without feeling or conscious thought. A gull chick pecks at a red spot above it. The parent has a red spot on its bill; the chick pecks the parent's bill. The gull parent feeds its chick when pecked on the bill. The baby gets fed. The interaction need have no emotional content.

At the same time, there is no reason why it cannot have such content. In mammalian animals and humans that have given birth, often milk is released automatically when a new baby cries. This is not under voluntary control; it is reflex. Yet this does not mean that feeding a new baby is exclusively reflex, expressing no feelings like love. Humans have feelings about their behaviour even if it is conditioned or reflexive. Yet since reflexes and fixed action patterns exist, and conditioned behaviour is widespread, measurable and observable, most scientists explain animal behaviour using only these concepts. It is considered simpler. The often appealed to principle of parsimony, or Ockham's razor, which holds that one should choose the simplest explanation for a phenomenon, or that entities are not to be multiplied without necessity, was modified by Lloyd Morgan to read, 'In no case may we interpret an action as the outcome of an exercise of a higher physical faculty, if it can be interpreted as the outcome of the exercise of one which stands lower in the psychological scale.' This rule of giving credence to only the lowest or simplest or most parsimonious explanation for behaviour is not unassailable. For one thing, there are many assumptions buried in the assessment of faculties as higher and lower. Emotions are typically considered higher faculties for no very clear reason. Moreover, the world is not necessarily a parsimonious place. As Gordon Burghardt has pointed out, 'The origin of life by creation is simpler than the indirect methods of evolution, and geological catastrophism is simpler than uniformitarianism'.[23]

Preferring to explain behaviour in ways that fit science's methods most easily, many scientists have refused to consider any causes for animal behaviour other than reflexive and conditioned behaviour. It is not necessarily the case, however, that emotional explanations for animal behaviour are impossibly complex or untestable. They are just more difficult for the scientific method to verify in the usual ways. The unwarranted step seems to have been taken that what cannot be readily measured or tested cannot exist, or is unworthy of serious attention.

Evolutionary biology offers further support for the view that animals feel. In this model, anything that enhances survival has

29

selective value. Emotions can motivate survival behaviour. An animal who is afraid of danger and runs away may survive over the one who does not. An animal that angrily defends its territory may live longer and better. An animal that loves and protects its offspring may leave more descendants. Happiness may motivate animal actions. An animal may derive happiness from the company of parents, siblings, a mate or offspring. It may take pleasure in successful foraging or hunting, in the ability to run swiftly, fly strongly or burrow deeply. The old German concept of *funktionslust* refers to the pleasure taken in what one can do best – for example, the pleasure a cat takes in climbing trees, or monkeys take in swinging from branch to branch. This pleasure, this happiness may increase an animal's tendency to do these things, and will also increase the likelihood of its survival. That is not to say that all actions driven by emotion have survival value. A loving animal may leave more offspring, thus making love an aid to survival; but a loving animal may care for disabled offspring or colleagues which have no chance of surviving. It may adopt the babies of others, not passing on its own genes. These actions would not enhance, would probably decrease, its own fitness. Yet lovingness could still have survival value, because a net effect would be the leaving of more offspring. This kind of phenomenon could represent a test for the existence of emotions. If a usually adaptive behaviour is manifested in an unadaptive situation, an overarching emotion, not a narrow adaptation, may drive the behaviour.

Biologists often point to the evolutionary advantage a behaviour confers as a way of avoiding recognition of emotions. Scientists sometimes argue that the songbird is not singing with joy, nor singing because he finds song beautiful, but because he is establishing territory and advertising his fitness to possible mates. Thus birdsong as an aggressive and sexual act provides a genetic and sufficient explanation for the behaviour. The bird's song may announce his territorial claims, and may indeed attract a mate, but that does not preclude the bird singing because he is happy and finds his song beautiful. As Frans de Waal points out, 'When I see a pair of parrots tenderly and patiently preening each other, my first thought is not that they are doing this to help the survival of their genes. This is a misleading manner of speaking, as it employs the present tense, whereas evolutionary explanations

30

can deal only with the past.'[24] Instead de Waal views the birds as expressing love and expectation, or, retreating a little, 'an exclusive bond'.

Similarly, human behaviour that can be viewed as increasing fitness often cannot be explained from that standpoint only, as sociobiologists sometimes attempt to do. When monogamous humans have affairs, they are not generally thinking about maximising reproductive chances by impregnating females other than the one with whom a substantial parental investment is being made, or about mating with genetically superior males for the benefit of their progeny. Indeed adulterers usually try to avoid reproduction. Sexual abuse of children has no survival value either, yet is common. If humans are subject to evolution but have feelings that are inexplicable in survival terms, if they are prone to emotions that do not seem to confer any advantage, why should we suppose that animals act on genetic investment alone?

It is clear that as human beings, we apply different standards to ourselves than we do to other animals. Humans are conceded to have emotions. The usual reason given is that feelings are expressed in language, using phrases like 'I love you', or 'I don't care', or 'I am sad'. People live much of their lives by what they or others say they feel. Although it is widely agreed that some people lie to gain an advantage, and some people make mistakes about their feelings, or do not know what they really feel, or express them without credibility, generally no one doubts that feelings exist – one's own and those of others. The primary reasoning seems to be analogy and empathy: we know we have feelings because we feel moved by them, and others appear to be like us, so we believe that they have feelings too.

This method is not without its difficulties. One can learn from personal experience that humans can feel gratitude because they say so and act as though they did. By itself, this sheds no light on whether a lion can feel gratitude. On the other hand, humans, even when embedded in intricate cultural environments, are a species of animal. The relation of physical to psychic determinants of emotions, whatever it is, may be a shared one. While emotions cannot be reduced simply to a blend of hormones, to whatever extent hormones contribute to emotional states in humans, they probably also do so in animals. Substances like

31

oxytocin, epinephrine, serotonin and testosterone are found in animals as well as in humans. Moreover, the part of the brain called the limbic system, which is thought to mediate emotion, is one of the most phylogenetically ancient parts of the brain, so much so that it is sometimes called 'the reptile brain'. Since grossly over-simplified explanations of human behaviour in terms of hormones have proved not only faulty but pernicious, there is no need to make the same mistake in explaining animal behaviour.[25] Unfortunately for those who hold that emotions are exclusively human products of our unparalleled mental powers, the physical pathways of human emotion are among the most primitive. From a purely physical standpoint, it would be a biological miracle if humans were the only animals to have feelings.[26]

Given this kind of information, could it be shown, say, that a cat loves her kittens or that kittens love their mother? If measurements showed hormone levels surging in the cat's bloodstream when she sees her kittens, and electrical activity spiking in certain parts of the cat's brain, would that be accepted as proof? Some would still say no, we can never know if a cat loves. Yet most observers already believe that the cat loves the kittens, simply on the basis of her behaviour. Scientists prefer not to say so.

Could it not be that the statement, 'the ape is clearly sad', is not different from 'John is clearly sad'? The 'clearly' signals an interpretation; it refers to clues that are socially agreed to indicate sadness. John is staring at the ground for hours and sighing. So is the ape. John may refuse to eat. So might the ape. John refuses to speak; when asked how he feels, he stares past the speaker. We do not, for that reason, say that he cannot feel sorrow or he would say so. We can be wrong about the ape. We can also be wrong about John. John might, in fact, be feeling something entirely different – apathy, perhaps. We may have misunderstood his actions, his facial expressions and his vocalisations. 'Clearly' is a statement about the kind of evidence we think we have, but our evidence may not be as good for people, and as poor for animals, as we think.

Humans do have the advantage of language, one of the biggest differences between humans and other animals. Animals, unlike people, cannot speak of their feelings in a way humans suppose they can reliably understand, although the language barrier between humans and animals is not entirely insuperable. Neither is language wholly trustworthy as a yardstick of feeling, even between humans. Verbal assertion of a feeling does not prove an emotion exists, nor does the inability to verbalise an emotion prove it does not. Some profoundly retarded humans cannot speak their feelings; this does not mean they do not have them. Mute humans feel. Intellectually sophisticated people can lie about their feelings or conceal them. This does not prove they cannot or do not feel. Human intellectual capacity may distinguish them from animals, even if only in degree, but even among humans, intelligence and emotion are not closely correlated.

The prejudice has long existed that only humans can have thoughts and feelings. Only humans, it is thought, can feel, because only humans can communicate thoughts and feelings in words, both written and spoken. Descartes, the seventeenth-century French philosopher, believed animals to be 'thoughtless brutes', *automata*, machines:

> There are [no men] so depraved and stupid, without even excepting idiots, that they cannot arrange different words together, forming of them a statement by which they make known their thoughts; while, on the other hand, there is no other animal, however perfect and fortunately circumstanced it may be, which can do the same . . . the reason why animals do not speak as we do is not that they lack the organs but that they have no thoughts.[27]

An unknown contemporary of Descartes put this position starkly:

> The (Cartesian) scientists administered beatings to dogs with perfect indifference and made fun of those who pitied the creatures as if they felt pain. They said the animals were clocks; that the cries they emitted when struck were only the noise of a little spring that had been touched, but that the whole body was without feeling. They nailed the poor animals up on boards by their four paws to vivisect them to see the circulation of the blood, which was a great subject of controversy.[28]

Voltaire responded that, on the contrary, vivisection showed that the dog has the same *organes de sentiment* that a human has. 'Answer me, you who believe that animals are only machines,' he wrote. 'Has nature arranged for this animal to have all the machinery of feelings only in order for it not to have any at all?'[29] Elsewhere, in *Le philosophe ignorant*, he criticises Descartes by saying that he 'dared to say that animals are pure machines who looked for food when they had no appetite, who had the organs for feeling only to never have the slightest feeling, who screamed without pain, who showed their pleasure without joy, who possessed a brain only to have in it not even the slightest idea, and who were in this way a perpetual contradiction of nature'.[30] As early as 1738, Voltaire talked about the humane feelings of the great English physicist Isaac Newton and how, like the philosopher John Locke, he was convinced that animals had the same sentiments man did. Voltaire writes: 'He [Newton] believed that it was a very terrible contradiction to believe that animals could feel, and yet cause them to suffer.'[31]

It is true that animals have no speech that humans yet understand. But is the absence of speech, after all, as important an indication of feelings as some philosophers have imagined it to be? Several chimpanzees and other great apes have American Sign Language (ASL) vocabularies of more than a hundred words. They communicate not only with humans but with members of their own species. Would it not be parsimonious to suppose that they had previously communicated some of these same thoughts to other apes via means other than human sign language? Why would they wait for scientists before doing something they were already capable of doing? The fact that apes do not have human vocal cords does not mean that they must remain uncommunicative. Following a first flush of excitement, the overwhelming response of the scientific community to signing apes has been to ignore or disbelieve them, both as individuals and as a species. Given that statements made by apes about food and toys are attacked, one can only imagine the reaction to statements about their feelings. It is all too convenient for rooted prejudice to say that animal feelings cannot be known because animals cannot speak, and then when they do speak in a human tongue, to claim that what they are saying cannot possibly be understood.

Even when animals speak our language, humans do not always take them at their word. For sixteen years Alex, an African grey parrot, has been trained by psychologist Irene Pepperberg, who is researching the bird's cognitive abilities. Alex is one of the few parrots in the world who has been demonstrated to understand

34

the meaning of the words he speaks. He knows the names of fifty objects, seven colours and five shapes. He can enumerate up to six objects and say which of two objects is smaller. Alex has also picked up many 'functional' phrases. He has learned, 'I'm gonna go now', something he hears people say in Pepperberg's laboratory. Pepperberg describes how, when Alex is scolded, 'We say, "No! Bad boy!" We walk out. And he knows what to say contextually, applicably. He brings us back in by saying, "Come here! I'm sorry!"' Alex learned to say he was sorry by hearing humans say it. He knows when to say it. Does he feel regret? 'He bites, he says "I'm sorry", and he bites again,' Pepperberg says somewhat irritably. 'There's *no* contrition!'[32] Just like many people.

Here is an animal who appears to be verbally reporting an emotional state – regret – but we don't believe him. If he were really sorry (in the way we understand the term) for biting, would he immediately bite again? Perhaps he would. Whatever is going on inside Alex, he feels something which makes him motivated enough to learn human words for human feelings – possibly to make humans into more satisfactory parrot companions. Alex may not feel contrition about hurting someone. Pepperberg may have no word for what Alex wants from her either; she may never have felt what Alex feels. Humans are surprisingly deficient in vocabulary for positive social emotions, and unduly successful at naming negative individualistic ones. Could there not be gradations of social affection at the top of the forest canopy for which Alex's owner is a functional emotional illiterate? Maybe we have something to learn.

In the last few years there has been an increasing interest, both among academics and therapists, in nonverbal communication among humans. Many complex mental states are more conveniently conveyed by gestures than sentences, while others appear to escape verbal language entirely. Attempts to convey subtle or elusive feelings leave everybody with a sense of the inadequacy of speech. Poetry, after all, is an attempt to convey feelings, moods, states and even thoughts that are hard to grasp and that seem to defy language in prose. And some feelings do in fact elude language, even poetry, altogether. The arts and silence pick up where words leave off.

There can be little doubt that humans communicate thoughts

and feelings *without* words; indeed, there is growing evidence that a great part of communication with others takes place outside verbal speech. Just as humans communicate through body language, gestures and expressive acts, consideration should be given to the nonverbal statements about feelings that animals make.

Animals communicate information through posture, vocalisations, gestures and actions, both to other animals and to humans who are attentive. Although study of these patterns is improving, even specialists can be rather poor at interpreting this information; this is especially true for those unfamiliar with the species. The animals themselves are much better at understanding these signals, even across species. Indeed, Elizabeth Marshall Thomas speculates that animals are much better at reading human body signals than humans are at reading animal signals of any kind, and that 'our kind may be able to bully other species not because we are good at communication but because we aren't'.[33] De Waal complains that anthropoid apes are so good at reading human body language as to leave people who work with them feeling transparent.[34]

Scientifically, the nonverbal communication of animals is seldom not accepted as proof of emotion, and yet scientists often speak as if it were. David Macdonald, after fifteen years of studying red foxes, raising them and sleeping with them, understands their body language. He can tell at a glance a happy fox, an excited fox, a nervous fox. He writes of them freely as playful, furious, besotted, fearful, confident, contented, flirtatious or humiliated. His *Running with the Fox* includes illustrations of fox body language, so that those less familiar with foxes can figure it out. Then, while discussing whether foxes enjoy killing, he issues the caveat 'assuming they are subject to emotions recognisable to humans . . .' He calls this question philosophically unanswerable.[35] It is no more philosophically unanswerable than the question of whether other humans have emotions, including sadism.

In Konrad Lorenz's *The Year of the Greylag Goose*, the caption to one photograph of a gander reads, 'After Ado [another gander] had appropriated Selma [his former mate], Gurnemanz went to pieces, as can be seen in this picture.' To a person only casually familiar with geese, this cannot be seen at all. It might as easily be a happy goose or a furious goose. A goose does not have a mobile face, so there is little in the way of facial expression. Lorenz, from long experience, knows a goose's body language and can read it. Ado's posture and neck position tell of his submission and demoralisation. Elsewhere Lorenz describes goose postures, gestures and sounds as victorious, uncertain, tense, glad, sad, alert, relaxed or threatening.[36]

The point is that a goose or other animal may be a quivering mass of emotion. Its feelings may be 'written all over its face'. It may take practice to read that writing, but once we can do so, it is information. We are restricted only by ignorance, lack of interest, desire for exploitation, wanting to eat them or by anthropocentric prejudices that preclude us, as if by divine fiat, from recognising commonality where it might exist. How can we be gods if animals are like us?

The standards for defining the existence of emotions in animals should be the same as those in common use for humans. One should demand no more proof that an animal feels an emotion than would be demanded of a human – and, like humans, the animal should be permitted to speak its own emotional language, which it is up to the beholder to understand.

At this point, it should be squarely faced that human emotions, too, escape exact scientific scrutiny. There is, in fact, no universally accepted scientific proof of human feelings. What one person *feels* is never entirely available to another. Not only is it uncertain our feelings are communicable; whether or not anyone understands the landscape of anyone else's inner life is ultimately unknowable.[37]

A history of human events in which fear, anger, love, pride and guilt played no part would be strangely inadequate. An ordinary person's life in which no one loves, is loved or wants to be loved; in which no one fears anything; in which no one becomes angry or makes anyone else angry; in which no one feels pride in anything they do; in which no one is ever ashamed to do anything or never feels guilty if they do – this would be an unnatural, unrealistic description. It would be neither believable nor accurate. It would be called inhuman. Equally, to describe the lives of animals without including their emotions may be just as inaccurate, just as superficial, just as distorted, and may strip them of their wholeness just as profoundly. To understand animals, it is essential to understand what they feel.

CHAPTER TWO

Unfeeling Brutes

T HROUGHOUT human history, there has been much concern with differentiating humans from beasts. *We* speak; *we*
reason; *we* imagine; *we* anticipate; *we* worship; *we* laugh. They
do not. The historical insistence on an unbridgeable gap suggests
that it serves some need or function. Why do we humans define
ourselves by distinction from animals? Why should the distinction
between man and beast matter?

Any dictionary of quotations reveals many attempts to make
this distinction, which fall largely into two categories. Many cite
human failings as unique, chief among which is fighting among
ourselves. Usually the writer is attempting to inspire his readers
with moral resolutions. In the first century AD, Pliny the Elder
in his *Natural History* admonishes: 'Lions do not fight with one
another; serpents do not attack serpents, nor do the wild monsters
of the deep rage against their like. But most of the calamities of man
are caused by his fellow men.' When, in 1532, Lodovico Ariosto

38

in *Orlando Furioso* says that 'Man is the only animal who injures his mate', this, too, is meant as an admonition. James Froude in his *Oceana* of 1866 claimed that 'Wild animals never kill for sport. Man is the only one for whom the torture and death of his fellow creatures is amusing in itself.' And even William James, in this century, wrote that man 'is simply the most formidable of all the beasts of prey, and, indeed, the only one that preys systematically on his own species'. Samuel Butler in the nineteenth century made a slightly different but equally admonishing distinction concerning man's relations to other animal species: 'Man is the only animal that can remain on friendly terms with the victims he intends to eat until he eats them.' In these examples, animals are not so much being observed as men are being exhorted to cease killing (usually) other men. They are intended to shame men into recognising that they behave worse than animals. This is perhaps what Carolus Linnaeus had in mind in a letter he wrote in 1747: 'What is the difference between man and ape, based on natural history? Most definitely I see no difference. I wish some one could show me even one distinction.'

The other – and by far the larger – category of man/beast contrasts cites human advantages: our intelligence, our culture, our sense of humour, our knowledge of death. In the nineteenth century William Hazlitt maintained that 'man is the only animal that laughs and weeps; for he is the only animal that is struck with the difference between what things are and what they ought to be'. And in our century, the philosopher William Ernest Hocking claimed that 'man is the only animal that contemplates death, and also the only animal that shows any sign of doubt of its finality'. Uniqueness is claimed for the human sense of humour, the ability to understand virtue, the ability to make and use tools. Again the authors seem more interested in making a didactic point for humans than in observing or understanding animals.

Contemporary renditions of this contrast have been scarcely more grounded in animal reality and have not shed much more light on animals – or humans. Recently N.K. Humphrey wrote that 'human beings have evolved to be the most highly social creatures the world has ever seen. Their social relationships have a depth, a complexity and a biological importance to them, that no other animals' relationships come near.'[1] Considering how

little is known about 'other animals' relationships', this seems
unwarranted. Until very recently it was held as a canon of
animal behaviour that only the human female experienced an
orgasm: non-human females did not. As recently as 1979, anthropologist Donald Symons pronounced that the 'female orgasm is a
characteristic essentially restricted to our own species'.[2] When the
question was actually investigated in the stump-tailed macaque,
using the same physiological criteria as used for humans, it was
found that the female macaques did appear to experience orgasm.[3]
Primatologist Frans de Waal notes that, from behavioural evidence, this is also true of the female bonobo (pygmy chimpanzee).[4]
The truth is that, like many questions specifically involving the
human female, not many scientists had ever considered the question
systematically, let alone done the necessary field observation
studies to find an answer. Perhaps it pleased most male scientists
to imagine that while animal females sought sex only during an
oestrus cycle, and hence had sex only for reproduction, human
females, due to their unique orgasmic capacity, wanted sex all the
time.

People have always exalted certain 'higher' feelings which
we claim single us out from animals. Only humans, it has
been claimed, feel the noble emotions, such as compassion, true
love, altruism, pity, mercy, reverence, honour and modesty. On
the other hand, people have often attributed so-called negative
or 'low' emotions to animals: cruelty, pride, greed, rage, vanity
and hatred. At play here appears to be the seemingly unbearable
injury to our sense of uniqueness, to our entitlement to the
nobility of our emotional life. Thus not only whether animals
can feel, but what they feel, is used to strengthen the species
barrier. What lies behind this 'us/them' mentality, the urge
to define ourselves by proving we are not only different,
but utterly different, including emotionally? Why should this
distinction between man and beast be so important to humans?
Examining distinctions humans draw among themselves may
provide a partial answer. Dominant human groups have long
defined themselves as superior by distinguishing themselves from
groups they are subordinating. Thus whites define blacks in part
by differing melanin content of the skin; men are distinguished
from women by primary and secondary sex characteristics. These
empirical distinctions are then used to make it appear that it is

40

the distinctions themselves, not their social consequences, that are responsible for the social dominance of one group over the other.

On this model, one could say that the distinction between man and beast serves to keep man on top. People define themselves either as distinct from animals, or similar when convenient or entertaining, in order to keep themselves dominant over them. Human beings presumably want to treat animals the way they do – hunting them, jailing them, exploiting their labour, living on their flesh, gaping at them and even owning them as signs of social cachet. Any human being who has a choice does not want to be treated like this. In this analysis, the distinction between man and beast serves to direct various forms of human aggression away from human beings and towards animals as such.

A blatant example of many of these prejudices, with a suggestion of some of their social consequences, can be found in the article on 'Animals' in the *Encyclopaedia of Religion and Ethics*, written in 1908:

> Civilization, or perhaps rather education, has brought with it a sense of the great gulf that exists between man and the lower animals . . . In the lower stages of culture, whether they be found in races which are, as a whole, below the European level, or in the uncultured portion of civilized communities, the distinction between men and animals is not adequately, if at all, recognized . . . The savage . . . attributes to the animal a vastly more complex set of thoughts and feelings, and a much greater range of knowledge and power, than it actually possesses . . . It is therefore small wonder that his attitude towards the animal creation is one of reverence rather than superiority.[5]

Only a lower man, one close to animals, would value them. The ingenuity of human rationalisations of this gap is analysed in an elegant book on hunting by Matt Cartmill:

> In policing the animal-human boundary, scientists have shown considerable ingenuity in redefining supposedly unique human traits to keep them from being claimed for other animals. Consider our supposedly big brains. Human beings are supposed to be smarter than other animals, and therefore *we* ought to have larger brains. But in fact, elephants, whales, and dolphins have

bigger brains than ours; and small rodents and monkeys have relatively bigger brains (their brains make up a larger percentage of body weight than ours do). Scientists who study these things have accordingly labored to redefine brain size, dividing brain weight by basal metabolic rate or some other exponential function of body weight to furnish a standard by which these animals' brains can thus be deemed smaller than ours. The unique bigness of the human brain thus turns out to be a matter of definition.[6]

Animals' presumed lack of feeling has provided a major excuse for treating them badly. If they have no feelings, humans need not respect those feelings or them. This has been so extreme that animals were long regarded as unable to feel pain, physical or emotional. When an animal is hurt in a way that would hurt a person, it generally reacts much as a person would. It cries out, it gets away, then examines or favours the affected part, and withdraws and rests. Few veterinarians can be found who doubt that it is pain that animals feel when wounded. The only criterion that an animal fails to meet for feeling physical pain as humans understand it is the ability to express it in words. Yet the fish on the hook is said not to be thrashing in pain (or fear) but in a reflex action. A lobster in boiling water or puppies whose tails are being docked are said to feel nothing. To rebut such rationalisations a recent German book on animal consciousness argues that 'The fact that we so immediately understand these signals is just a further sign that we share with other animals the grand construction of our pain apparatus'.[7] When the subject is actually researched, the findings are in line with common sense. The pain of the fish twisting on the hook is real. Even insects are found to be sentient and experience pain.[8]

In considering the role of the denial of sensate experience in the way animals have been made into a lesser form of life by many, it is important to observe that rationalising away the pain of others is practised on people too. Joseph Wood Krutch writes, 'Man has never denied anything of the animals without coming shortly thereafter to deny it of himself also'.[9] It is usually, in fact, a dominant group denying feelings in a subordinate group. And surely the feelings of animals have value whether or not their denial ultimately hurts people.

42

It has always been comforting to the dominant to assume that those in subservient positions do not suffer or feel pain as keenly or at all, so they can be abused or exploited without guilt and with impunity. That lower classes and other races are relatively insensitive has been a frequent assertion in the history of prejudice.[10] Similarly, until the 1980s, it was routine for surgery on human infants to be performed with paralytic agents but without anaesthesia, in the long-held belief that babies are incapable of feeling pain. It was believed, without evidence, that their nervous systems were immature.[11] The notion that babies do not feel pain is directly counter to their screams and can only be classified as scientific myth. Yet it has been a tenet of human medicine, only recently acknowledged to be false in the wake of studies showing that infants who do not get pain medication take longer to recover from surgery.

A similar bigotry has extended to the presence of emotions in the poor, the foreign, those raised in impoverished or unenlightened cultures, and in children, who supposedly have not yet learned to feel in fully human ways. It is often asserted that when an infant smiles, it is a physical response to gas in the intestines. The baby is said not to be smiling in response to other people, or out of happiness, but in response to digestive events. Despite the fact that adults do not smile as a result of discomfort in the stomach, this notion is widely repeated – though often not believed by the infant's parents. Studies showing that infant smiles are not correlated with burps, regurgitation and flatulence have made little impact on this idea.[12] Many people are gratified to think of infants as having diminished or no feelings.

If it is so easy to deny the emotional lives of other people, how much easier it is to deny the emotional lives of animals. In science, the greatest obstacle to investigating the emotions of other animals has been an extreme desire to avoid anthropomorphism. Anthropomorphism means the ascribing of human characteristics – thought, feeling, consciousness and motivation – to non-human things. When people say that their car is out to get them, or that a tree is their friend, they are anthropomorphising. Few believe their vehicle is plotting against them, but anthropomorphic ideas about animals are held with greater conviction. Outside scientific circles, it is common to speak of the thoughts and feelings of pets and of wild and captive animals. Yet many scientists regard even the notion that animals feel pain as the grossest sort of anthropo-morphic error.

Science considers anthropomorphism towards animals a grave mistake, even a sin. It is common in science to speak of 'com-mitting' anthropomorphism. The term originally was religious, referring to the assigning of human characteristics to God – the hierarchical error of acting as though the merely human could be divine – literally a sin. In science, the sin against hierarchy is to assign human characteristics to animals. Just as humans could not be like God, now animals cannot be like humans (note who has taken God's place).

Young scientists are indoctrinated with the gravity of this error. As animal behaviourist David McFarland explains, 'They often have to be specially trained to resist the temptation to interpret the behaviour of other species in terms of their nor-mal behaviour-recognition mechanisms'.[13] It is still treated as axiomatic that 'scientists must keep a constant vigil against anthropomorphic thinking and interpretation when performing animal research.'[14] In his recent book, *The New Anthropomorphism*, behaviourist John S. Kennedy laments that 'the scientific study of animal behaviour was inevitably marked from birth by its anthropomorphic parentage and to a significant extent it still is. It has had to struggle to free itself from this incubus and the struggle is not over. Anthropomorphism remains much more of a problem than most of today's neobehaviourists believed . . . If the study of animal behaviour is to mature as a science, the pro-cess of liberation from the delusions of anthropomorphism must go on.'[15] He ends his book hoping that 'anthropomorphism will be brought under control, even if it cannot be cured completely. Although it is probably programmed into us genetically as well as being inoculated culturally that does not mean the disease is untreatable.'[16]

The philosopher John Andrew Fisher has noted that 'The use of the term "anthropomorphism" by scientists and philosophers is often so casual as to almost suggest that it is a term of ideologi-cal abuse, rather like political or religious terms ("communist" or "counter-revolutionary") that need no explication or defense when used in criticism.'[17]

Women have been deemed especially prone to anthropomorphic empathy in a science dominated by men. Women, long considered inferior to men precisely on the grounds that they feel too much, were thought to over-identify with the animals they studied. This is one reason why male scientists did not encourage female field biologists for so long. They were too emotional;[18] they allowed emotions to sway judgments and observations. Women, it was felt, were more likely than men to attribute emotional attitudes to animals, to project their own feelings on to them. Thus did gender bias and species bias converge in a supposedly objective environment.

To accuse a scientist of anthropomorphism is to make a severe criticism. It is regarded as a species-confusion, an unprofessional merging, a forgetting of the line between who one is and what one is observing, between subject and object, womanish. To assign thoughts or feelings to a creature known to be incapable of them would indeed be a problem, but to ascribe to an animal emotions such as joy or sorrow only makes the error anthropomorphic if one knows that animals cannot feel such emotions. Many scientists have made this decision, but not on the basis of evidence.

The situation is not so much that emotion is denied but that it is regarded as so dangerous an area that it should not be part of the scientific agenda – such a minefield of subjectivity that no investigation of it should take place. As a result, none but the most prominent scientists risk their reputations and credibility by venturing into this area. Thus many scientists may believe that animals have emotions but are unwilling to say that they believe it, and unwilling to study it or encourage their students to investigate it. They may also attack other scientists who try to use the language of the emotions.

From the belief that anthropomorphism is a desperate error, a sin or a disease, flow further research taboos, including the appropriate use of language. A monkey is not angry; it exhibits aggression. A crane does not feel affection; it displays courtship or parental behaviour. A cheetah is not frightened by a lion; it shows flight behaviour. In keeping with this, de Waal's use of the word 'reconciliation' in reference to chimpanzees has been criticised: wouldn't it be more objective to say 'first post-conflict contact'?[19] What is really being sought here may be that part of objectivity which distance and disidentification provide.

The biologist Julian Huxley has argued, against this scientific orthodoxy, that to imagine oneself into the life of another animal is both scientifically justifiable and productive for knowledge. In 1961 Huxley introduced one of the most extraordinary accounts of a very deep and mysterious emotional tie between a human being and a free-living lioness, Joy Adamson's *Living Free*, as follows:

> When people like Mrs Adamson (or Darwin for that matter) interpret an animal's gestures and postures with the aid of psychological terms – anger or curiosity, affection or jealousy – the strict Behaviourist accuses them of anthropomorphism, of seeing a human mind at work within the animal's skin. This is not necessarily so. The true ethologist must be evolution-minded. After all, he is a mammal. To give the fullest possible interpretation of behaviour he must have recourse to a language that will apply to his fellow-mammals as well as to his fellow-man. And such a language must employ subjective as well as objective terminology – *fear* as well as *impulse to flee*, *curiosity* as well as *exploratory urge*, *maternal solicitude* in all its modulations in welcome addition to goodness knows what complication of behaviourist terminology.[20]

Huxley's argument ran counter to mainstream scientific thinking at the time, and still does so. A contemporary example is provided by Alex, the African grey parrot, who was being trained or tested by experimenters who varied the requests they made of him for several reasons, one being to avoid cueing, another to prevent Alex from becoming bored. When reviewers of a paper the researcher Pepperberg submitted to a scientific journal vetoed her use of the term 'boredom', she responded:

> I had a referee go ballistic on me. And yet, you've watched the bird, he looks at you, he says 'I'm gonna go away.' And he walks! The referee said that was an anthropomorphic term that had no business being in a scientific journal . . . I can talk in as many stimulus-response type terms as you want. It turns out, though, that a lot of his behaviours are very difficult to describe in ways that are not anthropomorphic.[21]

What is wrong with exploring the idea, based on many such observations in a research setting, that parrots and humans may have a shared capacity for boredom? The preconceived belief, the dogma, the unresearchable, has gone from the uncritical projection of human feeling-states on to animals to the refusal to recognise animal feeling-states even when ample evidence is produced over and over again.

A related taboo in the study of animal behaviour has been that the scientist should not name the animals. To separate individuals, they might be called Adult Male 36, or Juvenile Green. Most field workers over the generations have resisted this precept, naming the animals they spent their days watching, at least for their own use, Spot-Nose and Splotch-Tail, Flo and Figan, or Cleo, Freddy and Mia. In their published work, some reverted to more remote forms of identification; others continued to use the names. Sy Montgomery reports that, in 1981, anthropologist Colin Turnbull declined to provide a supporting statement for Dian Fossey's book of observations on mountain gorillas.[22] It is even more common not to name animals in laboratories, perhaps for the same reason that farmers often avoid naming animals they expect to slaughter: it is harder to kill a friend, and proper names humanise.

Rebutting the view that naming animals only causes one to assign them human traits, elephant researcher Cynthia Moss notes that the opposite happens to her: people remind her of elephants. 'When I am introduced to a person named Amy or Amelia or Alison, across my mind's eye flashes the head and ears of that elephant.'[23] The no-name norm has gradually changed, particularly among primatologists, perhaps because of the outstanding work of researchers who named – and admitted that they named – the subjects they studied. Yet as recently as 1987, researchers studying elephants in Namibia (then South West Africa) were instructed by park authorities to assign the animals numbers because names were too sentimental.[24] Granted that a number is more dehumanised than a name, does that make it more scientific? Assigning names to them – referring to a chimpanzee as Flo or Figan – can be called anthropomorphic, but so is assigning numbers. Chimpanzees are no more likely to think of themselves as F2 or JF3 than as Flo or Figan.

We do not know if animals name themselves or each other. We do know that they have and recognise individuality. Animals recognise other animals as individuals and distinguish between them; names are the way humans label such distinctions. Names make the same distinctions animals do. There is speculation that bottlenose dolphins may identify and imitate one another's signature whistles, something very close to a name.[25] Some animals clearly respond emotionally to being given a name. Mike Tomkies in *Last Wild Years* writes that 'only the ignorant pour scorn on this habit of mine of giving names to the creatures that, over the years, have shared my home. And also others that have not. So long as it is not a harsh sound, it matters little what the name is, but there can be no doubt whatever that an animal or bird will respond differently, become more trusting, once it is given a name.'[26]

If naming the animals one studies promotes empathy towards them, this may help rather than occlude insight. The essential fact glossed over in the attack on anthropomorphism is that humans are animals. Man's relation to animals is not a literary exercise in creating charming metaphors. As Midgley puts it: 'The fact that some people are silly about animals cannot stop the topic being a serious one. Animals are not just one of the things with which people amuse themselves, like chewing-gum and water-skis, *they are the group to which people belong*. We are not just rather like animals; we *are* animals.'[27] To act as if humans are a completely different order of beings from other animals ignores reality.

Even fierce opponents of anthropomorphism concede that it often works when trying to predict animal behaviour. By considering what an animal feels or thinks, we may improve our ability to project how it will act. Such guesses have a high success rate. It has frequently been pointed out that a successful prediction does not prove that the animal actually felt or thought what was imagined. But successful prediction is a standard test of scientific theories. J.S. Kennedy, the animal behaviourist who views anthropomorphism as a disease, concedes nevertheless that it is a useful way to predict behaviour. In fact, he advocates using 'mock' anthropomorphism for this purpose, although successful predictions are not to be construed as indicating that the basis for prediction had any value. Kennedy argues that anthropomorphism works because animals have evolved to act *as if* they thought and felt: 'it is natural selection and not the animal that ensures that what it does mostly "makes sense", as we are wont to say'.[28]

Even though Kennedy disavows what he calls the 'assumptions that they have feelings and intentions', he does acknowledge that empathy can be useful for generating questions and making predictions. Thus one might predict that a cheetah, fearing for the lives of her cubs, may run close to a lion to lure it away from them. Under Kennedy's formulation, if the cheetah does run close to the lion, it does not mean she fears for the lives of her cubs. It only means that she has evolved to act for survival *as if* she fears for their lives. To speculate that leaving more offspring is the ultimate cause of her behaviour is permitted. Not permitted is to speculate that fear for their lives is its proximate cause, far less about how she may feel seeing the lion grabbing them. Why is it so impossible to know what animals feel, no matter how much or what kind of evidence there is? How is knowing about their feelings different, in truth, from the assumptions made routinely about the feelings of other people?

Short of being another person, there is no way to know with certainty what another person is feeling, although few people, even philosophers, carry their solipsism this far. In learning of the feelings of others, people are not always led by words alone, but watch behaviour – gestures, the face, the eyes – and its patterns and consistency over time. Conclusions are based on this, and ground everyday life decisions. We love certain people, hate others, trust some, fear others, and act on this basis. Although belief in the emotions of others is indispensable to life in human society, some will argue that ultimately it cannot be proved. N. K. Humphrey writes that 'for all I know no man other than myself has ever experienced a feeling corresponding to my feeling of hunger; the fact remains that the concept of hunger, derived from my own experience, helps me to understand other men's eating behaviour.'[29]

On the question of humans knowing animals' pain, Mary Midgley has said: 'If a torturer excused her activities by claiming ignorance of pain on the grounds that nobody knows anything about the subjective sensation of others, she would not convince any human audience. An audience of scientists need not aim at providing an exception to this rule.'[30] She locates the basis of human assumptions of natural superiority underlying the position of the solipsist when she quotes an astonishing passage from the *Ethics* of the seventeenth-century Dutch philosopher Benedict de Spinoza:

It is plain that the law against the slaughtering of animals is founded rather on vain superstition and womanish pity than on sound reason. The rational quest of what is useful to us further teaches us the necessity of associating ourselves with our fellow-men, but not with beasts, or things, whose nature is different from our own; we have the same rights in respect to them as they have in respect to us. Nay, as everyone's right is defined by his virtue, or power, men have far greater rights over beasts than beasts have over men. Still I do not deny that beasts feel; what I deny is that we may not consult our own advantage and use them as we please, treating them in the way which best suits us; for their nature is not like ours, and their emotions are naturally different from human emotions.

Spinoza refrains from discussing how he knows that animal emotions are different from human ones, or from explaining how this justifies the human exploitation, plunder and murder of them. He simply says we have more power than they do. Might makes right. J. Ortega y Gasset's defence of hunting comes to the same conclusion, insisting that the victim is always asking for it:

[Hunting] is a relationship that certain animals impose on man, to the point where not trying to hunt them demands the intervention of our deliberate will . . . Before any particular hunter pursues them they feel themselves to be possible prey, and they model their whole existence in terms of this condition. Thus they automatically convert any normal man who comes upon them into a hunter. *The only adequate response to a being that lives obsessed with avoiding capture is to try to catch it* [Gasset's italics].[31]

Such delusional anthropomorphism is based on deep and hidden structural assumptions and interests. Ortega y Gasset's buried premise – that hunted beings seek their own demise – closely resembles rationales about rape. A common excuse of rapists is that women ask for rape, thus seeking and causing their own violation, especially when trying to avoid it. A similar exoneration of hunters is sought here by justifying the capture of animals by calling animal flight from capture an 'obsession' – meaning they most desire what they most strenuously flee.

More simple forms of anthropomorphism can also interfere with observation and distort understanding. Carolus Linnaeus, the eighteenth-century Swedish naturalist who developed the classification system of living things, wrote of the frog: 'These foul and loathsome animals are . . . abhorrent because of their cold bodies, pale colour, cartilaginous skeletons, filthy skin, fierce aspect, calculating eye, offensive smell, harsh voice, squalid habitation and terrible venom.' The words are all very emotive, referring to emotions Linnaeus felt when *he* saw a frog. They are pure projection. 'Calculating' is not a scientific term to describe a frog's eye. This passage describes little in the physical world, but powerfully conveys the scientist's subjective state. It is art.

Both cats and dogs are prime targets of anthropomorphism, for good and bad. It is common to ascribe unlikely thoughts and feelings to pets: 'She understands every word you say'; 'He sings his little heart out to show how grateful he is'. Many people seem to enjoy believing that cats are selfish, unfeeling creatures who heartlessly use their deluded owners, compared with loving, loyal and naive dogs. More often, however, people have what seem to be quite realistic views about their pets' abilities and attributes. The experience of living with an animal often provides a strong sense of its abilities and limitations – although even here, as for people living intimately with people, preconceptions can be more persuasive than lived evidence, and can create their own reality. Perhaps the richest source of actual anthropomorphic error is our thinking about wild animals. Since people live with domestic animals, erroneous theories about their behaviour are likely to be disproved in the course of events. But since most people's contact with wild animals is so limited, theories about them may never run up against actual facts, and we remain free to imagine ravening wolves, saintly dolphins or crows who follow parliamentary procedure.

Another problem with anthropomorphism has been that human views of gender – often as wrong as human views of animals – have been attributed to animals. A recent television nature programme featured a family of cheetahs in Tanzania's Serengeti National Park. The male cub was called Tabu and the female Tamu – Swahili for Trouble and Sweetness. One expects different things from a Sweetness than a Trouble. Surely the sentence 'Trouble is prowling around my tent' is more threatening than

'Sweetness is prowling around my tent'. Sociobiology has tended to encourage prejudices men have about women by insisting that they are 'natural', by which is meant they can be found among members of the animal kingdom. As already noted, one can prove almost anything by careful choice of species. It does not seem accidental that human society has for so long been compared to baboon society, despite the facts that baboons are far more sexually dimorphic than humans and that baboons do not form mated pairs. The idea seems to be to impose greater gender inequality on human females by enforcing a supposedly natural template.

One way to avoid such errors is to pretend that animals are neuter in gender. Writing about creative behaviour in dolphins for a scientific journal, researcher Karen Pryor was told to call the rough-toothed porpoise Hou 'it' rather than 'she', on the grounds that 'she' should be reserved for referring to humans.[32] Not that being called 'she' has humanised women with any security. Refusal to discuss observable facts (Hou was unquestionably female) is hardly scientific. Such language use springs from a desire to treat animals as things rather than beings. At the same time, by treating animals as creatures like ourselves we risk projecting unexamined assumptions about human gender on to observations and analysis.

A serious problem with careless and uncritical human-animal comparisons is the inadequacy of our present knowledge, especially of crucial matters like the role of culture in animal learning in the wild. Elephants, for example, learn from their elders which humans to fear based on the history of the herd with humans. Mike Tomkies describes watching an eaglet in the wild being taught to fly so as to hunt and kill by repeated demonstrations on the part of its parent, who was clearly showing the youngster what to do rather than engaging itself in search of prey. Evidently the eaglet is not born knowing this.[33] It is transmitted by learning – that is, by culture. That a skill has to be learned does not make it unnatural. The distinction between innate and natural, on the one hand, and cultural and learned on the other, loses much of its force in the light of more recent observations on what animals teach each other. To use the word natural to describe how the eaglet kills simply means that an animal was observed doing it.

The real problem often targeted by many of the criticisms of anthropomorphism is actually *anthropocentrism*. Placing humans at the centre of all interpretation, observation and concern, and dominant men at the centre of that, has led to some of the worst errors in science, whether in astronomy, politics or animal behaviour. Anthropocentrism treats animals as inferior forms of people and denies what they really are. It expresses a passionate wish to differentiate ourselves from animals, to make animals 'other', presumably in order to maintain humans at the top of the evolutionary hierarchy and the food chain. The notion that animals are wholly other from humans, despite our common ancestry, is more irrational than the notion that they are like us. But even if they were not like us at all, that is no reason to avoid studying them for their own sakes. The point has been made by J.E.R. Staddon that 'Psychology as a basic science should be about intelligent and adaptive behavior, wherever it is to be found, so that animals can be studied in their own right, for what they can teach us about the nature and evolution of intelligence, and not as surrogate people or tools for the solution of human problems.'[34] The knowledge obtained from this study, whether or not it contributes to the solution of human problems, is still knowledge.

Although not nearly as frequent as the denigration and demonisation of animals, idealising animals is another kind of anthropocentrism, the belief that animals have all the virtues to which humans aspire and none of our faults. It is anthropocentric because its core is an obsession with the ways of humans, negative in this case, which animals are used to highlight. In this view the natural world is a place without war, murder, rape and addiction. Animals, in this sentimental formulation, never lie, cheat or steal. This view is embarrassed by reality. Deception has been observed in animals from elephants to Arctic foxes.[35] Ants take slaves. Chimpanzees may attack other bands of chimpanzees, unprovoked and with deadly intent. Groups of dwarf mongooses battle against other groups for territory. The case of the chimpanzee murderers Pom and Passion, who killed and ate the infants of other chimpanzees in their group, has been well documented by Jane Goodall's research team. Orangutans have been seen to rape other orangutans. Male lions, when they join a pride, often kill young cubs who were fathered by other lions. Young hyenas, foxes and owls have been seen to kill and eat their siblings.

All is not as humans wish it to be among our evolutionary cousins. One has to sympathise with Jane Goodall's reaction to chimpanzee treatment of one old animal, his legs wholly paralysed by polio, who was lonely, shunned, and sometimes attacked by those who were still healthy. In the hope of inducing companions who were grooming each other to groom him as well, he dragged himself up into a tree:

> With a loud grunt of pleasure he reached a hand towards them in greeting – but even before he made contact they both swung quickly away and, without a backward glance, started grooming on the far side of the tree. For a full two minutes, old Gregor sat motionless, staring after them. And then he laboriously lowered himself to the ground. As I watched him sitting there alone, my vision blurred, and when I looked up at the groomers in the tree I came nearer to hating a chimpanzee than I have ever done before or since.[36]

It is hard to romanticise anything this ugly.

It has been a long time since anyone called the lion the King of Beasts, but in recent years dolphins have been portrayed as smarter, kinder, nobler, more pacific, and better at living in groups than people. This ignores the well-known fact that dolphins can be quite aggressive. Recently it has been discovered that some dolphins occasionally rape. At the same time, animal cruelty does not approximate the human standard. It is unlikely that dolphin rape rivals the human figures. One random sample survey in 1977 found that almost half of all the women in one U.S. city had been victims of rape or attempted rape at least once in their lives.[37] While abuse of young may occur among animals in the wild, nothing compares with more than one in every three girls being sexually abused as children, as another American study shows.[38] Physical abuse of others for pleasure is not recorded in the animal world. Torture, as it is performed by humans, is unknown in any other species. No other known animal attacks another merely to see it suffer.

If humans can misunderstand animals by assuming they are more like us than they are, can animals also wrongly project their feelings on to us? Do some animals commit what might be called zoomorphism, ascribing their attributes to humans? A cat who brings a human offerings of dead rodents, lizards and birds day after day, no matter how often these objects are greeted with loathing, commits zoomorphism. This is the equivalent of offering sweets to a cat, as children sometimes do. Similarly, in *The Hidden Life of Dogs*, Elizabeth Marshall Thomas writes, 'When a dog with a bone menaces a human observer, the dog actually assumes that the person wants the slimy, dirt-laden object, and is applying dog values, or cynomorphizing.'[39] Were a dog to give a history of the human race, some valuable attributes might be denied us, just as our history of any animal civilisation would doubtless miss many of its signal achievements.

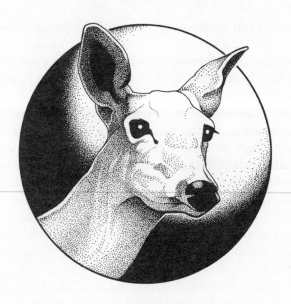

CHAPTER THREE

Fear, Hope and the Terror of Dreams

WILDLIFE biologist Lynn Rogers has spent decades studying black bears, following them through forests and swamps. He has accustomed bears to a human presence much as the chimpanzees studied by Jane Goodall or the gorillas studied by Dian Fossey have become accustomed to such a presence. He has discovered much that was unknown about their feeding habits, territoriality, habitat selection and social and maternal behaviour.

As a graduate student, he learned about black bears from his professor, Albert Erikson. One day they were trying to take a blood sample from an anaesthetised wild bear, when it suddenly woke. The bear lunged at Erikson. To Rogers' surprise, Erikson lunged back. The bear turned to Rogers. Erikson said 'Lunge!' Rogers obediently lunged at the bear, who turned and ran away. Rogers says, 'I was learning things that would help me interpret bears' actions in terms of their own fear rather than mine.'[1]

The error into which anthropomorphism can lead us is to see

bears through our own emotions: we fear them, so we perceive
them as angry and hostile. The equal and opposite error into
which the fear of anthropomorphism can lead us is to refuse to
recognise that bears can feel their own emotions. Rogers learned
to observe bears in terms of those emotions, discovering that the
bears themselves were often fearful. He learned what frightened
them and how not to frighten them: 'Once I started looking at
bears in terms of their fear, and interpreted all the things that
used to scare me and interpreted those in terms of the bear's fear,
it was easy to gain their trust and begin walking with them very
closely, sleeping with them – doing all the things that you have
to do to see how an animal really lives in its world.'[2]

So well has Rogers learned to understand the wild bears that
he can curl up for the night a few feet from their den or even
handle their cubs. Asked whether scientists don't usually avoid
using words like 'fear' and 'trust' to describe animal behaviour,
this maverick researcher replies, 'Yes. But I think that we miss
the mark more by ignoring those emotions than by taking them
into account. Those are basic emotions that animals and people
share.'

His description of a suddenly alarmed bear shows how humans
can learn to 'read' bears: 'You can be very close to a bear and
have things be calm, until some little unidentified noise happens
far off in the forest. Then the bear is suddenly keyed up, wary
. . . Whenever there's anything that makes the bear take a deep
breath, which is the first sign of their fear, and then you see its
ears prick up, you think, "Better give the bear a little bit more
room, don't be standing right on top of it, because there's a good
chance it'll whack you." It feels threatened by some other thing
and it wants room and the peace of mind from you to deal with
that. After being told in no uncertain terms by bears to get away
in that situation, after a while I learned.'

Of all emotions animals might feel, fear is the one that sceptics
most often accept, one of the few that comparative psychology
investigates. One reason is that it is easy to argue for an evolutionary advantage to fearfulness.

Fear can serve as a mechanism to trigger defensive behaviour, so
it has obvious survival value for any organism capable of defence.
Fear can set animals running, diving, hiding, screaming for help,
slamming their shells shut, bristling their quills or baring their

teeth. If an animal had no mode of defence, fear would confer no benefit. Yet fear has also been known to interfere with survival: the actions of a panicking person or animal are not always the wisest, as when a terrified soldier on a battlefield runs into the line of fire.[3]

People also find it easy to believe that animals feel fear because this emotion is one that humans often elicit from animals, and may even enjoy eliciting. An urban dweller who has never so much as visited a zoo has probably scattered birds into flight, seen cats flee from dogs or dogs flee from bigger dogs, and has no reason to doubt that animals feel fear.

Nor does a powerful intellect seem necessary to experience fright. Intellect may enable the detection of subtler reasons to fear, but the less intelligent still find plenty to fear. Those who wish to believe that a great gulf separates people from other animals seldom seem threatened by the notion of animal fear.

In animals it may not be called an emotion, however. Thus, while dictionaries call fear an emotion, animal behaviourists may prefer to call animal fear 'a state of motivation which is aroused by certain specific stimuli and normally gives rise to defensive behaviour or escape'.[4]

What may be the traces of fear are easy to find in a laboratory (indeed, what animal would not, with reason, fear a laboratory?). A small electrical impulse to a cat's amygdala (part of the brain's limbic system) produces alertness, a larger one produces the expressions and actions of terror.[5] A rat whose amygdala has been removed loses the fear of cats and will walk right up to one.

Researchers at New York University trained rats to expect an electric shock when they heard a tone, and discovered to their surprise that the nerve impulses in the rats taught to fear the tone went straight from the ear to the amygdala, instead of via the usual route through the auditory cortex. The theory is that the amygdala attaches emotional import to some forms of learning.[6]

Endocrine studies show that hormones such as epinephrine and norepinephrine help pass along fear messages. Geneticists say that in just ten generations of breeding, two strains of rats can be produced from a parental stock, one fearful, one calm.

But biologists concede that physiological symptoms do not

form a complete description of fear. Anthony Kenny has given the example of a person who fear heights and avoids them scrupulously, as compared to a relatively fearless mountain climber. The person who avoids heights may succeed in doing so and, as a result, seldom exhibit physiological symptoms of fear. The climber, more often at risk, may show such signs more often, yet cannot be said to be more afraid.[7]

Fearful behaviour has also been studied in the laboratory, with attention being given to such issues as the fearfulness in later life of birds, dogs or macaques reared in isolation; and what kind of parental contact is required to reassure frightened baby animals.

In *The Expression of Emotions in Man and Animals*, Darwin made a systematic study of how animals look when they are afraid. In both humans and animals, he found, some or all of the following may occur: the eyes and mouth open, the eyes roll, the heart beats rapidly, hairs stand on end, muscles tremble, teeth chatter and the sphincter loosens. The frightened creature may freeze in its place, or cower.

These rules hold true across a remarkable array of species. Somehow it is unexpected to learn that when dolphins are terrified, their teeth chatter and the whites of their eyes show,[8] or that a frightened gorilla's legs shake.[9] To see such familiar behaviour in a wild animal reminds us of our ultimate kinship. Melvin Konner has written: 'We are – not metaphorically, but precisely, biologically – like the doe nibbling moist grass in the predawn misty light; chewing, nuzzling a dewy fawn, breathing the foggy air, feeling so much at peace; and suddenly, for no reason, looking about wildly.'[10]

Other symptoms of fear may be more particular to a species. A frightened mountain goat, biologist Douglas Chadwick reports, flattens its ears, flicks its tongue past its lips, crouches and raises its tail. According to Chadwick, a kid raises its tail when it wants attention or to nurse. The adult continues to raise its tail when fearful. If the tail is partially raised, Chadwick says, it means 'I'm worried'; a completely erect tail means 'I'm scared', or maybe 'Help, Momma!'[11]

Aviculturalist Wolfgang de Grahl notes that frightened young grey parrots in new surroundings may not only flutter wildly at the approach of humans but may hide their heads in a far corner. In de Grahl's view, these birds probably believe, like the ostriches who were once said to hide their heads in the sand, that they cannot be seen when they do so.[12] This may be an error produced by overestimating the stupidity of birds, however. Humans who cover their eyes or turn their faces away from scary sights do not believe they cannot be seen. Perhaps, like humans, the parrots cannot bear the sight of what frightens them, or are trying to keep their feelings from overwhelming them.

Because people have lived and worked with horses for so long, some of the things that frighten them are fairly well understood. In addition to such obvious dangers as predators, they may be alarmed by unfamiliar motions, noises and smells. Changes in their environment often frighten horses. Skittish horses even appear to be alarmed by imagined changes: an object that a horse has passed countless times may suddenly cause a horse to shy although there has been no alteration. What frightens one horse will leave another horse unmoved, and some horses seldom display fear. Horses may also be afraid to go to places that do not smell as if horses have been there. A horse that goes happily in horse-trailers will sometimes refuse to go in a brand new horse-trailer.

These descriptions encompass many of the things that frighten animals in general. Personal history also plays a part in the genesis of fear for a particular animal. A horse can learn to fear something that it did not fear before. This is expressed in common sense beliefs. For example, if you pick up a stick to toss for a dog to retrieve and instead it cringes in fear, your first reaction is likely to be that the dog has been beaten. Animals form associations with objects that have been frightening to them in the past, although it is not always clear what associative pathways are taken. Memories can be triggered by resemblances, or perhaps even by wandering thoughts. Terror can return in dreams. From a Kenyan 'elephant orphanage' comes a report of baby African elephants who have seen their families killed by poachers, and witnessed the tusks being cut off the bodies. These young animals wake up screaming in the night.[13]

The laboratory rats described above fear pain – they learn to fear receiving an electric shock. Similarly, a coyote learns to fear getting a face full of porcupine quills or a monkey learns that a long fall is painful.

Fighting is one of the ways in which animals frequently

get hurt, either vying with a conspecific (member of the same species), fending off a predator or even, for predators, struggling with a particularly combative prey. Young animals that play-fight with other young animals have an excellent opportunity to learn what hurts when fighting. Thus, in many (though by no means all) species of animals, fighting with conspecifics has become stylised. Animals threaten, posture, call and generally display their strengths in an attempt to frighten off the other animal without actually having to do battle. Or fighting may take place, but in a ritualised manner which tests strength without causing injury.

Logically enough, most animals fear predators. How they recognise them as predators if they have never seen them in action is not always clear, but the reaction itself is clear enough.

In the Rockies, Chadwick one day saw a lynx stalking a large mountain goat billy. It sneaked above the billy, to a position which seemed perfect for pouncing, but then hesitated. Then the goat spotted the lynx, and backed off into a corner. After a while the goat came forward, stamped his feet, and began leaping up in the direction of the cat, hooking towards it with his horns. The lynx watched for a while, now and then dangling a paw towards the goat, before finally walking off.[14]

Here it appears that the goat was frightened of the predatory lynx at first, but then lost its fear and became aggressive. The lynx was mildly frightened of the goat – enough not to attack immediately and eventually to give up.

One factor in the recognition of predators may be an innate response to staring eyes. Birds have been found to be more likely to mob a stuffed owl if it has eyes. Young chicks who have never seen a predator avoid objects with eyes or eye-spots on them, particularly if the eyes are large. Wild birds at a feeder table are much more apt to flee when a design is highlighted on the table if the design resembles eyes, and the more realistic the eyes, the greater their panic.[15]

Fear of falling off high things also appears to be innate in many different animals. Infants of many species (including humans) show terror when confronted with a steep drop, or the convincing image of a steep drop, even if they have never been dropped or seen a drop.

The fear of heights is probably less easily triggered in some

species than in others. A creature that lives in high places cannot survive if it spends too much time quaking with alarm. Yet
the mountain goats observed by Chadwick also showed signs of
fear when searching for a foothold on cliffs too precipitous even
for them, or when loose rock underfoot started to slide towards
a drop. It is important to be wary of explaining things too readily
as innate or instinctive, when they might just as easily be learned
by hard experience, or even somehow taught by other members
of the species.

A brown bear cub who fell into the McNeil River in Alaska
and was carried out into the rapids showed signs of fear – flattened
ears and wide and rolling eyes. His mother saw him fall in but did
not seem alarmed, only going after him after he had been carried a
considerable distance away. Perhaps she did not realise that what
was safe for her was not safe for him. Or perhaps she realised, or
felt, that he was in no real danger. The cub succeeded in getting
out on his own.

For social animals, or for the young of most species, loneliness holds fears. The fear of being alone is sometimes hard
to separate from the fear of being lost. Wingnut, a particularly
timid brown bear cub observed on the McNeil River, was said
by Thomas Bledsoe literally to be afraid of his own shadow. He
was afraid of being left alone, and would call 'hysterically' every
time his mother left to fish, continuing until she returned.[16] Again,
it may well be that an earlier experience lies behind this reaction. A
Pacific bottlenose porpoise, Keiki, who lived in a marine park,
was released into a bay nearby. Separated from his companions
into a location he did not know, Keiki was stricken with terror,
teeth chattering and eyes rolling.[17]

Zoo keepers report that captive elephants are subject to 'sudden-
death syndrome' or 'broken-heart syndrome', which happens
(most often with young elephants) when they are separated from
their social group or put in a new enclosure by themselves. Jack
Adams of the Center for the Study of Elephants ascribes this to
'gripping fear'.[18]

Like the horses afraid of unusual things, captive but untamed
grey parrots are suspicious of change in their surroundings.
Rather than eat from a new bowl, they will go hungry for
days. Even once they have learned to trust and accept food from
a particular individual, a change of clothing can create alarm. One

aviculturalist reported that a group of mistrustful parrots would accept peanuts only from his mother – and only when she wore her usual apron.[19] The term 'neophobia' has been coined for this fear of the unfamiliar.

Neophobia can produce odd reactions in an animal raised in unusual circumstances. The Indian conservationist Billy Arjan Singh raised an orphaned leopard cub and a tiger cub. In each case, the young cat was terrified by its first glimpses of the jungle and had to be patiently soothed, repeatedly taken for walks in the jungle and generally convinced that it was worth visiting.[20]

Cody, an orangutan raised from infancy by humans, was stricken with terror on first beholding another orangutan. The hair stood up all over his body. He recoiled in fear and hid behind his human 'parent', clinging so hard that he left marks. The placid orangutan who frightened him so much happened to be his own mother.[21]

Jim Crumley has described watching a flock of two hundred whooper swans resting in a field in Scotland. As he looked on, a wave of disturbance passed through the flock. Sleeping birds raised their heads and stood looking to the west, but then the flock settled down. The swans gradually relaxed, and then suddenly became agitated again: all heads shot up, and they called to each other in alarm. This happened three times before the perplexed Crumley understood what was worrying the swans. A thunderstorm was approaching, and the swans had heard it coming before he did. He watched them through the ensuing storm, and saw that the flashes of lightning brought no reaction, but that the claps of thunder terrified them again and again.[22]

Much fear is learned. This accords with classical behavioural conditioning theory, in which animals learn to associate negative stimuli with particular events. Elizabeth Marshall Thomas notes some of the specific fears of a husky, Koki, she acquired as an adult animal. The sound made by an object whizzing through the air, such as a rope or a stick, would cause Koki to cower, with chattering teeth and hair on end. According to Marshall Thomas, 'the sound of alcohol in a man's voice' had the same effect. It is possible that Koki was reacting to scent rather than sound, since alcohol affects the odour of human perspiration; but in any case, she had learned to be frightened of men who had been drinking.[23] It is hard to avoid thinking she had been hit by a drunken man.

Classical conditioning theory was shaken up when it was discovered that some stimuli are far more easily associated with fear than others. Rats readily associate food with illness, and will avoid a food if they have been ill after eating it. But they are very unlikely to associate an electric shock or a loud noise with illness, no matter how often experimenters pair the two stimuli. Many people are afraid of snakes or spiders who have never had a bad experience with them and who seldom see them. Yet, as Martin Seligman has pointed out, very few people have phobias about hammers or knives, although they are much more likely to have been injured by these.

Mountain goats have learned to fear avalanches or rock slides and to take evasive action. When goats hear the rumble of a slide overhead, they put their tails up and their ears back and run for a sheltering overhang, if one is nearby. If not, they stamp, crouch and press themselves against the mountain. Some goats take off at the last moment.[24]

Everyone has experienced fear without an apparent object, the sense that an unknown misfortune impends. At other times, the fear is in response to the sense that we are on unfamiliar ground, like Singh's tiger and leopard cubs. Something bad could happen, though we don't know what. Fear can exist without an object, a vertigo of the morale.

In Hwange National Park in Zimbabwe the elephants are culled (systematically killed) annually. During this process, elephant family groups are herded by aircraft towards hunters who shoot all except the young calves, who are rounded up for sale. The elephant calves run around, scream and search for their mothers. One year a wildlife guide at a private sanctuary near the park noticed that eighty elephants vanished from their usual haunts on the day culling started at Hwange, said to be ninety miles away. He found them several days later, bunched at the end of the sanctuary as far from the park as they were able to get.[25]

It has been discovered quite recently that elephants can and do communicate over long distances by means of subsonic calls – sounds pitched too low for people to hear. So it is not surprising that the sanctuary elephants apparently received some frightening message from the Hwange elephants. But unless elephant communication is far more refined than anyone has yet speculated, the message cannot have been very specific. The sanctuary elephants must have known that something very bad was happening to Hwange elephants, but they can hardly have known what it was. Their fear was inchoate, but real.

In a description of gerenuks (slender African antelopes) in a zoo, author Michael Ventura writes, 'they stood straight and almost unbearably alert in a group, each facing a slightly different way, such that the field of vision of the little herd covered all possible threat from any side. They were beings who could not feel safe, never felt safe, even here, where if you coughed their flanks would twitch, if a motor revved far off, they'd register it, so with all the children's cries at this busy day at the zoo – the gerenuk constantly blinked, flicked their ears, twitched their flanks, and gave sharp little kicks with their impossibly thin legs, tiny hooves stamping the ground as though about to flee. Clearly anything in the wild could hurt them. They lived by virtue of their alertness – an alertness, a sensitivity, excruciating to watch. How could they bear it? And here, in this enclosure, they were denied the only act that could satisfy their fear, the all-out running for which they were made, for which they longed.'[26] While there are elements here that may involve human projection – wild gerenuks frequently satisfy their fear by freezing, hiding behind bushes or by fleeing in a 'stealthy, crouched trot'[27] rather than by all-out running – the basic observation of timid, vigilant animals confined in a small space with nowhere to hide or flee is poignant.

Humans not only fear for themselves, but may fear for others. This feeling borders on empathy, something people are much less likely to concede to animals than fear. While examples of animals frightened for themselves can easily be found, examples of fear for others are scarcer. Most such evidence, as one might expect, is of parents frightened for their young.

Wildlife biologist Thomas Bledsoe describes the actions of Red Collar, a mother grizzly brown bear whose cubs vanished while she fished for salmon in the McNeil River, a gathering place for bears. First she looked up and down the riverbank, then ran to the top of the bluff and looked there, running faster and faster. She stood on her hind legs to see farther, jerking her head around, panting and drooling. After some minutes Red Collar gave up the search and went back to fishing. Here her behaviour is puzzling and susceptible to varying interpretations, ranging from loss of interest (which humans would find difficult to identify with) to belief that no disaster had befallen them. It is worth noting that on the occasions when Red Collar's cubs disappeared from the river, they had invariably gone off with one of the other mother bears and her family, and they were in fact safe. According to Bledsoe, at one point two of Red Collar's cubs were with another bear for three days before she encountered and reclaimed them.[28]

Parents not only fear losing their young but also fear that they will be injured. Another brown bear Bledsoe observed, Big Mama, was alarmed when her two curious yearling cubs chose to investigate human observers, going after them uttering alarm calls until they left the humans alone.[29] Lynn Rogers, who studies the smaller black bear, says that when faced by danger, mother bears not only urge cubs up trees but also discourage them from climbing smooth-barked trees such as aspens in favour of rougher-barked pines (which are easier for small cubs to climb).[30] Paul Leyhausen observed several mother cats who would allow their kittens to chase mice, but would interfere if the kittens went after rats. Tested away from their mothers, the kittens proved quite capable of tackling rats, in the view of the humans.[31]

Mountain goat nannies vigilantly try to prevent their kids from taking dangerous or fatal falls. According to Douglas Chadwick, nannies try to stay on the downhill side of their kids, both when the kids are moving about and when they sleep. Due to the energy and exuberance of the kids, the nannies watch them constantly. Chadwick notes of one mountain goat, 'I could hear her literally cry out when the baby took a hard spill, and she would rush over to lick and nuzzle it, and then encourage it to nurse.'[32]

A peregrine falcon father was seen to attack one of his sons every time the young falcon came too close to human observers. This changed the young bird's behaviour and he invariably avoided the observers afterwards.[33]

Social animals may fear for other members of the group. One experimenter decided to investigate the reaction of some young chimpanzees to 'a bold man' and 'a timid man'. The chimpanzee Lia avoided the 'bold man', but the chimpanzee Mimi fought him. One day the 'bold man' bent Mimi's finger back until she screamed. Lia joined the attack, but stopped when she got punched (such is the elegance of experimental research). After that, Lia devoted her efforts to trying to hold Mimi back, by grabbing her hands and pulling her away.[34] In a group of caged chimpanzees at Oklahoma's Institute for Primate Studies, a female chimpanzee with an infant, whose previous babies had been removed, became apprehensive when approached by scientists. So did the other chimpanzees in the group in nearby cages. In this case, however, it is not clear whether the other chimpanzees were actually fearful; they may have been merely hostile.[35]

Fear at its mildest – a readiness to fear – may be characterised as caution or alertness and has obvious survival value. The alert worm hears the early bird coming, and escapes. When this feeling intensifies it is called anxiety, a painful uneasiness of mind. Psychiatry has made a good living from the fact that some people seem to be incapacitated by the degree of anxiety they feel while others think it unnecessary or exaggerated.

Very great fear, like very great pain, can produce shock. The term shock has a medical definition, and there is no doubt that animals can experience it. Hans Kruuk describes what looks like shock in wildebeests cornered by hyenas. These animals scarcely try to defend themselves once they have been brought to a standstill. They will stand in one spot, moaning, and be torn apart by the hyenas.[36]

Pandora, a two-year-old mountain goat trapped at a salt lick by Douglas Chadwick and his wife, to be fitted with a radio collar, at first made spirited attempts to escape. She tried to jump out of the enclosure, hooked a horn at Chadwick, and when tackled and brought down, attempted to get up again. While being blindfolded, she went into shock, falling limp. Pandora had injured herself only slightly in this struggle, so it seems the reaction was the result of her intense fear. (After being collared, she was revived with smelling salts and released, showing no ill-effects.)[37]

In Africa a buffalo was knocked down, but not injured, by a lion and simply lay on the ground in a state of shock while the lion (perhaps an inexperienced animal) chewed on the buffalo's tail. Such an instance is another demonstration that fear does not always lead to survival.[38]

Bravery, sometimes considered an emotion, is related to fearfulness. Unfortunately, bravery or courage is so poorly defined in humans that it is difficult to look for it in animals. Often it is considered to involve the overriding or setting aside of fear. Is a dangerous act a brave one if you aren't fearful when you do it? Or is it only brave if you are fearful? To stand fast or to be aggressive though fearful would define human bravery in the eyes of some people – can that also define animal bravery?

Hans Kruuk reports several instances in which cow and calf wildebeests were pursued by hyenas. In each case, when the hyenas caught up with the calf, the mother turned and attacked the hyenas, butting them so fiercely as to bowl them over.[39] Perhaps this counts as bravery. Without a calf, a wildebeest cow keeps running. Surely, fear is what makes her run. On the other hand, a human in a parallel situation may declare, 'I was so angry I forgot to be scared'. Perhaps a mother wildebeest is so angry she forgets fear. Not everyone will call this bravery.

On a nature television programme about cheetahs, a lioness was filmed killing a litter of cheetah cubs. While she was still there, the mother cheetah returned. Seeing the lion, the cheetah circled, hesitated and then darted close to the lion until the lion pursued her. The cubs had already been killed, though the cheetah probably didn't know this.[40] The mother cheetah feared that the lion would kill her cubs and also feared being attacked by the (much larger) lion herself. Her attempt to draw the lion away seems to qualify as a brave act.

Elephant calves, like mountain goat kids or bear cubs, do not always fear what their elders think they should. Cynthia Moss, who studies elephants in Kenya, reports that very young calves appear largely fearless. They may come up to her Land Rover and examine it – while people are in it. This often alarms their mothers and aunts, producing visible conflict, Moss says. Apparently they would like to hustle the calves away but are too frightened to come close enough to do so. They stand very tall, and shuffle back and forth or swing one leg. When the calf eventually wanders back, the adults pull it to them, feel it, and make threatening gestures at the vehicle.[41]

By the time elephant calves are grown, they are likely to fear a number of things besides people in Land Rovers. In most creatures' lives objects of fear appear in due course. What about an animal that is protected and sheltered, so that it never encounters anything frightening? What happens to its capacity for fear?

It is possible that such a creature will feel fearful anyway, that its capacity to fear will demand expression, and that it will fasten that fear to an object that seems arbitrary.

Koko, a gorilla born in a zoo and raised by humans in a sheltered, loving environment, is an example of such an animal. Koko has never been exposed to big older gorillas, to leopards, to hunters, or to anything that might frighten her. Yet she has fears. For instance, she has shown fear of alligators, though she has never seen a real one. For years she behaved as if toy alligators were frightening – unless their lower jaws were missing. Though not frightened of her alligator puppet, she would play chasing games with it, and it is reported that she once threatened an aide (in American Sign Language) with being chased by an alligator if she didn't make lunch faster. She also appeared to be afraid of iguanas, specifically a pet iguana which she saw often. Although the iguana (described as 'comatose') never made threatening moves towards her, Koko would run into her own room if the iguana was brought out.[42]

Possibly Koko's fear of lizards and alligators is instinctive, or partly instinctive, but perhaps it is strengthened by the lack of anything else to fear. It may be that fear demands an object, and that no matter how secure and protected a child is, vampires, werewolves or fire engines will be conjured up to serve as that object. In later years, perhaps because she received gifts of dozens of toy alligators of various descriptions, Koko seemed to lose her fear of them.

The chimpanzee Viki, raised by humans, had a fear of tarpaulins so severe that she could be kept from entering forbidden rooms by hanging pieces of tarpaulin on the doorknobs. The famous Washoe, while unimpressed by tarpaulins, has been reported to fear dusters. Moja, another chimpanzee in the same group, was unmoved by dusters but found the dividers from ice-cube trays so alarming that researchers kept ice-cube dividers hidden in drawers and cupboards so that, if Moja became unruly, they could punish her by taking out a divider and exhibiting it.[43]

Washoe and the other chimpanzees in her group were also led to fear an imaginary 'bogeydog'. This grew from an effort to get the easy-going young Washoe to sign 'no' more often. One evening, researcher Roger Fouts looked through the window of Washoe's trailer, and signed to Washoe that he saw a big black dog with long teeth that ate baby chimpanzees. He then asked

Washoe if she wanted to go out and got a most emphatic 'no'. On other occasions, when Washoe was playing outside and did not want to go in, researchers would sign that they saw the big black dog coming – and Washoe would hasten inside.[44]

If fear is the feeling that something bad is imminent, then its converse may be hope, the feeling that something good is imminent. In humans hope, like fear, can be unreasoning and irrational or logical and conscious. One of the most endearing traits of pet animals is their (quite reasonable) hope of being fed, and their unsophisticated joy at the prospect. Dogs whirl around in anticipation, cats purr loudly and rub against objects, people or other animals.

When Washoe grew older, she had a baby, who died four hours after birth because of a defective heart. Three years later she had a second baby, Sequoyah. Sequoyah was sickly, and despite excellent care from Washoe, died of pneumonia at the age of two months. Determined that Washoe should raise a baby, researchers made frantic efforts to find a replacement, and eventually procured Loulis, a ten-month-old chimpanzee. Fifteen days after Sequoyah's death, Fouts went to Washoe's enclosure and signed 'I have baby for you'. Every hair on Washoe's body stood on end. She displayed signs of great excitement, hooting, swaggering bipedally and signing 'baby' repeatedly. 'Then when she signed "My baby", I knew we were in trouble,' Fouts said.

When Fouts returned with Loulis, Washoe's excitement vanished instantly. Her hair flattened and she declined to pick Loulis up, impassively signing 'baby'. But after an hour had passed, Washoe began approaching Loulis, trying to play with him. That evening, she tried to get him to sleep in her arms, as Sequoyah had done. At first she was unsuccessful, but by the next morning, they were clasped together, and from that time Washoe has been a devoted mother to Loulis, who eventually acquired a vocabulary of fifty signs from Washoe and the other chimpanzees in the group.[45] It seems clear that when told she would get a baby, Washoe hoped to see Sequoyah again.

Ludwig Wittgenstein believed that animals may feel frightened but not hopeful. He wrote, in the 1940s, that 'One can imagine an animal angry, frightened, unhappy, happy, startled. But hopeful? . . . A dog believes his master is at the door. But can he also believe his master will come the day-after-tomorrow?'[46]

Wittgenstein argues that only those who have mastered the use of language can hope. Not only does this statement remain unproven to this day, but there seems no good reason to doubt that an animal can imagine or even possibly dream about happiness in the future. Animals may lack the language of hope, but the feelings that underlie it are probably shared by humans and animals alike.

CHAPTER FOUR

Rage, Dominance and Cruelty in Peace and War

ALTHOUGH humans are moved by anger and hostility with undeniable regularity, they generally wish to control or at least disguise these emotions. Yet people often are eager to point out aggression among animals, identifying it as 'animal', 'brutal' or 'savage'.

Animals do seem to become angry, commit aggressive acts against each other, fight for turf and hurt and kill one another. They may not, however, do this in exactly the ways people expect – something which can be difficult for observers to recognise.

A giraffe researcher reports that in the fifteenth century, when they were known in Europe as cameleopards, Cosimo de Medici shut a giraffe in a pen with lions, bloodhounds and fighting bulls to see which species was the most savage. As Pope Pius II looked on, the lions and dogs napped, the bulls quietly chewed their cuds, and the giraffe huddled against the fence, shaking with fear.[1] Although these European leaders were surely disappointed at the absence of carnage, all these animals can indeed be fierce in other circumstances.

Scientists too may find their expectations about animal aggression confounded at times. Ethologists seeking to chart dominance hierarchies in groups of wild animals occasionally become frustrated when they cannot tell whether one animal is dominant to another. Their conclusion is often that with a little luck or more work the observer will discover the true rank of the animals, and not that a hierarchy might not accurately describe their situation. It is as if they hope that the relations between animals gathered at a waterhole can be as neatly quantified as those of academics gathered before a granting agency.[2]

Some people maintain the hope that animals – and if not all animals, then the members of some particularly cherished species – do not display aggression except in self-defence, and that in the society of wolves, or the company of dolphins, or the murmuring of doves there is only harmony. If the lion does not lie down with the lamb, perhaps the lambs at least lie down together?

On the evidence, lambs may lie down together and then rise to butt heads. Doves, dolphins and wolves can treat each other very roughly. This is not to say that all their social life is marked by conflict, only that the hope for some saintly species to become our guru of peace, love and benevolence is unlikely to be fulfilled. Perhaps it is an unreasonable expectation to begin with, whether among animals or humans.

Aggression spans a range from attack to self-defence. When an animal pushes another away from food or refuses to be pushed, growls at another animal that comes near its young, chases away a potential rival, or perhaps even when it marks a territory, it is behaving aggressively. From the viewpoint of survival, such behaviour often has advantages. The aggressive animal gets more to eat, keeps its offspring safe, has a better chance to mate, faces less competition for food or has a larger area in which to raise a family, all of which may enable it to leave more descendants. Anger and other emotions related to aggression may produce such behaviour.

When humans take a critical view of violence in the animal world, the forms they are most apt to forgive are those of

73

self-defence and defence of young. A wolf attacking a deer may be called ferocious, savage and ravening, and the deer's defence may be called brave, heroic and noble. Protection of young is even more esteemed. The tigress or the bear defending her cubs is an archetype of justifiable rage. Animals like the red kangaroo, who may toss the larger of her joeys out of her pouch if she is too closely pursued, are viewed with great disfavour. Such an incident is no one's favourite animal story.

Animal behaviourists typically distinguish between offensive and defensive behaviours, and identify different mixtures of the two. The distinction seems to be real, yet typically the behaviours are not found in pure form. Paul Leyhausen, studying the behaviour of both domestic and wild cats, found it very difficult to get a cat to display purely offensive behaviour unmingled with defensiveness, noting that many people very familiar with cats had never seen this. Eventually, however, he felt that he had succeeded.

For his aggressor, Leyhausen selected a particularly large tomcat, M7, who regularly killed other cats, and who had been trapped and donated to science at the request of his human neighbours. For the unintimidating (but not submissive) victim, the experimenter used a small stuffed cat. M7's expressions, body language and gesture, Leyhausen said, spoke purely of attack. By drawing himself, he made himself look taller, but he didn't arch his back defensively. He bent his tail stiffly down. He pointed his ears outwards, but didn't flatten them as a fearful cat would. He stretched his neck forward, and, howling loudly, advanced on stiff legs towards the stuffed cat. He sprang, biting the dummy on the nape of the neck and kicking it with his hind legs. The dummy went flying and fell to the ground, and M7 stopped his attack, inhibited by the posture. He ignored the dummy unless Leyhausen stood it upright again, upon which the tomcat would resume the attack.[3]

Clearly this epic battle represents something uncommon in nature, an attack upon an unthreatening victim which does not defend itself, try to get away or submit. In many animals there are postures of surrender which usually inhibit the attacker of the same species. Lying down is such a posture in cats, which is why M7 didn't destroy the dummy after it toppled over. What does an aggressor feel when an attack is checked in this way?

Aggression is employed by many animals to obtain access to resources. Food is one such resource, and a principal delight of researchers on the African savannahs is keeping track of which hyenas killed a wildebeest, which lions stole the carcass from them (or vice versa) and which jackals and vultures managed to snatch a bite before being driven off.

Such interspecies competition makes for dramatic spectacle. Most animals do not usually clash in this way. The wildebeest being struggled over did not, in life, stage bloody battles with other wildebeest over which of them was going to eat that blade of grass. But wildebeest are aggressive towards one another in other contexts. Males, even when handicapped by the need to accompany the herd on its migrations, manage to establish temporary territories which they defend from one another.

When two animals or groups of animals are both trying to use the same resource, and it is in short supply, the result is competition. Competing requires a lot of energy, and many species appear to minimise competition. For many animals the creature that is likely to be its closest competitor, to want the same foods or the same nest sites, is another of its own species, and if it is an animal that forms pairs, the one it will compete with most often may be its own mate. For this reason, it has been suggested that in some species there may be an advantage if the males and females are of different sizes. A female osprey is larger than her mate: this means that they catch fish of different sizes, and this takes them out of competition with each other, so increasing the supply of food jointly available to them.

One important way in which some animals minimise the wear and tear of competition is to establish and patrol territories. Thus a pair of birds may have a territory which they defend against other birds of their own species (or, rarely, against birds of other species), ensuring that they will not face competition for food in that territory.

The concept of territory reminds people irresistibly of human ideas about their property. As a result we occasionally misinterpret the ways animals themselves view their territories. The term of 'territoriality' is not yet a precise one. Much remains to be learned and we may need a more subtle concept. Leopards are considered solitary animals, and it was long said that they maintained exclusive territories which they would defend against other leopards.

Later research indicated that leopard territories overlap, and that the term 'home range' may be more accurate.[4]

Territorial species of animals avoid fighting over their territories by advertising their presence, marking it by scent, clawing trees, howling or singing. Conspecifics often react by avoiding the area: researchers tracking pumas found that when a cat suddenly doubled back and went the way it had come, there invariably proved to be other pumas in the area, which it had apparently scented.[5] Tigers advertise their presence to other tigers by various means, including the calls that frighten other species. In this way, they can avoid each other, rather than meeting unexpectedly and perhaps having to fight.[6] Maybe their mutual fear tempers their mutual hostility.

Aggressiveness may also keep animals from gathering too densely and using up resources. Douglas Chadwick, who studied mountain goats in the Rockies, argues that if goats cluster in large groups, they will quickly overgraze. Their irritability, which is so great that they may kill each other if confined in close proximity, keeps flock size down. If mountain goats were more tolerant of one another, they might not get enough to eat.[7]

Tame parrots often take a strong dislike to individual humans or to classes of humans, often a whole gender. Many veterinarians are weary of hearing clients say, 'He hates all men. He must have been abused by a man in the past.' Parrots have been known to conceive hatreds of all redheads, all brunettes or all adults.[8] While it is inevitable of wild-caught parrots that they would all have been abused in the past due to the cruelty involved in their capture and transport, this is unlikely for all parrots born in captivity. But it remains unknown whether these kinds of eccentric dislikes are found in the wild.

Perhaps these parrots simply enjoy having enemies. This may promote flock solidarity, prevent interbreeding between different species, strengthen the pair bond or have some other valuable function.

Another possibility is that the quarrelsome nature of some parrots is connected with dominance struggles in the flock. Dominance hierarchies, real and imagined, have been the subject of much ethological research since the announcement in the 1920s that 'pecking orders' had been discovered in chickens. In recent years they have also been the subject of much controversy, as some scientists ask whether they describe anything real. 'Part of the problem with dominance in the past has been that people have tended to see it everywhere,' biologist N.R. Chalmers has noted.[9] It has also been pointed out that chickens in wild flocks do not exhibit rigid pecking orders as they do in poultry yards.

Some scientists argue that dominance relationships between two animals are real, but that dominance ranks assigned to individuals (as in 'the second-ranking male in the troop') are not, that they 'may reflect our own ability to count rather than any important variable in social organisations'.[10] Others point out that an animal may dominate another in one situation – competing for access to food – but not in another – competing for access to water. A cat may dominate a second cat near the first cat's den, but not further away. Still others point out that while dominance may be important in the relationship between two adult males of a particular species, it may not be a useful or realistic way to describe the relationship between an adult female and her adolescent daughter.

Thelma Rowell, working with baboons, has suggested that rank relationships may be better characterised as subordinance rather than dominance relationships, since it is the giving way by one animal that constitutes a decision not to fight. In her formulation a dominance rank does not express the social character of a baboon, but is what is 'left over' after his degree of subordination is accounted for.[11]

A serious blow to theories about dominance has been the discovery that a major assumption about its reproductive value can be false. It has been widely presumed and stated that dominant males in groups of social animals are able to mate with females more often and produce more offspring. Recent studies show that this is not necessarily the case.[12] In the hamadryas baboon, for example, female preference for a male may prove more significant to his reproductive success than his dominance status.[13] Shirley Strum found that the more high ranking and aggressive a male olive baboon was, the less likely females were to mate with him. Such aggressive males also had less luck getting favoured foods, apparently because they had fewer friends.[14] Leyhausen noted long ago that when domestic tomcats fight over a female in heat, the female is no more likely to mate with the winner than with the loser.[15]

In many species, an animal courting another tries to seem anything but dominant in order to avoid frightening the other. A courting male mountain goat lowers his back in a bid to look small, keeps his head back so his horns don't threaten and takes small steps. A male brown bear slouches, flattens his ears, takes care not to stare at the female and behaves more playfully than usual.

It has also been argued that one of the factors that dominance analysis fails to recognise is that of 'authority'. It is possible that some social animals who do not fit the usual definitions of dominant animals (other animals let them eat first, make submissive gestures towards them) still, by virtue of age or knowledge of the local terrain, are able to lead others.

In cases where dominance relationships have been observed, it is often unclear what makes one animal dominant over another. Some factors include size, knowledge, strength, age, ferocity, family background and perhaps even wisdom. Among some social animals status appears to be partially inherited from the mother.

One biologist, observing bears, defined a bear as dominant over another if the other 'deferred' in any way when it approached. While a bear that usually deferred to another at a fishing spot might not defer if it was particularly hungry, a rank order was produced by evaluating each bear's 'win–loss record' over the season. Despite this definition, when a previously deferential bear, Reggie, after the birth of her cubs attacked the largest male bear on the river and drove him away from a fishing spot, the experimenter ascribed this to 'tolerance' on the part of the male, not to lack of dominance.[16] This may indicate that human ideas about dominance in animals are more strongly influenced than we realise by our ideas about human behaviour, even when we think we are being rigidly scientific. In situations like these Frans de Waal distinguishes between 'real' dominance, 'formal' dominance and a third, unnamed form of dominance described in terms of generosity, respect and tolerance.[17]

The notion of observing a group of animals engaged in mysterious interactions and extracting a tidy hierarchy which generates testable predictions has great appeal for scientists. Sometimes the idea that hierarchies are inevitable and prove certain things about humans is also part of the appeal. Theorists may pay more attention to species with a high level of aggressive interaction than to more pacific ones, and more attention to species in which males tend to dominate females than to species in which females dominate males, as in the lemurs.[18] Human interest in dominance is so great that this seems to be a particularly fertile area for anthropomorphic error. Recreational hunters often seek out the biggest males as trophy animals. These are not usually the tastiest animals, or the easiest to find. People who do this are targeting what is likely to be identified as the dominant or alpha male, perhaps asserting dominance over them.[19]

Increasingly, the attempts of careful observers to fit theories of dominance to the actual behaviour of animals seems to require the use of such anthropomorphic terms as influence, power, respect, authority, tolerance, deference to age, prestige and leadership.

Yet the notion of dominance can describe real phenomena in animals as well as people. In a herd of scimitar-horned oryx living in a wildlife preserve in the Negev desert, a male called Napoleon had grown old and short of breath and had lost his former status. Rather than leave for a solitary life, like many old male oryx, he continued to challenge other males and pursue females. His challenges were ignored, but when he pursued females the other males would attack him, goring him seriously with their yard-long horns.[20]

To protect Napoleon, the preserve managers captured him, treated his wounds and put him in protective custody – a five-acre paddock with other hoofed animals (not oryx) for companionship. He escaped the next day, only to be injured again by the other oryx. He was recaptured and treated – and soon escaped again. After he had made eight escapes from the paddock, now festooned with bolts and other security devices, the preserve managers took a different approach. Since Napoleon could not be forcibly contained, they determined to remove his reason for escaping by giving him what he wanted in the paddock. Their conclusion, interestingly, was that what he wanted was not to attack other males, nor to be with females, but to be dominant. Every morning the preserve director – not someone Napoleon was pleased with, after all his captures – would enter the paddock with a bamboo pole. They would have a brief ritual battle in which the director clattered the pole on Napoleon's horns and Napoleon threatened and charged at the director until the director allowed Napoleon to drive him out of the paddock, thereby winning the battle. Napoleon stopped trying to escape and lived in the paddock until he died of old age the following year, still the top oryx of his enclosure, and apparently quite content.

Had Napoleon not been in a preserve, he would surely have been killed by a predator before reaching such an advanced age. The fact of his captivity provided the chance for him to exhibit his tremendous urge to achieve status, or as de Waal would call it if Napoleon were a chimpanzee, his ambition.[21] It is worth asking how an animal feels when it loses status. Do animals get depressed, do they adapt, or is it ever a relief?

It should be noted that dominance may be more important to some captive animals, who need to spend less time foraging for food and may lack other outlets for their energies, than it is for their wild cousins. Usually they are also forced into closer contact than they would be in the wild. To the extent that dominance relationships exist, they can be looked at as a way of reducing net aggression. If an animal knows which other animals in its group can eat before it and which must wait until after it, it reduces any need to compete over food. Whether hierarchies actually do reduce net aggression in this manner is unclear, however. Also, we do not know what emotions are connected with it.

Another form of aggression is rape and this has been observed in some animals. Biologists have observed cases of forcible rape in orangutans, dolphins, seals, bighorn sheep, wild horses and some birds. An attempted rape was observed in coatimundis, but the attacker was driven away by a group of females.[22] In none of these species does rape appear to be the norm. Nevertheless, in several it occurs regularly.

White-fronted bee-eaters (tunnel-nesting African birds) form mated pairs. But female bee-eaters leaving the nest must dodge males who pursue them and try to force them to the ground and rape them. The males preferentially attack females who are laying eggs and thus might lay an egg fertilised by the rapist, rather than by the mate.[23]

Among waterfowl, such as mallards, pintail, and teal, an unwilling female is occasionally pursued by one or more males other than her mate, and this can result in her death by drowning.[24] She will fight back and attempt to escape, and her mate will try to drive off the aggressors, but their efforts at defence do not always succeed.

The male of a pair of mallards will sometimes attempt to mate with the female immediately after a rape attempt by another male. These mating attempts may not be preceded by the usual displays of males in mated pairs. In most such cases 'the female visibly struggled, but in no case did she flee'.[25] The sociobiological explanation for such marital rapes is that it gives the mated male's sperm a better chance of competing with the rapist's sperm. It sheds no light on how the birds feel. Such behaviour does not provide any evidence whatsoever that human rape is 'natural', biologically determined or reproductively advantageous.

At one marine park, where newly captured dolphins would be given a companion who was accustomed to captivity, bottlenose dolphins could not be used as companions because they would torment and sometimes rape the newcomer, if it was of another species.[26] In the wild, bottlenoses, despite their saintly popular image, have been seen to form male gangs to sequester and rape females of their own species.[27]

Hans Kruuk witnessed a male spotted hyena attempting to mate with a female, who drove him off each time. Her ten-month-old cub was nearby, and the male hyena repeatedly mounted it and ejaculated on it. According to Kruuk, the cub sometimes ignored this and sometimes struggled 'slightly as if in play'. The mother did not intervene.[28]

One of the gravest charges against the human race is that of making war. At times, it has been humbling to reflect that animals do not make war. Yet some animals do go to war. The wars of ants are the best known, but insects are sufficiently dissimilar to us that people seldom take that to heart. In recent years it has become clear that animals as closely related to us as chimpanzees can go to war. The famous chimps of Gombe attack other bands with no provocation, and with deadly intent. They may kill and eat one another.

When a group of chimpanzees from Gombe's Kasakela group found a strange female and her infant in a tree they barked threateningly. After a few blows had been directed at her, there was a pause, during which some of the chimpanzees fed in the same tree. She approached one of the males submissively and touched him but he made no response. When she tried to leave several of the males blocked her way. She approached another male, Satan, submissively and again touched him. His response was to pick some leaves and use them to scrub the spot she had touched. Immediately several chimpanzees attacked her and grabbed her infant. For eight minutes she fought for her unsuccessfully, and finally escaped, badly injured. One of the Kasakela apes smashed the infant against trees and rocks and then tossed her down. She was not dead and Satan picked her up gently, groomed her and put her down. Over the next few hours, three different males, including Satan, carried the infant tenderly, supporting and grooming her, before she was abandoned to die of her wounds.[29] It is hard to know what to make of this strange story. Is it possible to attribute the feeling of regret to these chimpanzees?

In other encounters between bands, infants have been killed and eaten, but this incident shows the mixed feelings of the chimpanzees. Satan's xenophobia in trying to scour away the contaminating touch of the strange female is also noteworthy.

Bands of dwarf mongooses also join battle, apparently over territory. In these battles many mongooses are injured, and some even die. One such battle began with the appearance in one group's territory of another group. Each band gathered, twittered, groomed and marked each other with scent. Then the resident group advanced as a body, and was met by the other group. The two 'armies' advanced and retreated and then suddenly began sinking their teeth into one another. At one point both bands retreated as if in truce, then moved together to fight again. Eventually the invading band withdrew. None of the resident mongooses was killed in battle, though toes had been bitten off, ears chewed to stumps, a tail broken. One was injured so badly that she could no longer feed herself and died later. In their next battle (with a larger band) this same group lost.[30]

These mass battles seem to be over territory. One group invades another's territory and battle is joined. Hans Kruuk observed territorial battle between groups of spotted hyenas, which occurred when members of one clan killed a prey animal in the other clan's range. Such quarrels were usually won by the resident clan, after a lot of noise, threats and chasing, but on other occasions the conflict escalated, and hyenas were injured or killed. On one occasion, to Kruuk's horror, a hyena whose clan had killed a wildebeest on another clan's range was fatally injured. His attackers bit off his ears, feet and testicles, and left him bleeding, paralysed and partly eaten.[31]

In discussing aggression, animal behaviourists typically distinguish between attacks on conspecifics and predatory attacks, arguing that an animal attacking another animal it wants to eat is manifesting a motivation associated with hunger, rather than true aggression. While cases like that of the hyena mentioned above seem to have aspects of both kinds of attack, this may be a valid distinction.

In all these examinations of aggression, territoriality and dominance, nothing is said about anger or other emotions that might inhabit such behaviour. Unfortunately it is very difficult to tell when anger is or is not involved in aggression. Aggressive behaviour in humans is sometimes coolly calculated: whatever motivates it does not seem to be the same thing that makes people shout and fume. There is some belief that penguins may push one of their number into the water before they all go in, to see whether leopard seals are waiting there to eat them.[32] If this proves true, it would seem unlikely that penguins commit such aggressive acts out of anger.

Some instances of animal behaviour do resonate with human experience of anger and irritation, and perhaps are easier to understand in this way because they do not constitute stereotypical reactions. Giraffes seem to dislike cars. When a car honked at a giraffe standing in the road, the giraffe knocked the car over and kicked it vigorously. Another driver encountered two giraffe crossing a road at night, stopped and dimmed the headlights. One giraffe got off the road but the other walked over, turned its back and delivered a series of two-footed kicks to the radiator.[33] To any pedestrian who has ever been annoyed by a honking vehicle, this is the very picture of an irritated individual's behaviour, if not a fantasy of fulfilling a wish.

Karen Pryor notes that if you are teaching either people or porpoises to do a task and then stop rewarding them for it, they both seem irritated: the humans will grumble and look sour and the porpoises will jump out of the water and splash you from head to toe.[34]

Pryor also describes Ola, a young false killer whale, reacting to a bird called a booby. One day, during a show at the oceanarium, a booby landed next to Ola's tank. Ola stuck his head out of the water and looked at the booby. When the booby didn't move, Ola leapt up at it with gaping jaws. The booby still didn't move. By this time most of the audience was ignoring the show and watching Ola and the bird. Ola hurtled around the tank, raising big waves which splashed over the booby's feet. Still the booby didn't move. Ola submerged, took a mouthful of water, came up and squirted it directly on to the booby. The bird took flight, shaking water off its feathers, and the audience burst out laughing.[35] Such laughter contains an element of recognition. What did they recognise? Irritation, frustration or a biologically meaningless wish to dominate a bird?

One of the colleagues of the famous Ivan Pavlov was trying to discover how precisely a dog could distinguish between a circle and an ellipse. Food rewards were given along with the circle but not with the ellipse. Each time the experimenter found (apparently by observing the flow of the dog's saliva) that the dog could tell the shapes apart, new tests would begin, with a rounder ellipse. After three weeks the dog got not better, but worse at making the distinction. 'The hitherto quiet dog began to squeal in its stand, kept wriggling about, tore off with its teeth the apparatus for mechanical stimulation of the skin, and bit through the tubes connecting the animal's room with the observer, a behaviour which had never happened before. On being taken into the experimental room the dog now barked violently, which was also contrary to its usual custom; in short it presented all the symptoms of a condition of acute neurosis.'[36] This is the picture of an angry dog, not a neurotic one.

These animals present a much more recognisable picture of anger than does an elk bugling at another elk or a baboon taking food before another baboon. Difficult as it is to untangle anger and aggression in people, it is not surprising that it is also hard to do in the animal world. This difficulty is compounded with predatory animals, whose way of getting food is more direct than anything most people experience.

This brings up an issue associated with predation, the alleged cruelty of the predator. Nature is frequently charged with being cruel and the animals who form a part of the natural world are also liable to this accusation. It has been used to justify hunting certain species almost out of existence. The wolf and the tiger are charged with cruelty, as are lesser predators like the fox and the blue jay.

Viewed with especial horror are cases where predators begin eating their prey while it is still alive and cases where predators kill more than they can eat. Literature arguing against the protection of wolves, for example, is full of accounts of deer 'literally eaten alive' by wolves.[37] The whistling dog (Kipling's dhole) of India, because of its short canines, seldom kills its prey quickly, and is persecuted because it is accordingly perceived as treacherous and vicious.[38]

It is common for some predators to begin eating their prey before it is dead and it is routine for them to kill and eat baby animals before their mothers' eyes. Is this cruel? It is certainly uncaring, unempathic. In certain places and times the eating of certain live animals has been considered a delicacy by humans. However, the question is not whether humans can act cruelly – we know that we can. The question is whether animals can be cruel.

If animals are to be excused for cruel acts like eating the baby in front of the anguished mother, on the grounds that they simply cannot understand the feelings of the other, then they can also be acquitted of torture. To torture another requires understanding the feelings of another. But can we then believe that they are ever kind, compassionate or empathic, which also requires understanding the feelings of another?

Cruelty spans a continuum from mere lack of empathy to deliberate pleasure in the sufferings of others. This last is also called torture. Animals commit cruel acts. But are they cruel? Do they torment and torture? Do they like to make others suffer? (Those extremists who deny that animals can suffer must also deny that animals can be cruel, since it is not possible to delight in non-existent suffering.) A familiar instance of an animal torturing another is the cat with the mouse. On countless occasions a well-fed cat may be seen to catch a mouse which it doesn't eat. It may not kill the mouse at once. It may, instead, toss the mouse in the air, allow it to run off and almost escape – and then pounce on it again. It may hold the struggling creature down with a paw, and view its desperate attempts to escape with an expression that certainly looks like one of pleasure. A leopard has been seen to play with captured jackals in the same way.[39]

The experiments of Paul Leyhausen and others with domestic and captive wild cats show that a cat will go on chasing, catching and killing mice long after it has ceased to be hungry. Eventually it may stop killing them but will go on chasing and catching them. Then it may stop catching them, but will still stalk them. After a great while, it may give up on mice altogether (for the time being).[40] But the stage during which the cat is chasing and catching without killing and eating looks just like torture.

Note the significance of this in terms of what the cat likes best: it likes most of all to chase, then to catch, next to kill and least of all to eat. This hierarchy of appetites corresponds well to what a successful hunter needs. A predator may have to chase many animals before it catches one, is not able to kill all that it catches (some prey get away) and may have to catch more than it can eat (as when it is providing for the young). It has been estimated that a tiger catches prey once in twenty tries.[41] Many kittens practise their predatory skills with prey their mother catches but does not immediately kill. A lioness has been seen holding a live warthog in her paws while cubs looked on with fascination,[42] and cheetah have been seen bringing live gazelles to their cubs.

Does the cat who is sated with killing mice take pleasure in their suffering? How can this be tested? Consider prey that doesn't suffer. A cat can hardly take pleasure in the suffering of a ball of yarn or a wad of paper. A cat is attracted to certain attributes of prey – a scamper, an uneven gait. Mice usually manifest these attributes better than balls of yarn or wads of paper. But if a wad of paper could squeak and scamper as well, it might be just as attractive to the cat. Some cats have been seen to play with paper balls while mice run around underfoot.[43]

In addition to the movement of prey, cats are often fascinated by the idea of prey in hiding. Leyhausen reports that a captive serval (a tall, lynx-like African cat), when no longer hungry, will catch a mouse, carry it delicately over to a hole or crevice and release it. If the mouse doesn't take advantage of the chance to hide, the serval will actually push it into the hole with its forepaw – and then try to fish it out again. This can't be good for the nerves of the mouse, but servals also play the same game with pieces of bark.

Alternatively one may ask whether cats take pleasure in the suffering of prey if it does not involve flight behaviour. Would a cat enjoy seeing a mouse beaten or stretched on a rack? It seems unlikely – mice in traps are of only fleeting interest to cats. (If any person were to suggest actually doing such experiments, one would instantly have more data about cruelty in humans.) Let us assume that the answer is no. A cat quickly loses interest in a mouse who is too badly injured to scamper away. Perhaps the cat bats it with a paw to see if it can be induced to run again, but when it doesn't the cat is bored. The mouse may be visibly suffering, gasping and bleeding, but if it is not trying to escape, a well-fed cat is not interested.

Whence comes that glee that seemed to flash over the cat's face? The cat loves to hunt, to catch, to triumph. Many predators do. They may be said to enjoy killing their prey. They are uninterested in and unaware of how their prey feels. Catching prey is part of their work, and they enjoy being successful.

The issue of surplus killing brings this into sharper focus. Surplus killing is a phenomenon that has enraged shepherds and poultry keepers ever since people began husbanding animals. A weasel gets into a hen house and kills all the chickens there, more than it can possibly eat; or a fox jumps a fence and kills a whole flock of geese, making off with only one.

It happens in the wild, too. Orcas attack a school of fish and tear from one to another, leaving bodies floating. Bears, confronted by a river full of salmon, become more and more selective about which parts of the fish they eat, until, at times, they simply stand as if in a trance, catching and releasing salmon without even killing them.[44] Hyenas invade a flock of gazelles at night and kill dozens, far more than the pack can eat.[45]

Such surplus-killers are charged with cruelty, evil and wastefulness. The fact that predators may kill more than they need to eat is used to justify killing predators – which humans do not need to eat either.[46]

At the same time, it has been pointed out that predators which surplus-kill are very often animals that store food to eat later. Foxes and weasels cache food. Both wild and captive hyenas, interestingly, have been seen to store meat in shallow water, which keeps it from rotting as quickly as it would in air.[47]

A predator that stores food may have the capacity to surplus-kill because sometimes it is able to cache the excess. And it may still surplus-kill on occasions when it will be unable to store the excess, like the fox that kills a flock of geese when it can only carry off one. It has also been noted that when hyenas surplus-kill, other members of their pack, including pups, often eat some of the surplus carcasses.[48]

Orcas that dispatch many fish in a frenzy succeed in eating more than they would if they ate each fish as soon as they killed it, while the rest of the school escaped. They may not estimate closely how many fish will be eaten by the members of the pod, and so may kill extra fish. Or they may kill something large and eat only part. It is not clear that orcas are physically able to detach all of the flesh from a whale. It has been argued that they eat what they can.[49]

At the same time these are no more than arguments concerning survival value in surplus-killing. On the emotional side, the question is whether some creatures *enjoy* the surplus-killing. Probably some do enjoy the act of killing, not because they are killing more than they need, but because they are displaying their abilities to the fullest, exercising their capacities. This is *funktionslust*, delighting in one's powers. Scientist David Macdonald, author of *Running with the Fox*, says this: 'I have watched foxes surplus-killing. Certainly their postures and expressions were neither aggressive nor frantic. If anything they looked playful, or perhaps merely purposeful.'

A person eating a hamburger is not thought to be gloating over the suffering of cows. Hunters enjoy their marksmanship, their ability to find their prey. They may enjoy killing the pheasant or the deer, but most hunters would claim that they do not enjoy the suffering of the pheasant or the deer.

Is this a case of claiming nice emotions for animals and not nasty ones? Does it seem likely that animals can be kind but never cruel? Are we, as a species, alone in our capacity for cruelty?

If predators are not seen to torture and delight in the suffering of their prey, they might still enjoy the suffering of one another. It would not be straying from a known pattern to hypothesise that the target of real cruelty might be a creature's very nearest – its family or the members of its group. Rather than ask whether cats are cruel to mice, it can be asked whether they are cruel to other cats. Do foxes ever take pleasure in being cruel to foxes, hyenas to hyenas? Little evidence is available that addresses this issue. Certainly hyenas and foxes act cruelly to conspecifics at times. Even when young, littermates have been seen to attack and even kill each other. Chicks of the great egret may push their siblings out of the nest. It is easy to argue that there is an ultimate evolutionary benefit to the killer, but harder to guess the proximal cause, the emotional state of the killer.

Perhaps such animals feel hatred. The word hatred does not seem to describe the relationship between predators and prey. From an evolutionary standpoint, rabbits would gain no advantage by hating owls, and they do not appear to do so. Nor do owls appear to hate rabbits. However, something like hatred does seem to exist, evidently reserved for competitors of the same or other species.

As an example, the interaction between lions and hyenas seems to be at times deeply hostile. Even when they are not fighting over a kill, they watch one another, and will attack a weakened or isolated animal of the other species. George Schaller notes that a lion chasing a hyena, cheetah or leopard does not wear the impassive face of a lion hunting. Instead it bares its teeth and utters the calls it would employ against another lion.[50] Lions and hyenas eat the same prey and steal one another's kills: they are competitors.

Animals may also hate rivals of their own species. No one is better equipped to compete with an animal than a member of its own species – their need for food, mates and space may be identical. Other wolves might not only oust a wolf from her place in the hierarchy of a pack, but might viciously attack her, drive her away, treat her cruelly or even kill her.

Congo, a chimpanzee raised by humans from an early age, became deeply unhappy when he was moved to a zoo enclosure. It was hoped that the company of female chimpanzees would please him, but he hated them and rejected their friendly attentions. He began soliciting lighted cigarettes from zoo visitors and with these he would chase the other apes around the enclosure, trying to burn them. His spirits continued to decline and he eventually stopped tormenting the female chimpanzees. In a short time he died.[51]

Scapegoating, the identification of one animal as a target for aggression, can be observed in some social animals. This is especially noticeable where captive animals are confined in close quarters. Leyhausen experimented with confining many cats in small enclosures to see what relationships would form. In one, called the 'community of twelve', two cats became pariahs for no apparent reason. If they ventured down from a retreat on a pipe near the ceiling, the other cats attacked them. They dared not even come down for food unless Leyhausen stood guard. It is important not to succumb to the idea that such situations are inevitable, since Leyhausen found that in other such 'communities' no pariahs or top cats emerged at all.[52] In the wild, an animal in such a position could leave, either to live a solitary life or to seek another group.

Yet what drives wild animals away from their group sometimes looks like cruelty. I believe that to answer the question of cruelty in animals, we will have to look harder at how they treat members of their own kind and not at how they feed themselves.

One source of aggression in social animals is jealousy, which often produces anger in humans. The evolutionary approach encounters no difficulty in attributing a value to jealousy. Between siblings it can ensure the individual's access to food and parental care. Between mates it can ensure that one's offspring receive care.

In humans, jealousy is an emotion that is frequently repudiated. Jealous people are often admonished not to feel that way. Romantic jealousy is sometimes called unnatural, a cultural artefact. Without examining whether jealousy is wrong or unwise, it is possible to examine the statement that it is an artefact by asking whether animals are ever jealous.

The emotion of jealousy must be separated from simple dislike. Circus animal trainer Gunther Gebel-Williams describes the actions of the elephant Tetchie, saying she was jealous of his wife and daughter, who worked in the circus, although she never bothered any other workers. Though his deduction that Tetchie was jealous of the attention he paid family members may be correct, it is also possible that Tetchie simply didn't like them. If Tetchie had liked them except when they were near Gebel-Williams, that would have been a clearer demonstration of jealousy.[53]

Jealousy is most commonly thought of in relation to siblings and to mates, though it might be manifested in any situation where animals gather. Animal siblings can be quite vicious, going so far as to eat one another, but this need not involve jealousy.

Group members other than siblings may be the source of jealousy. William Jordan has described what happened when the first baby was born in a group of gorillas at a zoo. The group members became closer and seemed more unified – except for the mother's brother, Caesar, who displayed small evidence of hostility towards the baby: throwing branches at her, swatting her on the head. Ultimately he climbed out of the gorilla enclosure 'in what appears to have been a jealous snit', and was placed in another cage.[54]

In a Swedish animal park, Bimbo, a young male elephant, was shown special attention by Tabu, an older female. When a younger calf, Mkuba, arrived, Tabu lost interest in Bimbo. Bimbo responded by surreptitiously digging Mkuba with his tusks whenever possible, and Mkuba responded to that with loud histrionic shrieks for help from Tabu.[55] This is the sort of behaviour that is so reminiscent of human actions that strong scientists feel compelled to take a deep breath and start numbering the animals they observe instead of naming them.

Freud formulated his notion of Oedipal jealousy in reference to humans. It is amusing to consider Herbert Terrace's account of the chimpanzee Nim Chimpsky's upbringing in this light. After being taken from his mother at the age of five days, Nim was raised in a human household. His 'mother', Stephanie, observed that Nim displayed both affection and a certain hostility towards her husband. In one instance, Nim, Stephanie and her husband were taking an afternoon nap on a large bed, with six-month-old Nim in the middle. Nim appeared to be asleep, but when Stephanie's husband put his arm around her, Nim leapt up and bit him. Terrace was unable to resist describing Nim's behaviour as 'downright Oedipal'.[56]

Jealousy over food is easily observed. Nim enjoyed playing with dolls, and would pretend to feed them. One day a teacher brought her cat for Nim to play with. He offered the cat a spoonful of yogurt, just as he did with his dolls, but was shocked when the cat licked it up. After that, even when specifically instructed to feed the cat, Nim offered it only an empty spoon.[57]

This phenomenon is often exploited by animal trainers. Boots, a circus horse, would occasionally refuse to eat. If someone stood in front of Boots, offering sugar and carrots, Boots' favourite foods, he would just stare apathetically, but if Boots saw the horses in adjacent stalls being fed carrots and sugar, he would snatch at them eagerly the next time they were offered. In this way his trainers were able to end his hunger strike.[58]

The famous grey parrot Alex, who speaks words whose meaning he demonstrably understands, is not considered a parrot genius. His trainer has worked with at least one other grey parrot whose learning curve seems comparable. Asked why Alex has learned so much more than thousands of pet grey parrots over the decades, she ascribes his success to the model/rival method of teaching, developed by Dietmar Todt. (It may also be that some of those pet parrots did understand the meaning of some of the words they used, but that this was not credited.) With this approach, two humans work with the animal. One is the trainer, while the other acts as the model or rival. Thus, if Alex is to be taught the word green, the model (usually a graduate student) is shown a green object and asked what colour it is. When the graduate student names it correctly, the trainer praises her or him, and bestows the green object as a reward. When the graduate student gets it wrong, there is no reward.

Alex, who has watched this procedure, is asked to perform the same task. The graduate student may be thought of as a model, who demonstrates what is wanted and what the reward is for performing that task.[59] But the student may also represent a rival. Perhaps Alex doesn't really want the green object so very badly until he sees someone else get it. Perhaps he doesn't like to see someone else praised instead of him. This is presently only speculation: Irene Pepperberg's analysis of the model/rival system focuses on its referentiality, contextual applicability and interactivity, rather than on Alex's motivations.[60]

If parrots have a jealous nature, this might be expected to show up in their mating behaviour. Parrots (who form enduring pairs) often seem jealous of anyone who approaches their mate or desired mate. A tame parrot may suddenly become hostile to humans if it acquires a mate.[61] Parrot behaviour consultant Mattie Sue Athan estimates that a third of the calls for help she receives arise from 'love triangles' when a parrot falls in love with one member of a human couple and tries to get rid of the other with displays of hostility.[62]

At a California oceanarium three orcas were kept, two females and one male. When Nepo, the male, reached sexual maturity, he showed a strong preference for the female called Yaka. The other female, Kianu, repeatedly interrupted their mating by leaping out of the water and falling on them. Ultimately she attacked Yaka during a performance.[63]

Scientists composing classifications of animal mating systems have defined a number of systems in which it would be in an animal's genetic interest not to allow its partner to mate with others. They speak in terms of 'monopolising', 'defending' or 'guarding' mates, not in terms of love and jealousy.

Jealous behaviour can certainly have genetic effects. In the famous chimpanzee colony at the Arnhem Zoo, high-ranking males have some success in preventing females from mating with other males. To achieve this, they attack both the females and the males. Frans de Waal reports that, during the day, a female may decline invitations to mate from certain males. When the chimpanzees are brought in at night they are put in separate cages. Females may then mate with these same males without fear of attack from the high-ranking males, and will sometimes even rush over to their cages to mate through the bars. If it were not for the separate cages, the females might never dare mate with the lower-ranking males.[64] Wild chimpanzees sometimes leave the group in pairs, in 'consortships', and this may provide relief from jealous attacks.

The possible evolutionary function of jealousy must be separated from the emotion. Leyhausen kept two tree ocelots, the female imprinted on humans. When in oestrus, she was attracted to women, and would rub herself on their feet and legs and address courtship behaviour to them. When the male ocelot approached, she would drive him back energetically. 'Finally, however, the male did succeed in mating: At the peak of her courtship around my assistant's leg, the female worked herself up into such an ecstasy that she no longer noticed what was going on, and the male learned to take advantage of this.' This became standard for these cats, who raised six litters of kittens. The female tolerated the male, except when a human was in the room. Leyhausen notes, however, that whenever the female was in oestrus, the male became aggressive towards women and tried to bite their legs.[65]

If some animals show romantic jealousy, can they also show romantic fidelity? Significant rates of infidelity in some songbirds (both male and female) have been demonstrated by genetic analysis of parents and offspring and by field observation of the parent birds.[66] Not surprisingly, scientists have not indulged in comic opera experiments to see if these songbirds ever resist romantic temptation, though it is known that some animals do seem to reject opportunities for infidelity. For example, male prairie voles who have formed a pair with a female chase away other voles of either sex.[67]

Female African elephants in oestrus sometimes form consortships with males, but it is not clear whether they simply prefer a certain male and desire only his company, or whether by staying with one male – who vigorously attacks other males that come near – they gain protection from the pursuit of other males. According to Cynthia Moss, consort behaviour is something that female elephants learn. Young females who do not form a consortship may be 'chased and harassed' by many males.[68]

In other species females may not be as vulnerable. Rhinos in the Serengeti, despite their reputation as loners, sometimes do seem to form pair bonds during oestrus. An observer saw the male of one pair wander off, whereupon another male appeared and sought to mate, only to be rebuffed by the female. The preferred male then wandered back on the scene and they immediately mated, which seems to indicate that it was not simple lack of interest in mating that caused the female to reject the second male.[69]

Dogs, whose sexual behaviour is considered by most people to be synonymous with promiscuity, are very closely related to monogamous wild canids such as the wolf. In *The Hidden Life of Dogs*, Elizabeth Marshall Thomas has described the changed behaviour of her husky, Maria, after she had paired with another. 'So carefully did Maria save herself for Misha that when she went outside to urinate, she didn't mark, as female dogs in oestrus often do, by squatting partway down, raising a leg, and directing their urine to the base of some large wayside object such as a tree so that the scent can be carried far and wide on the feet of passers-by. In later years, when she no longer had Misha, she advertised her sexual condition. And in later years she showed a willingness to accept other dogs . . .'[70]

In the light of such observations, it seems possible that among

94

the songbirds whose infidelity has been so carefully studied, those birds who are not unfaithful to their mates might be exhibiting fidelity, rather than lack of opportunity.

While jealousy, anger and cruelty are not usually considered fit subjects for behaviourists to study, aggression is a most respectable subject, and a great deal of money and attention has been devoted to it. As Frans de Waal has pointed out, comparatively little study has been made of the avoidance of aggression and of peacemaking and reconciliation in animals or humans, despite the fact that these are vital parts of social life.[71]

Watching chimpanzees in the Arnhem Zoo in 1975, de Waal witnessed an attack by one chimpanzee on another, an altercation in which other group members immediately took part, resulting in shrieking pandemonium. There was a pause, and then the two apes involved in the original quarrel embraced and kissed, while the others hooted excitedly. Pondering the episode, de Waal suddenly perceived it as an instance of reconciliation. 'From that day on I noticed that emotional reunions between aggressors and victims were quite common. The phenomenon became so obvious that it was hard to imagine that it had been overlooked for so long by me and by scores of other ethologists.'[72]

De Waal has since studied the mechanisms of reconciliation in rhesus monkeys, stump-tailed monkeys and bonobos. Not only do these primates strive to make peace with each other after hostile encounters, but they bring about reconciliations between others who have quarrelled. Mama, the oldest female in the Arnhem colony, once ended a conflict between Nikkie and Yeroen, two dominant males. She went to Nikkie and put her finger in his mouth, a reassuring gesture. Simultaneously she beckoned to Yeroen and when he came over gave him a kiss. When she moved from between them Yeroen hugged Nikkie and the breach between the two was ended.[73]

De Waal's argument is not that the primates he studied are unaggressive, but that the ways in which they handle and dispel aggression are as important as the antagonism and deserve commensurate attention. A full understanding of reconciliation awaits evidence on the emotions felt by the peacemakers.

CHAPTER FIVE

Family, Friends and Lovers

ONE EVENING in the 1930s, Ma Shwe, a work elephant in Burma, was trapped in rising floodwaters in the Upper Taungdwin River, along with her three-month-old calf. Elephant handlers rushed to the river when they heard the calf screaming, but could do nothing to help, for the steep banks were twelve to fifteen feet high. Ma Shwe's feet were still on the river bottom, but her calf was floating. Ma Shwe held it against her body and, whenever it began to drift away, used her trunk to pull it back against the current. The fast-rising water soon washed the calf away and Ma Shwe plunged downstream for fifty yards and retrieved it. She pinned her calf against the bank with her head, then lifted it in her trunk, reared up on her hind legs, and placed it on a rocky ledge five feet above the water. Ma Shwe fell back into the torrent and disappeared downstream. The elephant handlers turned their attention to the calf, which could barely fit on the narrow ledge where it stood shivering. The ledge was eight feet below the top of the bank. Half an hour later, J.H. Williams, the British manager of the elephant camp, was peering down at the calf wondering how to rescue it, when he heard 'the grandest sounds of a mother's love I can remember. Ma Shwe had crossed the river and got up the bank and was making her way back as fast as she could, calling the whole time – a defiant roar, but to her calf it was music. The two little ears, like little maps of India, were cocked forward listening to the only sound that mattered, the call of her mother.' When Ma Shwe saw her calf, safe on the other side of the river, her call changed to the rumble which elephants typically make when pleased. The two elephants were left where they were, and by morning, Ma Shwe had crossed the river (no longer in flood) and the calf was off the ledge.[1]

Humans, perhaps as social primates, believe they know what love is and esteem it highly. The human capacity to love is traditionally admired, although people sometimes suspect that others do not really know what love is. Humans frequently declare that animals do not know this feeling, which is regarded as ennobling. Had Williams been an animal behaviourist describing Ma Shwe and her calf, he would probably have felt constrained from using the word 'love' to describe her behaviour. He might have written of a 'bond' between Ma Shwe and her calf instead.

In a critique of Harry Harlow's deprivation experiments in which young rhesus monkeys grew up without mothers, biologist Catherine Roberts has written: 'Does he not know that human love differs qualitatively from animal love? Does he not know that a human mother is unique because she has an abstract idea of the Good and that therefore human love, unlike animal love, has its ontogenetic beginnings in a spiritual bond between mother and child?'[2]

Jane Goodall, whose work has illuminated the emotional life of chimpanzees, has nevertheless argued that chimpanzees don't know true romantic love. She describes the chimpanzees Pooch and Figan, who repeatedly showed a preference for one another when Pooch was sexually active, leaving the group and going off together into the forest for a few days (this is in contrast to chimpanzees who remain with the larger group while sexually active). Goodall writes: 'I cannot conceive of chimpanzees developing emotions, one for the other, comparable in any way to the tenderness, the protectiveness, tolerance and spiritual exhilaration

that are the hallmarks of human love in its truest and deepest sense
. . . The most the female chimpanzee can expect of her suitor is
a brief courtship display, a sexual contact lasting at most half a
minute and, sometimes, a session of social grooming afterward.
Not for them the romance, the mystery, the boundless joys of
human love.'[3] Perhaps this is true. And yet we do not fully grasp
what chimpanzees do feel, or whether there are joys chimpanzees
feel that we do not.

The evolutionary approach can produce very different analyses
of the possibility of love. The writer of one book for a popular
audience has noted that there is general approval of animals that
mate for life, and added, 'It's important to remember . . . that
these animals are not displaying "true love", but simply following
the dictates of their genes. They are survival machines, and their
mission is to multiply their own genes in the gene pool. If a male
felt that his partner could raise young without him, he'd be off in
a flash. But this would not be abandonment in our terms, and we
need not feel sorry for the female. Both are pursuing their own
game plan that will lead to the best positioning of their genes – a
pursuit that is adaptive and, therefore, beautiful.'[4] Whatever their
scientific view of human coupling may be, most people would
not accept this as an accurate way of looking at their own loves
and families, far less of their emotional motivations, yet where
the difference on this point lies between animals and people is
not stated. The fact that an animal is described as a machine on the
one hand, and as a creature that may ponder whether its partner
can raise young alone on the other, is only one inconsistency in
this passage.

The intersection between evolutionary genetics and love is also
observed by Elizabeth Marshall Thomas of two dogs, Misha and
Maria:

> Popular prejudice might hold that romantic love, with its
> resulting benefit of fidelity, sexual and otherwise, is not a
> concept that can be applied to dogs, and that to do so is
> anthropomorphic. Not true. Fully as much as any human love
> story, the story of Misha and Maria shows the evolutionary
> value of romantic love. The force that drove Romeo and Juliet
> is no less strong or important if harbored by a nonhuman spe-
> cies, because the strength of the bond helps to assure the male

that he, instead of, say, Tybalt or Bingo, is the father of any children born and that both parents are in a cooperative frame of mind when the time comes to raise those children.[5]

Even though she offered a scientific rationale for the emotion, Thomas has been castigated for using the word 'love' rather than the word 'bond' in writing of dogs.[6]

Many theorists of affect considered love a 'drive', like hunger, rather than an emotion. Because it has an object, it has also been called a 'sentiment'. Most people think of it as an emotion, but whether emotion or drive, there has been a reluctance to apply it to animals.

Who do people love? Among those we may love are parents, siblings, other relatives, playmates, friends, teachers and leaders, lovers and spouses, children and pets. Who do animals love? There is good evidence that some animals sometimes love parents, siblings, other relatives, playmates, friends, teachers and leaders, lovers and spouses, children and pets. Love and friendship can be treated as points on a spectrum of affection.

One primary form of love is parental love. The evolutionary approach suggests that it makes urgent sense for animals to watch over their young. Parental care allows more young to survive; expressing care can well mean love. If parents protect their young, the young can grow bigger before they have to fend for themselves. A baboon can even inherit its mother's status in the troop and an adult female black bear can use her mother's territory while her mother is still occupying it. If a young animal needs to learn things, it can do so safely while it is under the protection of its parent. Perhaps – this is debated – the parent will even teach it some of those things.

Not all creatures protect their young. A turtle lays eggs in the sand and departs. Presumably it would not recognise, let alone love, its offspring. But if an animal lays eggs and guards them, as crocodiles do, there must be something that motivates it to do so, and then prevents it from eating the young when they hatch. This might not necessarily be love – it could be brought about by such simple mechanisms as an inhibition against eating eggs and young alligators. Yet more elaborate parental exertions are found in surprising places. Crocodiles, in fact, care for their young, digging them out of the nest when they hatch, guarding

99

them while small, carrying them in their jaws and responding vigorously to their distress calls. Females of a South East Asian diadem butterfly, apparently guard their eggs by standing over them. This probably increases their chances of survival. Remarkably, a female will sometimes continue with this behaviour even unto death, her rooted corpse standing guard over a batch of as yet unhatched eggs.[8]

Mother wolf spiders not only tend their eggs, but carry their babies on their backs. Perhaps the babies need to learn hunting skills. More likely, they just need protection while they grow. J.T. Moggridge tells the story of a trap-door spider he had collected and decided to preserve in alcohol. While spiders twitched for a long time after being put in alcohol, it was then believed that this was mere reflex action. Moggridge shook the baby spiders off her back and dropped her into alcohol. After a while, supposing her to be 'dead to sense', he dropped her twenty-four babies in too. To his horror, the mother spider reached out her legs, folded the babies beneath her, and clasped them until she died.[9] After this, Moggridge switched to the use of chloroform.

Can a spider love her babies? Was it a mere reflex that caused the trap-door spider to reach for her young? In this case it seems possible, but it is difficult to feel certain. One can imagine a simple instinct to draw close to anything that looks like a baby spider. Or she might have seized any objects that happened to be floating in the alcohol. A mother wolf spider is just as welcoming to strange baby wolf spiders as to her own. This might or might not be accompanied by an emotional state.

Does a spider love its eggs, something the naturalist John Crompton compares to loving a box of billiard balls? It is so hard to have any insight into a spider's mind that it is almost impossible to guess, based on present knowledge.

Yet spiders have evolved to produce complex venoms and digestive fluids, and spin silks of varying types from six different kinds of silk glands. The building of a spider's web is an extremely complicated behaviour. One can argue that a spider is not really simple and that the development of maternal love might well be a shorter evolutionary step than web-building.

Perhaps one day we will know. What if it were discovered that when a mother wolf spider sees young spiders, her body is flooded with a hormone whose presence is associated with feelings of love in higher animals? Would that be evidence that the spider loves her young? What if it were a hormone peculiar to spiders? Would that mean it wasn't love? When trying to comprehend the inner lives of creatures so unlike human beings it may be more useful and accurate to think not of a hierarchy (with *homo sapiens* at the top) but of a spectrum of similarity. A spider might have a rich inner life with a riot of emotions – but so different from our own that anthropomorphism fails and they are unintelligible. But this does not mean that the search for such emotions, no matter how difficult, is not worthwhile.

The question of whether a spider can feel parental love is baffling, but there is less doubt for 'higher' animals. Their behaviour is so complex that to dismiss it as the result of inhibitions and reflex and fixed action patterns seems fantastically implausible. Parental care manifests itself in feeding the young, washing them, playing with them and protecting them from external dangers and from their own inexperience.

Mammals, even 'primitive' ones such as platypuses and spiny anteaters, suckle their young. The suckling mother is extremely vulnerable, in a way that she will seldom allow herself to be with adult animals, in a way that many protective instincts would advise against.

Young mammals are safest in their own nests. In a series of classic experiments on rats, researchers put baby rats on cage floors, and mother rats (and in some cases females who were not mothers) proved zealous at retrieving the babies and bringing them into their nests. They would cross an electrified grid to get to the babies, and would retrieve unrelated babies as quickly as their own. Curious to see how long this would be kept up, the experimenters offered one rat fifty-eight babies, each of whom she picked up and crammed into her nest: '. . . the female appeared to be as eager at the end of the experiment, which had to be interrupted because we had no more young at our disposal, as she had at the beginning'.[10]

In contrast to this zealous rat, Nubian ibex who give birth to triplets instead of the usual twins are reported to reject one fawn.[11] Presumably the doe cannot produce enough milk for three, so that if she kept them all, they would all be malnourished. When most of a lioness's cubs die or are killed, she may abandon the last cub. Some biologists postulate that it is not energetically efficient for her to put all the effort of raising a litter into just one cub, when she can breed again sooner if she does not, and that her 'instinctive sense of investment' tells her so.[12] What an instinctive sense of investment may be or feel like is not clear. Human parents have been known to take similar actions. What goes on in the mind of an ibex doe or a lioness in this situation is unknown.

As young mammals grow older, their parents often feed them. Some animals simply let the young steal pieces of their own food. Others bring food to the young. An ocean bird may begin by regurgitating partially-digested food for its chick. When the chick is older, the parent shifts to bringing whole fish, which it holds until the chick manages to grab it properly.

Baby animals have also to be kept clean. Some birds carry the chicks' droppings away from the nest. Animals frequently lick their young, and for many species this is so essential that the babies may die if they are not washed, since washing triggers their excretion. As baby animals grow bigger, most of them play, sometimes with their littermates and sometimes with their parents. As anyone who has observed kittens or puppies knows, the parents can take quite a beating before they begin to protest.

One of the most important tasks of parents is to protect the young. Baby animals are typically small, inept, and defenceless, and make desirable meals for predators. Some parents protect their young by hiding them. At other times parents must fight to save their young.

In a typical instance, a lion was seen to attack a herd of six giraffe. Most of them ran away, but one calf was in danger because it was too slow. Its mother tried to push the calf to run faster, but when she saw this would not work, she stood over it and faced the lion. The lion circled the giraffe, and the mother wheeled round to face him. Whenever he got close, she kicked at him with her forelegs. After an hour the lion gave up and left. The two giraffe rejoined the herd. Since lions frequently succeed in killing giraffe, the mother was in real danger.[13]

The willingness of animal parents to fight in defence of their young is well known, since it is often humans who are the threat. Humans are so menacing, however, that such encounters seldom develop into actual fights. The last known whooping crane nest in the United States was found by ornithologist and egg-collector J.W. Preston in Iowa. Preston wrote, 'When I approached the nest, the bird, which had walked some distance away, came running back . . . wings and tail spread drooping, with head and shoulders brought level with the water; then it began picking up bunches of moss and sticks which it threw down in a defiant way; then, with pitiable mien, it spread itself upon the water and begged me to leave its treasure, which, in a heartless manner, I did not do.' This might have been either a male or a female crane, since both of them sit on the eggs.[14]

Animals will also try to rescue their young from dangers other than predators, as in the case of a cat who had never entered water but was observed jumping into a swimming pool to rescue her kittens.

To the north of Hudson Bay, the explorer Peter Freuchen came across a family of six wolves, two adults and four cubs. The wolves were howling. One of the cubs was caught in a trap that had been set at a cairn of stones over a food cache. The other wolves had overturned many of the large stones and scraped at the frozen earth around the stone to which the trap was fastened in their determined efforts to set free the cub.[15]

Since so many examples given of parental love are of motherly love, it is worth stressing that fatherly love is apparent in some species. It has been estimated that direct paternal care is found in ten per cent of mammalian genera.[16] Gerald Durrell has described the birth of cotton-topped marmosets at the Jersey Zoo. After the mother had delivered the usual marmoset twins, the father took them, washed them, and carried them with him everywhere he went, often one on each hip, only returning them to the mother to suckle. As they grew older, they would leave his side to explore. If he felt there was a threat to their safety, he would rush over and snatch them up.[17] Wild marmoset fathers of various species behave in the same way. Often they assist at the birth itself. Lion-headed marmoset fathers have been seen to mash fruit in their fingers for the babies when they begin to wean. Owl monkey males are also the ones to carry the babies.

103

Red fox researcher David Macdonald describes a new father wriggling with eagerness to care for his children:

> Smudge was almost comical in his husbandly diligence. Before eating a scrap for himself, he gathered as much food as he could wedge into his gaping jaws, and lugged it to Whitepaws' earth. There he would warble at the entrance. If she did not emerge, he would use his nose like a billiard cue to poke the lumps of food through the entrance and into the den.

When the cubs were older, Smudge's ambition was to play with them, something the mother and her sisters did not always allow: 'Smudge would skulk in the vegetation, waiting for Big Ears [their maternal aunt] to fall asleep, whereupon he would quietly warble to the cubs who would sneak off to gambol with him. Soon their exuberance led to squeals and snirks that awoke Big Ears who would vigorously reprimand Smudge.'[18]

Father zebras remain on good terms with their grown sons, who eventually leave the herd not because they are driven out but because they are looking for others to play with. Researchers studying wild zebras once decided to mark a stallion who was still living in his father's herd at the age of four and a half years, so that they could follow his subsequent travels. To their sorrow, the anaesthetic dart killed him. The young stallion's father came over to the body repeatedly and tried to rouse him. Later that day he spent hours roaming from herd to herd, calling for his son.[19]

In a pack of wild dogs, the mother of nine pups died when they were five weeks old. Apparently they were old enough to switch to solid food, for the rest of the pack, consisting of five males, reared them successfully.[20]

Direct paternal care is seen in many species of birds, including the kiwi, in which case the father incubates the egg and raises the chicks without help from the mother. In many other instances – the father beaver playing with his children; the father wolf letting his cubs chew his tail; the father dwarf mongoose taking the kits foraging with him – it appears that they love their children, or at least enjoy their company.

In these and other ways parents act out of love for their young. To argue that it cannot be compared to human love is unrealistic, a classic example of what Roger Fouts calls the rubber ruler, in which the standards are changed depending on whether the behaviour being mentioned is human or nonhuman. Consider the argument that it is impossible to know whether a mother ape loves her baby and then ask if it is possible to know whether the people down the street love their baby. True, they feed it and care for it. True, they tickle it and play with it. True, they defend it with all their might. But that is not considered proof in the case of the ape.

Unlike the ape, the people down the street may *say* they love their baby, but how do we know they are telling the truth? How can we know what they mean by the word love? Ultimately we cannot know exactly what other people mean when they speak of love. Yet in reality, we are usually quite sure they love that baby. If we see parents with a baby they don't love, we are shocked. When we learn of child abuse, we are outraged, in part because we believe that a relationship of love is violated. In truth, most people believe that the ape loves her baby, that the dog loves her puppies and that the cat loves her kittens. Most scientists probably believe it, too, though they may be hesitant to say so, at least in a scientific document.

A sceptical observer might still object that an ape with her baby is acting out of mere instinct. Could it not be that the people down the street are acting out of instinct as well? It must depend on whether love is defined as an instinct. Even if it is called instinct in either case, does that negate their love as an emotion?

Why has the idea of love as an emotion been so neglected? Why are we reduced to the rather tedious explanations offered by the evolutionary approach? This is the approach taught in universities, where its wider implications go almost unnoticed. It suggests that the more elaborate the parental tasks an animal performs, the more advantageous it is to have an overarching emotion like love driving them. If all parental behaviour consists of is nothing more than refraining from eating the children, no great emotional drama is necessary. But to feed them, wash them and risk your life for them – or (perhaps even harder) to let them chew on you, to let them snatch your dinner and to put up with their noise – you had better love them deeply, at least for the time being. Yet, in this approach, love, however it feels, is a device by which subsequent generations are produced. Rather than the

105

reason it exists, this could be one function it serves. Freeing ourselves from the tyranny of a purely biological explanation might widen the horizon. Love might even appear as mysterious and baffling in animals as it has in humans over the centuries.

Parental love has its complement, filial love, which is harder to pin down. To almost any demonstration of attachment and preference on the part of an animal for its parent, to the tiger cubs licking their mother, to the wolf cubs running to greet their father, the sceptic can simply argue that this is self-interest. The younger animal may simply wish to be around the source of food, warmth and safety. Young animals do not, as a rule, appear to fight to protect their parents. Nonetheless, Paul, an adolescent baboon, tried to defend his mother against large adult males in the troop. He didn't have great success, but a scientific observer felt that he was risking a great deal in his mother's defense.[21] When they grow older, many young animals are driven away by their parents. They often go with much reluctance, but this alone cannot prove that they love their parents. They might be reluctant to depart from safety and their accustomed habits, to go into unknown territory. Not all young animals are driven away. Chimpanzees usually remain in the same group as their mothers. They spend time with each other, and the young apes may help their mothers care for the next generation. Elephants, too, live in stable maternal herds and cooperate in extraordinary ways with one another. Elephant aunts play important roles in child-care.

In a captive baboon colony, experimenters isolated female baboons as soon as they began to exhibit menstrual cycles after the birth of an infant. The babies were usually about six months old and were left behind. Other females in the colony took over their care. Seven or eight months later, the original mothers were returned to the colony, often anaesthetised. Each time an unconscious baboon was carried in, her baby began to utter 'lost baby' calls. When she was returned to the enclosure the baby went to her and the mother-child relationship resumed. Baboons are individuals, however, and one baby chose to remain with its foster mother.[22]

Jane Goodall describes the reaction of a male chimpanzee called Flint, who was eight years old when his mother, Flo, died. Flint sat over Flo's body for many hours, occasionally tugging at her hand. As the days passed, he behaved in an apathetic and lethargic manner. In one remarkable instance, three days after his mother's death, Flint was seen to climb a tree and stare at the sleeping nest he had shared with his mother a few days before. He became more and more listless, and died within the month, probably of gastroenteritis. Goodall's scientific conclusion was that 'It seems likely that psychological and physiological disturbances associated with loss made him more vulnerable to disease'. Sy Montgomery quotes Goodall's poignant common-sense rendering of the same idea: 'Flint died of grief'.[23]

Besides parents and children, love can extend to other family members. One young wild elephant seemed to be as fond of his grandmother, Teresia, as he was of his mother. Often he would suckle from his mother and then go to Teresia, who was more than fifty years old, and stand with her or follow her.[24] In many species, young animals may remain with their parents and help raise the younger offspring. Young coyotes often remain with their parents and help raise subsequent new pups. These elder brothers and sisters may feed, wash, protect and simply baby-sit the pups. The arrangement clearly benefits the parents, who need all the help they can get with raising the pups; and benefits the pups, who have more adults looking after their welfare. If the parents are killed, the older siblings can successfully raise the pups if they are not too young.

Avoiding any mention of fondness, evolutionary biologists have identified a number of ways in which this benefits the older offspring. Possibly they have more time to learn hunting skills. If there are no good coyote hunting territories available, they are spared the necessity of going out and either fighting for one or being attacked by occupants of neighbouring territories. They also increase the chances of their genes being passed on, since they share many genes with their young siblings.

Year-old beavers typically remain with their parents and help take care of their younger siblings. Françoise Patenaude, who observed wild beavers in Quebec, saw the yearlings grooming the babies and fetching food for them. During the winter, the entire family was largely confined to the lodge. On more than one occasion, when an infant beaver fell into the water in the entrance to the lodge, a yearling picked it up and carried it in its arms to the dry floor of the lodge (beavers can walk on their hind legs and carry things, including very small beavers, in their forelegs). The yearlings later played with their younger siblings and helped perform every aspect of parental care except, of course, suckling.[25]

A social animal, who lives in a group, will often behave in a friendly way towards other members of the group, even when they are not relatives. Troops of baboons and herds of zebra or elephants are not just crowds of strangers. This can go far beyond toleration to a kind of need: it has been pointed out that a monkey kept alone will work for the reward of seeing other monkeys just as a hungry one will work to get food.[26] The animals in a social group have relationships with each other, some of which are affectionate. Lionesses baby-sit for one another. In baboon troops, many baboons have alliances with other baboons, on whom they can count to take their side in squabbles.

Elephants appear to make allowances for other members of their herd. One herd always travelled slowly because one of its members had never fully recovered from a broken leg suffered as a calf. A park warden reported coming across a herd with a female carrying a small several-days-dead calf, which she placed on the ground whenever she ate or drank: she travelled very slowly and the rest of the elephants waited for her.[27] This suggests that animals, like people, act on feelings as such, rather than for purposes of survival. It suggests that the evolutionary approach is not entirely adequate to explain animal feelings any more than it is, actually, to explain human ones. A single example such as this one, no matter how well documented, may not challenge the entire evolutionary paradigm for feelings, but it certainly does raise questions that biologists have yet to face. There appears to be so little survival value in the behaviour of this herd that perhaps one has to believe that they behaved this way just because they *loved* their grieving friend and wanted to support her.

Sociobiological prejudices about how males must behave have not always proven correct. They sometimes show, in what scientists call 'familial behaviour', evidence of love. In large social groups, males are often attracted to the young of the group, show responsibility for their protection and tolerate behaviour on their part that would earn an adult a fierce attack. Male lions often drive females away from kills but allow cubs to eat alongside them. In such groups, chances may be good that the male is related to the young, even if he is not their father, but there is no evidence that the males calculate degrees of relationship.

In wolf packs, researchers report that adults – and not only the parents – are so tolerant of pups climbing over them, chewing on them and generally manhandling them that they must leave the den area when they want to sleep. Wolves also display what appears to be admiration for the dominant (or alpha) wolves in their pack. In the wolf's close relative, the dog, this capacity to admire leaders has made domestication a success. The average dog treats its owners the way a wolf treats an alpha wolf.

Other social animals are often willing to accord humans this kind of status. Researcher Jennifer Zeligs, who studies and trains sea lions, appears to be in this position with her experimental subjects. Her success in training them to retrieve objects under water and to perform other tasks seems to be the result of their desire to please her and receive her praise and attention. She does not reward them with food, working with them only after they have eaten.

One could object that this is not love, because the sea lions get pleasure from Zeligs: attention, grooming and fun. That is why they give her the attention they do. But is human love any different? Must love be unrewarding to be real? The point is that sea lions seem capable of love and affection. That they can, under special conditions, extend these feelings beyond their own kind, to an alien species, merely demonstrates some of the conditions of those feelings. Two sea lions can feel an affectionate bond for one another, and Zeligs benefits from the extension of that feeling to a human.

Friendship is marked by singling out individuals, a mutual sharing of preferences for another's company. In social animals, friendships in this sense occur often between members of the group. Friendship can also extend outside the group, making it easier for new animals to join it. The membership of the chimpanzee bands at Gombe, for example, has some fluidity; a chimpanzee may leave one band and join another. This reduces inbreeding, among other functions served.

In general, animals are friendly only towards animals of their own species. One significant exception to this is captive animals, who are often isolated from others of their kind or forced into association with them. Some animals make friends with animals of other species or with humans. Friendship with an individual of another species does not guarantee friendship with an entire species: a hand-reared leopard was raised with a dog and loved to play with her, but tried to kill other dogs, even dogs that closely resembled her friend.[28]

John Teal, who experimented with raising endangered musk oxen, was once shut in a pen with them when some dogs came running up. To his alarm, the musk oxen snorted, stamped and thundered towards him. Before he could move, they formed a defensive ring around him and lowered their horns, pointing at the dogs. This is how musk oxen protect their calves from predators.[29]

Even an animal not usually considered social may make friends in captivity. Ocelots, usually considered solitary animals, can become quite friendly with humans. Perplexed by the amicability of his ocelot, Paul Leyhausen speculated that such cats have a capacity to be friendly from their juvenile days, but that once adult they cannot help seeing other cats as rivals or intruders. Humans, he hypothesised, are similar enough to be friends with, yet sufficiently dissimilar that we do not provoke rivalry: 'Thus genuine and lasting friendship, of a kind which may never occur between cats themselves, is possible between humans and members of various species of solitary cats. In other words, if the above hypothesis is correct, the individual wild cat would really "like" to be friendly with other cats, but feels toward them much like the eccentric who offends everyone and then, asked why he has no friends, replies in amazement, "I wish I did, but everyone else is so horrible!"'[30]

It is rare for animals to make friends with humans when they are not captive, for their own species make more suitable friends, and humans are usually feared. Beavers, given time, will tolerate well-mannered humans. If the humans supply favoured beaver food, the beavers will associate with them, even to the point of climbing into their laps to get particularly tasty food. They distinguish humans they know from strangers.[31] Yet there is no reason to suppose that the beavers actually enjoy the company of the humans. Lack of fear does not equal friendship.

Though friendship is typically seen in social animals, it seems that some animals who are normally solitary may retain the capacity for friendship. The male brown bear normally leads a solitary life as an adult (females usually have cubs with them). In the Casa de Campo Zoo in Madrid, up to nine brown bears were kept in one enclosure, and some of the male bears formed strong bonds with each other. They sought one another out to play and to rest together. Such a bear would notice what his friends were doing, and if they got into fights, would intervene or join his friend in the attack. They did not compete for female bears, but tolerated each other's presence around them. As a result of these alliances, the bears who had friends were higher in the social hierarchy. Those who were able to make friends were the younger bears.[32]

An advantageous result – high status and the support of his friends in fights – is achieved through such friendship. Yet it seems unlikely that bears calculate survival advantages when they make friends. More likely the friendliness has emotional roots, but may also confer evolutionary advantages.

What is the relevance of such friendliness, surely one aspect of love, in wild male bears? Although they are solitary, they may meet other male bears when they seek out female bears in oestrus or when they gather at an abundant food source such as a salmon run. Whether they form alliances at such times is unknown. Perhaps the capacity for friendship with other bears is a remnant of youth, when they lived in company with their mother, and possibly one or two siblings.

Friendship between animals and people often occurs when the animal is a pet. Animals also have pets occasionally – usually captive animals, since having a pet is a luxury. Lucy, a chimpanzee reared by humans, was given a kitten to allay her loneliness. The first time she saw the little cat, her hair stood on end. Barking, she grabbed it, flung it to the ground, hitting out and trying to bite it. Their second encounter was similar, but at their third meeting she was calmer. As she wandered about the kitten followed her and after half an hour Lucy picked it up, kissed it and hugged it, marking a complete change of attitude. Subsequently she groomed and cradled the kitten, carried it constantly, made nests for it and guarded it from humans. The kitten 'never appeared anxious to be transported by the chimpanzee' and was unwilling to cling to Lucy's stomach, so she either carried it in one hand or urged it to ride on her back.[33] Koko the gorilla showed great tenderness

111

towards a pet kitten she herself named All Ball. This is strikingly like love, the real thing, because it is chosen without regard for survival value.

It is common for horses to make friends with other animals such as goats. They are careful not to hurt the goats. Accounts of race horses who mope and do not run well when separated from their goat friends are not infrequent. These goats may well be the equivalent of pets. The horses are not confused about species: they know that the goat is not a horse, but they like it anyway. It has been reported that as a matter of routine one captive elephant put aside a little of its grain for a mouse to eat.[34]

Admirable as humanity considers friendship and familial love, perhaps the highest esteem is accorded to romantic love, and thus this is the kind of love that is considered the most suspect to ascribe to animals. Many people consider romantic love so rarefied that not only animals, but even other cultures, do not know it. It has been claimed both that the whole idea was invented in medieval Europe and that it is only a pastime of the privileged. In any case, anthropologists studying human beings had not deemed it a fit subject for study until the American Anthropological Association held its first session on the anthropology of romance in 1992. Anthropologist William Jankowiak said it took him three years to organise the session: 'I would call up people and they would just laugh'. When asked why romantic love had been ignored, Jankowiak said researchers had assumed that 'this type of behaviour was culture-specific'. He also pointed to a linguistic hegemony on cultural analysis. 'The dominant model was a linguistic one that said if it isn't in the language it's not important.' Not only do some cultures lack words for romantic love, but it is undefined in the anthropological lexicon. 'They themselves don't have the categories for this.'

Jankowiak said that when he asked colleagues for contributions to the session on love and was told in reply that romantic love didn't exist in the cultures they studied, he would ask whether people in those cultures ever had clandestine affairs, ever refused arranged marriages, ever eloped or ever committed suicide over love. The answer was always yes, such things did occur, but that they hadn't examined it or followed up on it.[35]

Another reason for ignoring romantic love in other cultures is the assumption that it is a luxury. As Charles Lindholm, a pioneer in this field, told me, 'The general paradigm in anthropology, as in all social sciences, is utilitarian, maximising gain. Romantic love doesn't seem to fit the paradigm very well . . . When you have people sacrificing their lives for each other, it doesn't seem like you're maximising gain.' He laughed. 'Another part of it is that it's embarrassing! You're asking people about personal relationships and anthropologists, like everybody else, aren't comfortable asking people about that.' He added that the general academic milieu has not favoured the study of love. 'It's sort of a woman's type of thing, you know. It's not good for your career.'[36]

When anthropologists saw instances of romantic love, they paid little attention. Anthropologist Leonard Plotnicov said that 'Romantic love would interfere with the nice neat structures that anthropologists – particularly based on the work of Claude Levi-Strauss – have been able to develop. We found what we looked for! Nice lineage structure, nice marriage arrangements, the exchange of women between well-defined groups over time, so that these structures are replicated over the generations. Under such conditions romantic love would be ill-fitting, to say the least.' Going back over his extensive interviews with men in Jos, Nigeria, when he had not asked informants about love 'as it seemed not significant then', Plotnicov found many accounts of romantic love among both Westernised and traditional interviewees, including the culturally conservative man who said of his third wife, 'When I saw her, she took my life away'.[37] The general lack of belief in the utility of documenting or analysing romantic love has affected generations of students of human cultures. As Plotnicov remarked, 'You don't go looking for what isn't there, and you certainly go looking for what will be marketable when you publish your reports'.

All these factors – the denigration of love as a luxury or as feminine, the absence of linguistic evidence, the stress on utility, the embarrassment, the lack of a theoretical framework, even the career concerns – may help to explain the parallel lack of the study of romance among animals.

Mating is not love *per se*, but it raises some considerations. Some animals mate for life, staying together for as long as they both live. Some animals pair off for a season, and others mate and separate at once. Among animals who form relationships

113

of significant duration, some form pairs and others form larger groups, such as trios, or the elephant seal 'harem'.

In the case of animals who do not form partnerships, but mate and then separate, is affection involved? A. J. Magoun and P. Valkenburg, who tracked wolverines from a small airplane, have described the mating of these rare and solitary animals. To an observer, they write, most wolverine mating appears to be a matter of aggressive males and reluctant females. They were surprised, however, by the behaviour of the female wolverine they called F9 and an unidentified male. F9 and the male joined in exploring a rock outcropping on the tundra. They played. They rolled on the ground. Like an exuberant dog, F9 crouched and lashed her tail, then bounded away. At one point, when the male did not respond to her sniffing him, F9 turned and bumped him with her hip. After playing, they rested and then mated. Two days later they separated, perhaps never to meet again (although it is not impossible that this same male was the one later captured and labelled M20, with whom F9 mated the following year).[38]

This describes a friendly, playful interaction, not one-sided lust or a convenient arrangement. Is it reasonable to call it love? Liking? Mutual interest? F9 was just a year old, so her playfulness might be ascribed to youth. Even if her emotions – and those of the male – sprang from her youth, that does not mean they did not exist.

It might be argued that whatever one wolverine feels for another, it cannot be love because the encounter is so brief. While it may be true that these two wolverines did not love one another, duration is not a valid measure of love. That would rule out much human love.

> After all, my erstwhile dear,
> My no longer cherished,
> Need we say it was not love
> Just because it perished?[39]

It is consistent with their behaviour to say that F9 and her consort enjoyed one another's companionship for those few days, that they liked each other. They had no need to play together: they did so because that was what they wanted to do.

If it seems suspect to grant romance to wolverines and their brief affairs, what about the animals who do mate for life? These are animals who court, mate, raise young and accompany each other when not raising young. Sometimes they are in a larger group of animals, such as a flock of swans. At other times they may leave the group, as when swans are actually nesting. Mates commonly sleep together, groom one another and in some cases forage together. Usually they feed one another only when courting or when one is staying with very young offspring. In most species sexual activity is confined to a brief period.

The most common proof offered of love between mates is the sorrow they exhibit when one of the pair dies. Konrad Lorenz describes as a typical example the behaviour of the gander Ado when his mate, Susanne-Elisabeth, was killed by a fox. He stood silently by her partly eaten body, which lay across their nest. In the following days he hunched his body and hung his head. His eyes became sunken. His status in the flock plummeted, since he hadn't the heart to defend himself from the attacks of the other geese. (A year later, Ado had pulled himself together and met another goose.)

The onset of love may also be considered notable. Karen Pryor describes an animal trainer asking Lorenz whether it wasn't anthropomorphic to speak of geese falling in love. 'It is the accurate term for a real phenomenon for which there is no other name. I consider the term appropriate to any species, if that is in fact what they do,' Lorenz replied, adding that two greylags are most apt to fall in love when they have known each other as youngsters, been separated and then met again. He made the comparison to an astonished human asking 'Are *you* the same little girl I used to see running around in pigtails and braces?', and went on, 'That's how I met my wife'.[40] According to parrot behaviour consultant Mattie Sue Athan, it is common for some of the larger species of parrots to fall in love at first sight, and this is known as 'The Thunderbolt'.[41]

Neither are such bolts indiscriminate. Seeking a mate for a male umbrella cockatoo, Athan purchased a young female cockatoo with beautiful plumage and put them together. 'He acted like she wasn't even in the room.' A few months later Athan was given an older female in bad condition. She had been plucking her feathers out, an effect of captivity. 'She didn't have a feather from the neck down. The skin on her feet was all gnarly. She had wrinkles around her beak. He thought she was the love of his life.' The two birds immediately paired off and began rearing a series of baby cockatoos.[42]

Zoo keepers know to their despair that many species of animals will not breed with just any other animal. Orangutans are among the notoriously selective, even though they do not form lasting pairs in the wild. No doubt wild animals are selective too, but this is less obvious since they are not locked up with uncongenial partners.

The devotion that members of pairs lavish on one another also gives evidence of love. Some birds are famous examples of fidelity. Geese, swans and mandarin ducks are all symbols of marital devotion, and field biologists tell us this image is accurate. Coyotes, who are considered symbolic of trickery, would make equally good symbols of devotion, since they form lasting pairs. Observations of captive coyotes indicate that they begin to form pair attachments before they are sexually active. Coyote pairs observed by Hope Ryden curled up together, hunted mice together, greeted each other with elaborate displays of wagging and licking, and performed howling duets. Ryden describes two coyotes mating after howling together. Afterwards the female tapped the male with her paw and licked his face. Then they curled up together to sleep.[43] This looks a lot like romantic love. Whatever distinctions can be made between the love of two people and the love of two animals, the essence looks the same.

Lovingness – which may have evolved because animals that had it were more successful and left more children than those that did not – is a flexible thing. Instinct may urge the animal to love but does not say who it will love, though it may drop heavy hints. Lovingness instructs an animal to protect and care for its young but does not identify the young. Or it instructs an animal to fall in love and mate but does not say who the mate will be.

The flexibility of parental love is seen in those animals who adopt unrelated babies. Bear researcher Lynn Rogers was given an orphaned twelve-week-old black bear cub. Accompanied by a photographer, he took her out into the woods and presented her to Terri, a wild female black bear with two cubs, who was used to human presence. Terri wanted the cub as soon as she heard her squalling, but the cub ran away from the strange bear, and climbed the (alarmed) photographer's leg. Terri went to the photographer, took the cub in her mouth and carried her into the den with the two other cubs. The cub, Gerri, grew up to use part of Terri's territory and have cubs of her own.[44]

Researchers in Africa kidnapped infant and juvenile hamadryas baboons and released them near unrelated troops. Invariably these young monkeys were promptly adopted by young adult male baboons, who cared for them tenderly.[45] In general, the younger a baby animal is, the more apt it is to be adopted.

Even greater flexibility in parental love is demonstrated by instances of animals adopting young of other species. The experimenters who gave the mother rat the opportunity to adopt fifty-eight babies went on to offer mother rats odder babies. The rats readily adopted baby mice. If they were strong enough to drag a baby rabbit to their nest, they did so. They also retrieved young kittens and tried to keep experimenters from taking them out of the nest again. But since kittens nurse from a mother who is lying down, and mother rats nurse from a standing position, the rats could not suckle the kittens despite their vigorous attempts to shove them into position. Curious to know how far this would go, the experimenters procured two bantam chicks, and the rats 'eagerly and repeatedly' tried to tuck these into their nests. This was an even worse match, however, as the chicks 'became very loud and flapped' when the rats tried to grab them by the neck and drag them home.[46]

There are of course innumerable cases of dogs or cats who have adopted orphaned skunks or piglets, and pictures of such odd families are often seen in the newspapers. There is an old story of an unusual adoption that was not initiated by humans:

At Northrepps Hall, near Cromer, the seat of the late Sir Fowell Buxton, a large colony of parrots and macaws had been established, for whom a home had been provided near the house in a large open aviary, with hutches for them to lay in. But the birds as a rule preferred the woods . . . only coming home at feeding-time, when, on the well-known tinkling of the spoon on the tin containing their food, a large covey of gayly plumaged birds came fluttering down to the feeding-place, presenting a sight not often to be seen in England. The hutches being then practically deserted, a cat found one of them a convenient place to kitten in. While the mother-cat was away foraging, one of the female parrots paid a chance visit to the place, and finding the young kittens in her nest, at once adopted them as her own, and was found by Lady Buxton's man covering her strange adopted children with her wings.[47]

Other species seem not to adopt. According to researchers, a wildebeest calf who loses its mother among the vast herds will not be adopted and will perish.[48] This raises the question of how selectivity in love is esteemed. We are not likely to be favourably impressed when parents cannot tell whether or not a baby is their own, but we also don't like to see parents discriminating too harshly against the babies of others. Yet there seems to be no reason why either response should be considered incompatible with parental love.

Ducklings and goslings will grow attached to and follow whatever creature they see during a short period after they hatch. They become 'imprinted' on that creature. In this sense, a mallard is not born to love only a mallard, and a teal is not born to love only a teal. They love whomever seems to be their primary caretaker. For a mallard, this is usually a mallard, and for a teal a teal, but it is common for mallards raised by humans to become attached to their human foster parents. It is often said of animals raised by humans, 'He thinks he *is* a human'. This shows the flexibility built into the animal's readiness to love a parent.

An animal raised by another species will often want a member of that species as its mate when it grows up. A bird, if it is of a species that forms pair bonds, may have the capacity to love a mate. It may also have very specific instincts to court the mate in certain ways. When Tex, a female whooping crane hand-reared by humans, was ready to mate, she rejected male cranes. Instead she was attracted to 'Caucasian men of average height with dark hair'. Since whooping cranes are so close to extinction, it was considered vital to bring Tex into breeding condition so that she could be artificially inseminated. To do this, International Crane Foundation director George Archibald, a dark-haired Caucasian man, spent many weeks courting Tex. 'My duties involved endless hours of "just being there", several minutes of dancing early in the morning and again in the evening, long walks in quest of earthworms, nest building, and defending our territory against humans . . .' The effort was successful and eventually resulted in a crane chick.[49]

118

If the whooping crane dance and nest building are fixed action patterns, the lovingness seems to be a more diffuse impulse. The crane has made an error through no fault of its own. If Tex had been raised by cranes, she would have fallen in love with one, as most cranes do. If George Archibald had been raised by a crane, with whom would he have fallen in love?

Tibby, an otter described in Gavin Maxwell's book, *Raven, Seek Thy Brother*, was raised by a man who lived on an island off the coast of Scotland, and who got around on crutches. When he became seriously ill, he brought Tibby to Maxwell and asked him to care for her. He never returned for her as he died not long thereafter. Tibby did not care for life in the enclosure Maxwell provided for her, and made a habit of escaping and visiting the nearest village. There she found a man who also used crutches, and she decided to live with him. She tried to build a nest under his house, but he didn't like this idea and chased her away. Tibby disappeared shortly thereafter. Some time later Maxwell received a telephone call from a person who had been alarmed by an otter that had acted strangely, even trying to follow him into his house. Maxwell wrote, 'Acting on a sudden inspiration I asked, "You don't by any chance use crutches, do you?" "Yes," he replied, with astonishment in his voice, "but how in the world could you know that?"'[50] Tibby may have been imprinted on humans who used crutches or she may just have been fond of such people because they reminded her of the affectionate man who had vanished from her life.

In general, people believe humans can and do feel love, but in any given case it is possible to be uncertain that one human loves another, no matter what they say. Parents who do not love their children exist, as do people who hate their parents, husbands and wives, and brothers and sisters who do not love each other. Yet we continue to believe that there are parents, children, spouses and siblings who do feel love. It makes sense to use the same standard for animals.

Nearly every 'scientific' statement ever made about love has proven, over the years, to be false. What remain are the personal disclosures, the poems, the novels and the letters. Love between a woman and a woman, between a man and his father, between people and the animals they live with, and love from animal to animal is rarely susceptible to more than wonder and delight.

119

CHAPTER SIX

Grief, Sadness and the
Bones of Elephants

W HEN non-scientists speak of sadness in animals, the most
common evidence given is the behaviour of one of a pair
when its mate dies, or the behaviour of a pet when its owner dies
or leaves. This kind of bereavement receives notice and respect.

Mourning for a mate has been observed in wild animals
on some occasions. According to naturalist Georg Steller,
the sea cow named after him, and now extinct, was a monogamous species, with families consisting usually of a female, a
male and two young of different ages – 'one grown offspring,
and a little, tender one'. When the crew of the ship Steller was
on killed a female, whose body was washed up on the beach, the
male returned to the body for two consecutive days, 'as if he were
inquiring about her'.[1]

A wildlife biologist was observing a peregrine's nest when the
female disappeared. The male called for her for three days, both
when bringing food back to their eyrie and when empty-taloned.

His behaviour changed: he spent as much as an hour at a stretch waiting by the eyrie, which he had never done before. Late on the third day, while perched by the eyrie, he suddenly uttered a moan. Then he did not stir from his perch for a full day thereafter. On the fifth day after his mate's disappearance, the falcon bestirred himself to a frenzy of hunting, bringing food to his nestlings from dawn to dusk, without pausing to rest (before his mate's disappearance, his efforts had been less frenetic). When biologists climbed to the nest, a week after the female's disappearance, they found that three of the nestlings had starved to death, but that two had survived and were thriving under their father's care.[2]

As the fate of the three dead nestlings shows, it can be disastrous for a wild animal to manifest its grief. There is no survival value in moping, not eating and grieving. While love can be more readily reduced to evolutionary function, grief over loss of a loved one – another expression of love – often threatens survival, or simply has nothing to do with it, calling for an explanation of emotions on their own terms.

The sorrow of bereavement is more easily observed in captive or pet animals who are under the human eye. Elizabeth Marshall Thomas gives a moving account of Maria and Misha, two huskies who had formed a pair bond, when Misha's owners gave him away:

> Both he and Maria knew that something was terribly wrong when his owners came for him the last time, so that Maria struggled to follow him out the door. When she was prevented, she rushed to the windowseat and, with her back to the room, watched Misha get into the car. She stayed in the window for weeks thereafter, sitting backward on the seat with her face to the window and her tail to the room, watching and waiting for Misha. At last she must have realized that he wasn't going to come. Something happened to her at that point. She lost her radiance and became depressed. She moved more slowly, was less responsive, and got angry rather easily at things that before she would have overlooked . . . Maria never recovered from her loss, and although she never forfeited her place as alpha female, she showed no interest in forming a permanent bond with another male . . .[3]

Maria only knew that Misha was gone from her. Her behaviour

cannot be seen as anything but reminiscent of human grief.

Most domestic dogs aren't seen to form such pairs. But wild canids, such as wolves and coyotes, to whom dogs are very closely related, do form pairs. The conditions in which dogs are kept are very different from those in which wild canids live. Probably dog behaviour is more flexible than has been realised, and more strongly dictated by the conditions humans provide for them. For instance, both female and male dogs symbolise promiscuity to many humans, yet this behaviour has been created by the way humans breed and maintain dogs.

Some animals who do not form pairs in the wild are housed in pairs in captivity and grow deeply attached to each other. Often the mate is the only companion the animal has. Ackman and Alle, two circus horses, were stabled together. No particular attachment between them was noticed until Ackman's sudden death. Alle 'whinnied continually'. She scarcely ate or slept. In an effort to distract her, she was moved, given new companions and offered special foods. She was examined and medicated, in case she was ill. Within two months she had wasted to death.[4]

Two 'kiko' dolphins in a marine park, Kiko and Hoku, were devoted to one another for years, often making a point to touch each other with a fin while swimming around in their tank. When Kiko suddenly died, Hoku refused to eat. He swam slowly in circles, with his eyes clenched shut. He was given a new companion, Kolohi, who swam beside him and caressed him. Eventually he opened his eyes and ate once more. Although he became attached to Kolohi, observers felt that he never became as fond of her as he had been of Kiko.[5]

Researchers who had captured a dolphin by means of a fish hook and put her in a holding tank soon despaired for her life. Pauline, as they named her, could not even keep herself upright and had to be supported constantly. On the third day of her captivity a male dolphin was captured and placed in the same tank. This raised her spirits, and the male helped her swim, at times nudging her to the surface. She appeared to make a complete recovery, but two months later died quite suddenly from an abscess caused by the fish hook. The male refused to eat and died three days later. An autopsy revealed a perforated gastric ulcer, which was surely aggravated by his fasting.[6]

In the wild, too, animals grieve for companions other than

mates. Lions do not form pairs, yet a lion has been known to remain by the body of another lion that had been shot and killed, licking its fur.[7]

It would be the end of most species if every bereaved animal died of grief. Such cases must be extreme and unusual. Dying of grief is not the only proof of love and affection in animals, but these incidents do illuminate an emotional range and emotional possibilities. As is so often the case, elephants offer examples that seem uncannily similar to human feelings.

Cynthia Moss, a researcher who has studied wild African elephants for many years, describes mother elephants who appear in perfect health, but who become lethargic for many days after the death of a calf, trailing behind the rest of the family.[8]

An observer once came across a band of elephants surrounding a dying matriarch as she swayed and fell down. The other elephants clustered around her and ran through every piece of behaviour that might get her up again. A young male tried to raise her with his tusks but could not, tried putting food into her mouth and even tried sexually mounting her. The other elephants stroked her with their trunks and one calf knelt and tried to suckle. At last the group moved off, but one female and her calf stayed behind. The female stood with her back to the dead matriarch, now and then reaching back to touch her with one foot. The other elephants were calling to her and finally she walked away slowly.[9]

Moss describes the behaviour of an elephant herd around a dead elephant, of how they circle it 'disconsolately several times, and if it is still motionless they come to an uncertain halt. They then face outwards, their trunks hanging limply down to the ground. After a while they may prod and circle again, and then again stand, facing outwards.' Finally (perhaps when it is clear the elephant is dead), 'they may tear out branches and grass clumps from the surrounding vegetation and drop these on and around the carcass'. The curious detail of standing outwards suggests that the elephants may find the sight painful to see, or perhaps that this might even have ritual significance, whose meaning we do not yet comprehend.[10]

It was once thought that elephants went to special elephant graveyards to die. While this has been disproved, Moss speculates that elephants do have a concept of death. Elephants are strongly interested in elephant bones, and not at all in the bones of other species. Their reaction to elephant bones is so predictable that filmmakers have no difficulty in getting shots of elephants examining bones. Smelling them, turning them over, running their trunks over the bones, the elephants pick them up, feel them and sometimes carry them off for a distance before dropping them. They show the greatest interest in skull and tusks. Moss speculates that they are trying to recognize the individual.

Once Moss brought the jawbone of a dead elephant – an adult female – into her camp to determine its exact age. A few weeks after the elephant's death her family happened to pass through the camp area and made a detour to examine the jaw. Long after the others had moved on, the elephant's seven-year-old calf stayed behind, touching the jaw and turning it over with his feet and trunk. One can only agree with Moss's conclusion that the calf was somehow reminded of his mother – perhaps remembering the contours of her face. It is certain that the calf's memory is at work here. Whether he experienced a feeling of melancholic nostalgia, sorrow, perhaps even a positive feeling tied in to the memory of his mother, or was prey to some emotional experience we might not even be able to identify, it would be difficult to deny that deep feelings were involved.

A chimpanzee at the Arnhem Zoo, rather confusingly named Gorilla, had several babies who died despite her tender care. Each time an infant died she would become visibly depressed. Gorilla would sit huddled in a corner for weeks on end, ignoring the other chimpanzees. At times she would burst out screaming. This story had a happy sequel, when Gorilla was given the care of Roosje, a ten-week-old baby chimpanzee, and was taught to bottle-feed her.[11]

The death of a loved one is not the only source of sorrow. Tatu, a wild dwarf mongoose observed in Kenya, appeared to become depressed when denied the chance to be close to her mother, Diana. Although her siblings had become independent, Tatu preferred to remain at her mother's side. When her mother came into oestrus, her possessive father made Tatu stay away from Diana. During this time Tatu played less than she had previously, spent more time sitting by herself and was uninterested in grooming other animals.[12]

Loneliness seems to be a source of sorrow and sadness in animals which live in social or family groups. It is probably one of the factors causing the death of many captive animals. The presence or absence of a companion is an important factor in the survival of captive beavers. One wildlife biologist noted that yearling beavers, 'if they do not get companionship, may simply sit where they are put down until they die'.[13] More often loneliness is observed in captive animals, since it is a frequent by-product of confinement and domesticity. A lonely wild beaver could presumably set off in search of other beavers.

Animals seek each other out more than biologists once assumed, perhaps in an effort to avoid feelings of sadness, loneliness and sorrow. Many animals are rather sweepingly described as solitary. Careful field studies of animals famed for their solitary natures – tigers, leopards, rhinoceros and bears – often reveal that they spend more time associating with each other than previously thought. Female bears, for example, spend most of their lives in the company of their young. Both females and males spend their youth with their mother and with siblings, if any. Both females and males may gather at fishing spots. In zoos, bears confined together may show a surprising capacity not only to get along but to play and form alliances.[14]

In some species, males who have been 'kicked out of the nest' by their mothers form bachelor herds. African elephants gather in groups in 'bull areas'.[15]

Both the European wildcat and the fishing cat have been said to be solitary species in which the female and male separate after mating, and the female rears the kittens alone. Female and male are often housed as pairs in zoos, however, with occasional interesting results. Usually the male is removed from the cage before the birth of kittens, in case he should harm them. But when this precaution was omitted in the Cracow Zoo, the male wildcat carried his meat to the entrance of the den and made coaxing sounds. Similarly, in the Magdeburg Zoo, the male wildcat lay outside the den day and night, and, though normally peaceful, attacked the keeper if he came too near. He carried food to the mouth of the den and waited until the female came out or hissed at him, upon which he withdrew. Later, the male threatened any zoo-goers who startled his kittens.

Fishing cats at the Frankfurt Zoo also cooperated in raising their kittens. The male not only brought food, but often curled up in the nest box with the rest of the family. If he was out and the female also left the nest box, the male became restless and went in the nest box with the kittens.

Possibly zoological beliefs about how these species behave in the wild are mistaken, and these species are less solitary than has been assumed, or perhaps this is another demonstration of the flexibility of animal behaviour. Paul Leyhausen, who observed these cats, speculates that while males in the wild may have nothing to do with their erstwhile mates and with their kittens, males in captivity may be 'subjected to stimuli which awaken normally dormant behavior patterns'.[16] If so, we are led to wonder whether a male fishing cat, wandering by a South East Asian stream or through a forest, ever feels a twinge from those normally dormant patterns and feels lonely.

Even when captive animals are not confined in solitude, their imprisonment may make them sad. It is often said of zoo animals that the way to tell if they're happy is to ask whether the young play and the adults breed. If they do, they're happy. I suspect most zoo keepers would not accept this standard of happiness for themselves, however. As Jane Goodall has noted, 'Even in concentration camps, babies were born, and there is no good reason to believe that it is different for chimpanzees'.[17]

Captivity is undoubtedly more painful to some animals than others. Lions seem to have less difficulty with the notion of lying in the sun all day than tigers do, for example. Yet even lions can be seen in many zoos pacing restlessly back and forth in the stereotyped motions seen in so many captive animals.

Recall the concept of *funktionslust*, the enjoyment of one's abilities. This allows us to imagine the opposite, the feeling of frustration and misery that overtakes an animal when its capacities are prevented from being expressed. If it is possible that the animal enjoys using its natural abilities, it is also possible that the animal *misses* using them just as much. Most zoo animals, particularly the large ones, have little or no opportunity to use their abilities. Eagles have no room to fly, cheetahs have no room to run, goats have but a single boulder to climb. A gradual trend in zoo construction and design is to make the 'cages' better resemble the natural habitat.

There is no reason to suppose that zoo life is not a source of sadness to most animals imprisoned in them. They have been compared to displaced persons in wartime. It would be comforting to believe that they were happy there, that they felt delighted to receive medical care and grateful to be sure of their next meal. Unfortunately, in the main, there is no evidence to suppose that they do. Most will take every opportunity to escape. Most will not breed.

Some captive animals die of grief when taken from the wild. Sometimes these deaths appear to be from disease, perhaps because an animal under great stress becomes vulnerable to illness. Others are quite obviously deaths from despair – near suicides. Wild animals may refuse to eat, killing themselves in the only way open to them. We do not know if they are aware that they will die if they don't eat, but it is clear that they are extremely unhappy.

In 1913, Jasper Von Oertzen described the death of a young gorilla imported to Europe. 'Hum-Hum had lost all joy in living. She succeeded in living to reach Hamburg, and from there, the Animal Park at Stellingen, with all her caretakers, but her energy did not return again. With signs of the greatest sadness of soul Hum-Hum mourned over the happy past. One could find no fatal illness; it was as always with these costly animals: "She died of a broken heart".'[18]

Marine mammals have a high death rate in captivity. This is not always apparent to visitors to marine parks and oceanariums. A pilot whale celebrity at one oceanarium was actually thirteen different pilot whales, each successive one being introduced to visitors by the same name, as if it were the same animal.[19]

It doesn't take much reflection to see the great difference in a marine mammal's life when it is kept in an oceanarium. Orcas grow to twenty-three feet long, weigh up to 9,000 pounds and roam a hundred miles in a day. They are believed to have a life expectancy as long as our own. Yet at Sea World in San Diego, the oceanarium with the best track record for keeping orcas alive, they last an average of eleven years.[20]

If a person's life-span were shortened this much, would one still speak of happiness? When I asked a number of dolphin trainers whether their animals were happy, they all said yes: they ate, engaged in sexual intercourse (though it is extremely rare for an orca to give birth in captivity) and were almost never sick. This could well mean that they were not depressed, but does it mean they were happy? The fact that people ask this question again and again is indicative of some deep malaise, some profound guilt at confining these lively sea-travellers.

Which animals will suffer the most in captivity is not always easy to predict. Harbour seals often thrive in oceanariums and zoos. Hawaiian monk seals almost invariably die. Sometimes they refuse to eat, and sometimes they succumb to illness. One way or another, one observer noted, they have generally 'just moped to death'.[21]

The issue of the effects of captivity is most painful when one considers animals that can live nowhere but in captivity because their habitat is gone – as is the case for an increasing number of species – or because they are physically incapacitated. When fewer than a dozen California condors were left in the wild, arguments raged about whether to capture the remaining birds for captive breeding or to let the species perish freely, without undergoing the ignominy of captivity. The condor is a soaring bird which can easily fly fifty miles in a day, a life which can hardly compare to that in a cage. In the end, the birds were captured, and so for a time there were no California condors in the wild. Since then, captive-bred birds have been released in an attempt to re-establish the species.

The fact that animals can be sad must be acknowledged if it is to be examined and understood. Zoo keepers ask whether animals are healthy, whether they are likely to breed. It is rare that zoos ask 'What would make this animal *happy*?' Nor have the studies of animal behaviourists been of much help. *The Oxford Dictionary of Animal Behaviour* notes: 'It seems reasonable to allow that animals may be distressed by being unable to feed and drink, to move their limbs, to sleep and to have social interaction with their fellows, but the difficulty of defining distress in an objective and convincing way has been a stumbling-block in the formation of animal welfare legislation even in countries where there is wide-spread public interest in the way that animals are treated.'[22]

In humans, extreme sadness is called depression. The standard psychiatric dictionary defines it as 'A clinical syndrome consisting of lowering of mood–tone (feelings of painful dejection), difficulty in thinking and psychomotor retardation'.[23] As used by psychiatrists and psychologists, it is a catch-all diagnosis, referring to melancholy springing from a number of sources. In the quest to validate the medical model of psychiatry, scientists have sought to produce clinically depressed animals in the laboratory. Pursuant to this, some experimenters have gone to work to provide animals with spectacularly unhappy childhoods.

Among the most widely reported experiments in the history of animal behaviour are those psychologist Harry Harlow performed on rhesus monkeys. The baby monkeys who preferred soft huggable dummy mothers to hard wire surrogates, even when only the wire ones dispensed milk, are famous and have been used as evidence that psychological studies on animals – really forms of torture – can teach humans about their emotions. But surely this gruesome experiment was gratuitously emotionally cruel as well as unnecessary to prove this point.

Other rhesus monkeys, at the age of six weeks, were placed alone in the 'depression chamber', or vertical chamber, a stainless-steel trough intended to reproduce a psychological 'well of despair'.[24] Forty-five days of solitary confinement in the chamber produced permanently impaired monkeys. Even when months had passed since their experience, the chambered monkeys were listless, incurious and almost completely asocial, huddling in one spot and clasping themselves.[25] No knowledge gained, no point proved, can justify this abuse.

Similarly, dogs, cats and rats in the laboratory have been induced to feel the global pessimism known as 'learned helplessness'. In the paradigmatic experiment, dogs were strapped into a harness and given electric shocks at unpredictable intervals. Afterwards they were placed in a divided chamber. When a tone sounded, the dogs needed to jump into the other side of the chamber to avoid being shocked. Most dogs learned this quickly, but two-thirds of the dogs who had been given inescapable shocks just lay still and whined, making no attempt to escape. Their previous experience had apparently taught them despair.[26]

This effect wore off in a few days. Yet, if the dogs were subjected to inescapable shocks four times in a week, their 'learned helplessness' was lasting. In related studies, rats subjected to unavoidable shock developed stomach ulcers, while rats that received as many shocks but could take action to avoid shock did not develop ulcers. Psychologist Martin Seligman, the principal figure in the study of learned helplessness, argues that the shocked animal is frightened at first, but when it comes to believe it is helpless, sinks into depression.[27] In his explanation of how he came upon the notion of doing experiments on learned helplessness in animals, Seligman cites the research of G. P. Richter during the 50s, 'who reasoned that for a wild rat, being held in the hand of a predator like man, having whiskers trimmed, and being put in a vat of hot water from which escape is impossible produces a sense of helplessness in the rat'. The animal research really shows nothing about humans that one cannot learn by talking to battered women about their lives in detail.

Learned helplessness has been experimentally produced in humans, though not by means of shock. People given tasks at which they repeatedly fail quickly come to believe that they will fail at other tasks and do poorly at them, compared to those who have not been put through a sequence of failures. In the real world, battered women may be unable to leave their batterers, although the risks of leaving and the lack of anywhere to go may be as important as their perception that any action on their part to save themselves from continued abuse is pointless.

Having produced depressed dogs, Seligman wanted to cure them. He placed 'helpless' dogs in the chamber and removed the partition to make it easy for them to cross and avoid shock, but the despondent dogs made no effort to get away and so did not discover escape was possible. Seligman got in the chamber and called them, and offered them food, but the dogs didn't move. Eventually he was reduced to dragging the dogs back and forth on leashes. Some dogs were dragged back and forth two hundred times before they discovered that this time they could escape the electric shocks. According to Seligman, their recovery from learned helplessness was lasting and complete.

Many other experimenters have produced learned helplessness in the laboratory by various means, with sometimes fiendish results. One experimenter raised rhesus monkeys in solitude, in black-walled isolation cages, from infancy until six months, to induce 'social helplessness'. Then he taped each young monkey to a cruciform restraining device and placed it, for an hour a day, in a cage with other young monkeys. After initial withdrawal, the unrestrained monkeys poked and prodded the restrained monkeys, pulled their hair, gouged their eyes and prized their mouths open. The restrained monkeys struggled, but could not escape. All they could do was to cry out. After two to three months of this abuse, their behaviour changed. They stopped struggling, though they still cried out. And as the experimenter noted, 'no advantage was taken of numerous opportunities to bite the oppressor which thrust fingers or sex organs against or into its mouth'.[28] These monkeys were lastingly traumatised, and were terrified of other monkeys even when unrestrained. Like the other experiments, this one is distinguished by its cruelty.

Comparatively few depressed humans became so by being placed in solitary confinement for half their childhood, or by being raised in solitary confinement and then tortured by peers. Oddly enough, the argument on the part of the scientists conducting these experiments has been that animals are so similar to us in their feelings, that we learn about human depression by studying animal depression. But this raises an important ethical question: if the animals can suffer the way we do, which is the whole point of the experiments, is it not sadistic to conduct them? Clearly the animals can be made deeply unhappy, but this fact could have been observed under naturally occuring conditions, without subjecting sensitive creatures to unnecessary cruelty.

Through all these griefs and torments, animals display sorrow through their movements, postures and actions. Often animal vocalisations provide evidence of sadness. Wolves seem to have a special mourning howl or lonesome howl that differs from their usual convivial howling.[29] Other animals are said to wail, moan or cry. When Marchessa, an elderly female mountain gorilla, died, the silverback male of her group became subdued and was heard to whimper frequently, the only time such a sound had been heard from a silverback. These two wild gorillas may have spent as much as thirty years of their lives together.[30] As one observer wrote of orangutans, 'In disappointment the young specimen quite commonly whimpers or weeps, without, however, shedding tears'.[31]

The shedding of tears is an evidence of human sorrow which often makes a great impression. Newborn infants cry, and their eyes may water if irritated, but they do not usually shed tears. By the time they are a few months old, tears appear when they cry. Adults cry less, and some adults never shed tears.

Tears have several functions. Continuous tears keep the eye moist. Reflex tears flush foreign objects or irritating gases out of the eye. Humans also shed emotional tears – tears of grief, tears of happiness or tears of rage. Emotional tears contain a higher percentage of protein than other tears.[32] The subject is curiously little studied, but emotional tears may have both physical and social or communicative functions. It is unclear how tears of pain should be classified.

No one knows for certain why humans weep at all. One human-centred theory has been that 'the ability to weep might be related to the ability to conceptualize . . . internally. Animals cannot conceptualize nor do they weep.'[33]

Since it is possible for people to feel great unhappiness and not weep, it is not clear why tears communicate so profoundly. It may be that our reaction is instinctive, and perhaps part of the respect accorded to tears comes from the possibility that they are ours alone. It has been suggested that almost every human bodily secretion is considered disgusting, and its ingestion is taboo (faeces, urine, mucus, etc.) with one exception: tears. This is the one body product that may be uniquely human and hence does not remind us of what we have in common with animals.[34]

Perhaps it isn't only humans who are impressed by tears, however. The chimpanzee Nim Chimpsky, who regularly sought to comfort people who looked sad, was particularly tender when he saw tears, which he would wipe away.[35] Since Nim was raised by humans, he may have learned the connection between tears and unhappiness.

It would be interesting to discover whether any animals who have not had the opportunity to learn about tears respond to tears as evidence of sadness in humans or even in other animals. This could be answered experimentally. If a chimpanzee reared with other chimps saw another who appeared to be shedding tears, would it react as Nim did? If a chimpanzee accustomed to humans saw a person cry for the first time, would it behave as though it was a sign of distress?

Tears keep the eyes of animals moist. Their eyes also water when irritated. Tears may spill from the eyes of an animal in pain. Tears have been seen in the eyes of animals as diverse as an injured horse and an eggbound grey parrot.[36] Some animals are more tearful than others. Seals, which have no nasolacrymal ducts into which tears drain, are especially apt to have tears rolling down their faces. This is thought to help them cool down when they are on land.[37]

Charles Darwin, in researching *The Expressions of the Emotions in Man and Animals*, looked for evidence that animals did or did not shed emotional tears. He complained that 'The Macacus maurus, which formerly wept so copiously in the Zoological Gardens, would have been a fine case for observation; but the two monkeys now there, and which are believed to be of the same species, do not weep'.[38] He was not able to observe animals shedding emotional tears, and called weeping one of the 'special expressions of man'.

Darwin noted one exception, the Indian elephant. It was reported to him by Sir E. Tennant that some newly captured elephants in Sri Lanka (then called Ceylon), tied up and lying on the ground, showed 'no other indication of suffering than the tears which suffused their eyes and flowed incessantly'. Another captured elephant, when bound, sank to the ground, 'uttering choking cries, with tears trickling down his cheeks' (a captured elephant is usually also an elephant that has been separated from its family). Other elephant observers in Sri Lanka assured Darwin that they had not seen elephants weep, and that Sri Lankan hunters said they had never seen elephants weep. Darwin put his trust in Tennant's observations, however, because they were confirmed by the elephant keeper at the London Zoo, who said he had several times seen an old female there shedding tears when her young companion was taken out.

In the years since Darwin's observations, the balance of the evidence has been the same: most elephant watchers have never seen them weep, or have, rarely, seen them weep when injured, yet a few observers have claimed to have seen them weep when not injured. An elephant trainer with a small American circus told researcher William Frey that his elephant, Okha, does cry at times, but that he had no idea why. Okha sometimes shed a tear when being scolded, it is reported, and at least once wept while giving children rides.[39] Iain Douglas-Hamilton, who has spent years working with African elephants, has only seen elephants shed tears when in pain.[40] Tears fell from the eyes of Claudia, a captive elephant, having a difficult labour with her first calf.[41]

R. Gordon Cummings, a nineteenth-century hunter in South Africa, described killing the biggest male elephant he had ever seen. He first shot it in the shoulder, so that it could not run away. The elephant limped over to a tree and leaned against it. Deciding to contemplate the elephant before killing it, Cummings paused to make coffee and then chose to determine experimentally which were an elephant's vulnerable spots. He walked up to it and fired bullets into various parts of the head. The elephant did not move except to touch the bullet wounds with the tip of his trunk. 'Surprised and shocked to find that I was only tormenting and prolonging the sufferings of the noble beast, which bore his trials with such dignified composure,' Cummings wrote, he decided to finish him off and shot him nine times behind the shoulder. 'Large tears now trickled from his eyes, which he slowly shut and opened; his colossal frame quivered convulsively, and, falling on his side, he expired.'42 This elephant must have been in great pain, however, and that alone would have been cause enough for him to shed tears. Other than humans, no animal documented runs torture experiments on other animals.

In his book *Elephant Tramp*, George Lewis, an itinerant elephant trainer, reported in 1955 that in the years he had worked with elephants he had only seen one weeping. This was a young, timid female named Sadie, who was being trained along with five others to do an act for the Robbins Brothers Circus. The elephants were being taught their acts quickly, since the show would start in three weeks, but Sadie had trouble learning what was wanted. One day, unable to understand what she was being told to do, she ran out of the ring. 'We brought her back and began to punish her for being so stupid.' (Based on information Lewis gives elsewhere, they probably punished her by hitting her on the side of the head with a large stick.)

To their astonishment, Sadie, who was lying down, began to utter racking sobs, and tears poured from her eyes. The dumbfounded trainers knelt by Sadie, caressing her. Lewis says that he never punished her again, and that she learned the act and became a 'good' circus elephant.43 His fellow elephant trainers, who had never witnessed such a thing, were sceptical. Victor Hugo wrote in his diary on 2 January 1871: On a abbatu l'éléphant du Jardin des Plantes. Il a pleuré. On va le manger. (The elephant in the Jardin des Plantes was slaughtered. He wept. He will be eaten).44

That elephants weep emotional tears is widely believed in India, where elephants have been kept for many centuries. It is said that when the conqueror Tamerlane captured three thousand elephants in battle, snuff was put in their eyes so they would appear to be weeping at the loss. Douglas Chadwick was told of a young Indian elephant shedding tears when scolded for playing too boisterously and knocking someone down, and also of an elephant that ran away and, when found by its mahout, wept along with him.[45]

Elephant handlers say that the eyes of elephants water heavily, presumably to keep their eyes moist. Fluid may also stream from their temporal glands, which are between the eye and ear, but anyone familiar with elephants would not be confused by this. Possibly there is some significance to the fact that most of the elephants shedding tears were lying down, not a usual position for an elephant. Perhaps the position somehow prevents drainage of tears.[46] For all we know elephants often shed tears of grief, but if standing, the tears run through nasolacrymal ducts and down the inside of their trunks.

Emotional tears have been reported in some other species. Biochemist William Frey, who studies human emotional tears, has received reports of dogs – particularly poodles – shedding tears in emotional situations, such as being left behind by their owner, but despite repeated efforts, he has been unable to confirm this in the laboratory. No one but their owners has witnessed these tears, and poodles are a particularly damp-eyed breed even at their most cheerful.

It has been reported that tears rolled from the eyes of adult seals who saw seal pups clubbed by hunters. This is undoubtedly true. But since tears often roll from seals' eyes, there is no proof that these were emotional tears.

Beavers have also been suspected of crying emotional tears. Trappers have said that a beaver in a trap sheds tears, but such beavers may be crying in pain. However, one biologist has reported that beavers also weep copiously when manually restrained.[47]

Dian Fossey reported tears shed by Coco, an orphaned mountain gorilla. Coco was three or four years old when her family was killed before her eyes to secure her capture. She had spent a month in a tiny cage before coming into Fossey's possession and was very ill. She was released into an indoor pen with windows. When Coco first looked out of the window of her pen at a forested mountainside like the one on which she grew up, she suddenly began 'to sob and shed actual tears'. Fossey said she had never witnessed a gorilla do this before, nor did she afterwards.[48]

Montaigne, who may be the first Western author to express distaste for the hunt, wrote in his 1580 essay 'Of Cruelty':

> For myself, I have not even been able without distress to see pursued and killed an innocent animal which is defenseless and which does us no harm. And as it commonly happens that the stag, feeling himself out of breath and strength, having no other remedy left, throws himself back and surrenders to ourselves who are pursuing him, asking for our mercy by his tears . . . that has always seemed to me a very unpleasant spectacle.[49]

It is possible that elephants and a few other animals weep. It is also possible that only humans weep for emotional reasons.

In the end, it hardly matters whether stags, beavers, seals or elephants weep. Tears are not grief, but tokens of grief. The evidence from other animal behaviours is strong. It is hard to doubt that Darwin's sobbing elephants were unhappy, even if their tears sprang from mechanical causes. A seal surely feels sad when its pup is killed, whether it is dry-eyed or not. Just as a psychiatrist cannot pronounce with any authority when a person has crossed the border of 'normal' grief to 'pathological' mourning, so too should we resist any temptation to declare the deep and mysterious world of sorrow beyond the emotional capacities of any animal.

CHAPTER SEVEN

A Capacity for Happiness

THEORISTS of human joy have sought to categorise it in terms of active and passive joy, active and receptive joy, or magic joy and real joy, and to analyse the causes of joy in terms that range from a 'sharp reduction in the gradient of neural stimulation' to 'what obtains after some creative or socially beneficial act that was not done for the express purpose of obtaining joy or doing good'.[1] Such theorists tend to ignore the possibility of animal joy.

No one who has ever had a dog or cat can doubt the animal capacity for happiness. Beholding and sharing their open joy is one of the great pleasures people take in animals. We see them leap or run, hear them bark or mew, and put words to their delight: 'You're home!' 'You're going to feed me!' 'We're going for a walk!' Like uninhibited human happiness, the pleasure is contagious, and pets serve as a conduit to joyful feelings. Many of us have to go a long way to find a person as openly ecstatic

137

as a cat about to be fed or a dog about to go for a walk. If such joy were a figment of our anthropomorphic projections, it would constitute a remarkable collective delusion.

Happiness can be a reward, a response of pleasure in accomplishment. As one psychologist who takes the evolutionary approach argues, 'Presumably, sentient organisms could just as well be constructed without mood – complex computers are. What selective pressure produced feeling and affect? I suggest that joy accompanies and motivates effective responding; and . . . in the absence of effective responding, an aversive state arises, which organisms seek to avoid.'[2] If an animal feels good from doing things that have selective value, certainly the happiness also can be said to have selective value. But that does not necessarily mean that the happiness exists only because it has selective value. Few people would recognise their own happiness in the above description. The grim tasks of survival, even surviving well, do not make a lot of people happy. Part of happiness is often its lack of relation, or even its perverse relation, to any rational end, its utter functionlessness. The evidence is good that animals as well as people do feel such joy.

There are many signs by which joy in animals can be recognised, including vocalisations. Pet cats are admired for purring, a sound which usually indicates contentment, though it may sometimes be used to appease another animal. Big cats purr, too. Cheetahs purr loudly when they lick each other, and cubs purr when they rest with their mother. Lions purr, though not as often as house cats (and only while exhaling). Both young and adult lions also have a soft hum they utter in similar circumstances – when playing gently, rubbing their cheeks together, licking each other or resting.[3]

Happy gorillas are said to sing. Biologist Ian Redmond reports that they make a sound – something between a dog whining and a human singing – when they are especially happy. On a rare sunny day, when the foraging is particularly good, the family group will 'sing', eat and put their arms around each other.[4] Howling wolves may be asserting territorial rights or cementing social bonds, but it also appears to make them happy, observers say.[5]

Black bear cubs express their emotions more clearly than adults, says wildlife biologist Lynn Rogers: 'When a cub is very comfortable, particularly when it's nursing, they give what I call a comfort sound. I used to call it a nursing vocalization until I saw cubs doing it when they were not nursing.' He imitates the sound, a low squeal. 'A pleasing little sound that they make. One time I gave a big bear a piece of warm fat. It just really seemed to like it. In fact, it made that same sound in a deeper voice. So I don't know – is that happiness or not? Is it just comfort? It was pleased, anyway.'[6]

Joy can be expressed in silence and observers of almost any species will quickly learn to know the body language of a happy animal. Darwin cited the frisking of a horse turned out to pasture, and the grins of orangutans and monkeys being caressed. In a personal letter he also gave a charming account of animal joy:

> Two days since, when it was very warm, I rode to the Zoological Society, & by the greatest piece of good fortune it was the first time this year, that the Rhinoceros was turned out. – Such a sight has seldom been seen, as to behold the rhinoceros kicking & rearing, (though neither end reached any great height) out of joy. – The elephant was in the adjoining yard & was greatly amazed at seeing the rhinoceros so frisky: He came close to the palings & after looking very intently, set off trotting himself, with his tail sticking out at one end & his trunk at the other, – squeeling and braying like half a dozen broken trumpets.[7]

Signs of happiness are no doubt as subject to misinterpretation as those of any emotion. One of the many factors contributing to the fascination with bottlenose dolphins is their permanent 'smile', created by the shape of their jaws rather than by emotional expression. Since a dolphin doesn't have a mobile face, it may be 'smiling' even when furious or despondent.

Despite this, biologist Kenneth Norris believes that people and dolphins can recognise the emotional freight of many of each other's signals. That is, the two species can recognise or learn to recognise friendliness, hostility or fear across the species barrier, even if we do not understand each other's vocalisations. He cites a spinner dolphin's 'peremptory' barks, which indicate boisterous behaviour, as compared with soft chuckles that indicate friendly contact, often between female and male. The body language of human and dolphin mothers with their babies, Norris says, is not only comparable, but easily understood by both species.[8]

When the ice finally melted from a New England beaver pond in spring, a male beaver and his yearling daughter swam over to look at their dam. On the way, they 'porpoised', swimming over one another's backs. Afterwards they swam across the pond together, rolling, diving, popping up again and turning somersaults in a display of delight with which even a non-swimmer could identify.[9]

In an example of more literal 'body language', several apes have been taught the sign 'happy'. Nim Chimpsky used the word when he was excited, as when he was being tickled.[10] Koko, asked what gorillas say when they're happy, signed 'Gorilla hug'.[11] Whether Nim and Koko would understand one another's use of 'happy' is unknown.

One rainy day the chimpanzees Moja and Tatu were offered a chance to go outside into an exercise area. Moja, who hates rain, went out but scurried into a cave. Tatu climbed to the top of a play structure and sat in the rain, signing 'Out out out out out out'. A researcher said 'It looked like she was singing in the rain'.[12]

A behaviour called 'war-dancing' is seen in mountain goats and chamois. One animal starts rearing, leaping, tossing its horns and whirling about. One after another, the whole band takes it up. Goats war-dance most often in the summer, when food is plentiful. The sight of a slanting snow bank can start a war-dance and send the band bucking, twirling and sliding downhill, kicking up the snow. They expend so much energy in their dance that some goats have been seen to make almost two full turns in the air in one jump.[13]

What have these goats got to be happy about? They haven't heard news of an inheritance, received the offer of a job or seen their names in the newspaper. They have nothing to be pleased about except life, sunshine and being well fed. They jump for joy.

Sometimes the source of the joy is obvious and one we immediately recognise, such as the excitement displayed by a group of wild chimpanzees finding a large pile of food. 'Three or four adults may pat each other, embrace, hold hands, press their mouths against one another and utter loud screams for several minutes before calming down sufficiently to start feeding,' Goodall and Hamburg reported. The implications seemed obvious. 'This kind of behavior,' they wrote, 'is similar to that shown by a human child, who, when told of a special treat, may fling his arms ecstatically around the bearer of the good news and squeal with delight.'[14] Nor are apes the only animals in which cooperation and emotion seem to reflect consciousness.

A principal source of joy for social animals is the presence of their family and the members of their group. Nim Chimpsky was raised in a human family for the first year and a half of his life. When he was about four years old, a reunion was arranged with the family which had raised him. When he spotted them, in a place where he had never seen them before, Nim smiled hugely, shrieked and pounded the ground for three minutes, gazing back and forth at the different members of the family. Finally he calmed down enough to go and hug his foster mother, still smiling, and shrieking intermittently. He spent more than an hour hugging his family, grooming them and playing with them before they left. This was the only occasion on which Nim was seen to smile for more than a few minutes.[15]

Two male bottlenose dolphins at an oceanarium did not have the adversarial relationship seen between many male dolphins confined together. One was removed to another exhibit for three weeks. When it was returned, the two seemed very excited. For hours they hurtled around the tank side by side, occasionally leaping out of the water. For several days they spent all their time together, ignoring the other dolphin in the tank.[16]

The meeting of two related groups of elephants seems to be a very emotional time. Cynthia Moss has reported the meeting of two such groups, one led by the old female Teresia, the other led by Slit Ear. From a quarter of a mile away they began calling to each other (since elephants can communicate over long distances with sounds too low for us to hear, they might have been aware of each other before they started calling audibly). Teresia changed direction and began walking fast. Their heads and ears were up, and fluid poured from the temporal glands of all the elephants in the herd. They stopped, called, got a response, changed course slightly and sped ahead. Slit Ear's group appeared out of some trees, running towards them.

The groups ran towards each other, screaming and trumpeting. Teresia and Slit Ear rushed together, clicked tusks and twined trunks together while rumbling and flapping their ears. All the elephants performed similar greetings, spinning around, leaning on each other, rubbing each other, clasping trunks and trumpeting, rumbling and screaming. So much fluid streamed from their temporal glands that it ran down their chins.

Moss writes: 'I have no doubt even in my most scientifically rigorous moments that the elephants are experiencing joy when they find each other again. It may not be similar to human joy or even comparable, but it is elephantine joy and it plays a very important part in their whole social system.'[17] Elephantine joy is recognised as joy because it resembles human joy. Yet we should not assume that it is identical joy. After all, we have no idea how one feels when one's temporal glands are streaming fluid. There may well be forms of joy in elephant society unrecognisable, unintelligible or simply unknown to human experience.

A principal source of delight for many animals is their young. Certain features signal 'baby animal', such as big eyes, uncertain gait, big feet and large head. Humans respond to these traits not only in baby humans but in baby animals, as well as in some adult animals. Some animals react to youthful traits with affection, others by being unaggressive towards babies. Such recognition of baby features is considered to be largely innate, and presumably animals may at times be feeling what people feel when they say a baby, whether human or animal, is adorable. The presence of such traits in baby dinosaurs has caused paleontologist John Horner to aver that some dinosaurs must have found their babies 'cute'.[18]

When a young sparrow crash-landed in the chimpanzee cage at the Basle Zoo, one of the apes instantly snatched it in her hand. Expecting to see the bird gobbled up, the keeper was astonished to see the chimpanzee cradle the terrified fledgling tenderly in a cupped palm, gazing at it with what seemed like delight. The other chimpanzees gathered and the bird was delicately passed from hand to hand. The last to receive the bird took it to the bars and handed it to the astounded keeper.[19] Was it joy or compassion or a combination of both that the chimpanzee felt?

Biologist Lars Wilsson observed that Tuff, a beaver, looked grim when watching over her baby as it swam, looked deeply unhappy if a stranger came near it, but when she was nursing it or grooming it, 'radiated pure maternal happiness'.[20]

Another source of human happiness is pride, the feeling that we have done something well. Wilsson described the changed demeanour of Greta and Stina, captive beavers who managed to build a dam in their enclosure. These yearling beavers had been captured as infants and had never seen a dam. Until they built theirs, they had not been particularly friendly and snarled at one another if they got too close. After the dam was built they began eating side by side, uttering friendly 'talk' sounds. Not only did they no longer object to one another, each sought the other out to vocalise or groom. Greta and Stina also spent more time out of their nest box, swimming and diving in the water which their dam had deepened.[21] The pride in accomplishment also seemed to create friendship.

One observer described wild beavers whose dam had been severely damaged by human vandals at a season when material to repair it was hard to find. The observer arranged for suitable branches to be deposited in the pond while the beavers were asleep. The male of the pair was removing wood from his lodge to transfer to the dam when he discovered the branches. He began to swim among the branches, sniffing them and uttering loud excited cries. One observer thought that the beaver was 'rejoicing', the other that he was 'marvelling', but then, coming to their scientific senses, they agreed that the beaver's 'subjective feelings . . . were beyond our power to ascertain'.[22]

Some captive animals experience little joy in life. For some, performing may be a chance to work, to display prowess, to feel proud. A tiger who cannot hunt, cannot mate with other tigers and cannot explore and survey its territory has little chance of feeling self-esteem. Perhaps, for some tigers, a chance to jump through a flaming hoop is better than nothing. But why should tigers have to settle for something that is better than nothing? To turn these magnificent animals into slaves, and then degrade them further by making them perform tricks for human amusement shows as much about human abasement as it does about theirs. It is sad that a tiger is reduced to wanting to perform because otherwise it is condemned to slow death by boredom.

The results of this distorted behaviour affect the animals and their trainers. Animal trainer Gunther Gebel-Williams had a tiger named India in his act for over twenty years. When he felt she was too old and deserved a rest, he stopped using her in the act. But every time he passed her cage while bringing the other tigers into the ring, she 'cried'. Gebel-Williams felt so sorry for India that he put her back in the act, with unfortunate results, as she was later attacked and injured by another of the tigers. Her performance may have been a source of pride, but that it was the only one she had was hardly of her own choice. Along with the pride, it is important to recognise the loss of dignity. We have not spoken of dignity much in this book, possibly because the history of human dealings with animals does not give much occasion for it.[23]

Arguing that dolphins may be on the verge of 'accepting domestication', Karen Pryor says that they enjoy performing tasks humans set for them. 'I have seen a dolphin, striving to master an athletically difficult trick, actually refuse to eat its "reward" fish until it got the stunt right.'[24] It is difficult to maintain that the dolphin 'enjoys' the challenge, unless we know what its alternatives are. Would a wild dolphin ever find pleasure in such a task? Perhaps this incident speaks for dolphins having a notion of justice, but it is difficult to say. It is provocative, even fascinating, but it was artificially induced. Observing something similar in wild dolphins would tell more about their society.

Horse trainers commonly observe that some horses feel pride. Secretariat, who won the Kentucky Derby in 1973, was said to be proud. As evidence it was noted by trainers and jockeys that he refused to run unless he was allowed to run the race his way, despite the fact that he was usually a docile, biddable horse.[25] When I asked whether a dog that performs well in an obedience competition is proud of itself, animal trainer Ralph Dennard cautiously replied, 'It seems like it's proud of itself. They look like they're proud. They're confident; they're happy; they stand up there,' and he threw out his chest as such a dog might.

People experience pride of possession, and perhaps animals can too. The chimpanzee colony of which Washoe is a member recently moved into a large new facility, with indoor and outdoor exercise areas. When one of Washoe's human companions visited for the first time since the move, Washoe took her by the hand and led her from room to room, carefully showing her every nook and cranny. Washoe may have had other motivations, but she may simply have been proud of her spacious new quarters.[26] It was also a sign of her feelings of friendship.

An important source of joy is freedom. It has been argued that if all an animal's needs are met, it will not care whether it is free or not, but many well-fed, well-treated captive animals regularly endeavour to escape. Freedom is relative. In spring, when the chimpanzees at the Arnhem Zoo are allowed out of their winter quarters for the first time, there is a scene of exultation as they scream and hoot, clasp and kiss one another, jump up and down and pound one another on the back. They are not actually free, but the additional space is thrilling to them. It looks as if it gives them joy.[27]

In a related issue, it has been argued that animals (and people) have a need for control. One experimenter gave captive white-footed mice an opportunity to change light levels in their cages by pressing a switch repeatedly. He found that the white-footed mice preferred dim light rather than bright light or darkness, and if left to their own devices would adjust the illumination to varying levels of dimness. But if he turned the lights up bright the mice would frequently respond by making the cage completely dark. Conversely, if he made the cage completely dark, the mice would frequently make the light as bright as possible.

If he turned their exercise wheels on automatically, and the mice had a way to turn them off, they would always do so within seconds. If he turned the wheel off, they would turn it on again. He found that if he disturbed sleeping mice, so that they came out of their nest boxes to investigate, they would soon go back inside, but if he put them inside by hand, they would come out again at once, no matter how many times he replaced them. In other words they wanted to be in the box only if it was by their own choice.[28] When given the opportunity to manage their environment, these white-footed mice battled fiercely for control. In the wild, white-footed mice have a great deal more control over their surroundings and activities than in a laboratory, so presumably this becomes an issue only to a captive animal. Even if a zoo animal is supplied with all its material wants, there may be something vital lacking.

Thus one of the joys of freedom may be the ability to control one's environment, and the ability to evade compulsion. In a related vein is the story of Charles, a small octopus who was the subject of an experiment to see whether invertebrates could learn conditioned tasks as vertebrates do. Along with two others, Albert and Bertram, each housed in a small tank, Charles was to be trained to pull a switch so that a light went on, and then swim over to the light to be rewarded with a minute piece of fish. Albert and Bertram learned to perform this task and Charles seemed at first to be doing the same. After some days, however, Charles rebelled. He began anchoring himself to the side of the tank and yanking on the lever so fiercely that he eventually broke it. Instead of waiting under the light to receive his smidgen of a fish, Charles reached out of the water, grabbed the light and dragged it into the tank. Finally, he took to floating at the top of the tank, with his eyes above the surface, accurately squirting water at the experimenters. 'The variables responsible for the maintenance and strengthening of the lamp-pulling and squirting behavior in this animal were not apparent,' noted the experimenter primly.[29]

Observing a captive breeding and release site for thick-billed parrots located in an Arizona forest revealed the captive parrots as healthy, glossy and well fed. Well supplied with food, water, safety and companionship, they looked like the best-treated captive parrots. All the same, the free-flying parrots looked startlingly better. It was hard to pin down the difference. Both groups of birds had glossy plumage and bright eyes. The demeanour of the two groups probably conveyed the difference. The captive parrots were not hunched or pathetic, but the wild parrots looked ten times better: stronger, happier and more confident. Even as they eyed the sky for hawks, they seemed to be revelling in life. In F. Fraser Darling's classic *A Herd of Red Deer*, a similar observation is made of deer kept in paddocks compared to wild deer: something is missing.[30]

Observations like these might lead one to wonder whether animals can ever be happy in captivity. Can there be a good zoo? Since animal behaviour is so often flexible, it seems that this ought to be possible, but then most animals are not held captive by people who are asking what it would take to make the animal happy. They ask what it would take to make the animal docile, or to make a good exhibit, or to breed. We do not study the art of making zoo animals content, thrilled or joyous.

Wolves will breed in captivity, but it seems unlikely that a wolf who is constantly being stared at from near by, a wolf with no place to hide, a wolf who cannot see the moon, can be a contented wolf. It may be true that a wolf cannot be happy while making a good exhibit. A raccoon might be less likely to have this problem. It may have other problems, however, no less distorting of its nature.

A happy animal needs to feel safe most of the time. If it is a social animal it needs company. It needs something that it can accomplish. A dish of food three times a day may be nutritionally equal to four hours of foraging, but not emotionally equal.

When Indah, an orangutan, escaped from her enclosure at the San Diego Zoo in June 1993 and clambered up on to the viewing deck, she neither headed for the hills nor attacked people. Instead Indah chose to go through a dustbin, put a bag on her head, taste what she found and dump an ashtray – while surrounded by an interested audience. In other words, she indulged her curiosity about what happens on the other side of the viewing deck, and her need to act on her world in her own way.[31] This seems to indicate that, in her enclosure, Indah was bored. She was not happy, in this sense.

An animal also needs room to wander over a range appropriate to its species. For some small animals who cherish the vicinity of a burrow or nest, an ordinary zoo cage, if appropriately complex, might be big enough. No cage is big enough for a polar bear or a cougar. Whether an animal without freedom to choose its own environment, no matter how small, can be happy is a question that needs to be asked. Is not freedom to choose inextricably tied into the very notion of what it means to be happy?

It is not surprising that a favoured task for captive animals to be taught is the miming of happiness. Dolphins, confined in tiny spaces, deprived of most companionship, and denied the use of many of their capacities, are trained to burst into the air in a shower of spray, to dance across the surface of the water and to leap in apparent joy. The joy may even be real, but it is momentary and does not reflect the overall reality of the captive animal's life.

George Schaller describes a two-year-old panda at a Chinese breeding centre being given a rare chance to go into an outdoor enclosure. The panda burst from its darkened cage, trotted up a hill with a high-stepping gait, and somersaulted down. Again and again it raced up the hill and rolled back down. It 'exploded with joy', Schaller wrote.[32]

The panda's joy expressed itself in play, a form of behaviour many animals indulge in, often even as adults. It seems to be both a sign and a source of joy. Play has been increasingly studied in recent years, following a long period when the subject was a less than respectable one. One reason for this, according to Robert Fagen of the University of Pennsylvania, was a reaction against the work of Karl Groos, who wrote at the end of the nineteenth century. Groos argued for a link between play and aesthetics, and depicted play as a simplified form of artistic endeavour. Fagen notes that 'the study of animal play has never quite overcome its embarrassment at Groos' attempt to unite animal psychology with aesthetics'.[33] Biologists continue to be dismayed by the lay public's interest in possible links between animal play and human art, language and recreation.[34]

Some researchers also feel that the study of play has been neglected because play behaviour has been inadequately defined. Various definitions have been propounded, more or less ponderous. Frustration is apparent in Robert Hinde's definition: 'Play is a general term for activities which seem to the observer to make no immediate contribution to survival.'[35] That is, play is something done for the joy of doing it, and for no other reason, and with little other observable benefit.

Fagen defines animal play behaviour as 'nonagonistic fighting and chasing maintained by social cooperation; solo locomotor and rotational movements performed in the absence of threatening predators, parasites and conspecifics; developing locomotor or manipulative behavior repeated with slight variation at a previously established level of mastery; and diversive effector interactions with an inanimate object subsequent to the termination of an initial phase of sensory and mastery activity, including exploratory manipulation directed toward the object'.[36]

Play is important to animals, although it carries risks with it, since animals can be injured or killed while playing. A variety of evolutionary functions have been proposed. Perhaps it is a form of practice, of learning to perform tasks, theorists suggest; perhaps it exercises developing social, neurological or physical capacities; or perhaps it does all these things. Cynthia Moss may have spoken for many biologists when, watching African elephants play in the rain – running, twirling, flapping ears and trunks, spraying water at each other, flailing branches, uttering loud play trumpets – she wrote in her notes, 'How can one do a serious study of animals that behave this way!'[37]

Hans Kruuk, studying spotted hyenas, complained that play 'is an anthropomorphic term, negatively defined; I have merely used it as a label for some activities which in our own species would be named that way'. An example of these activities was given by four adult hyenas swimming in a river, jumping in and out, splashing and pushing one another underwater. Kruuk adds that the hyenas made a substantial detour to reach the pool.[38]

Elephants, both Indian and African, are particularly playful animals. A travelling circus once pitched its tents next to a school playground with a set of swings. The older elephants were chained but Norma, a young elephant, was left loose. When Norma saw children swinging she was greatly intrigued. Before long she went over, waved the children away with her trunk, backed up to a swing and attempted to sit on it. She was unsuccessful but determined, even using her tail to hold the swing in place. Finally she flung the swing about irritably and returned to her companions. The children began to swing again, and Norma had to try again. Despite trying periodically for an hour, she was never able to swing.[39] Norma may have been looking for entertainment because she was bored. There seems no reason to doubt that animals can be bored. Nim Chimpsky often appeared to his sign language instructors to be bored and would demand to be taken to the toilet or to go to bed when his teachers felt strongly that he was just looking for a change.[40]

The life of many herbivores strikes humans as intrinsically boring. Grazing animals eat the same foods all day long every day. This would bore omnivores like us, but maybe buffalo have a higher tolerance for monotony. Maybe they find their life exciting. Maybe each blade of grass seems vastly different from the blade before. Perhaps their life is a rich tapestry of excitement and intrigue. In any case, to assume that a wild buffalo is bored with its life is true anthropomorphism.

Animals can play in complete solitude. Bears are playful throughout their lives and will slide on snow banks after the fashion of otters (head first, feet first, on the stomach, on the back, while somersaulting). Two grizzly bears in the Rockies were seen to wrestle for possession of a log. The bear who triumphed lay on its back and juggled the log on its feet while roaring with delight. A quieter grizzly floated in a mountain lake on a hot day. It ducked its muzzle beneath the water to blow bubbles –

and then reached out to pop them with its long claws.[41] Tiger cubs and leopards love to jump off branches into water and will do so repeatedly.[42] Bonobos in the San Diego Zoo play solitary games of blindman's bluff. The bonobo covers its eyes with a leaf or bag or simply puts its fingers or arm over its eyes, and then staggers about the climbing frame.[43]

At one time the gold leaf on the domes of the Kremlin was being scratched off by hooded crows. The crows were not indulging their fabled penchant for theft in this instance. They had simply discovered that it was enormous fun to slide down those onion domes, and their claws were doing significant damage. Eventually they were driven away by a combination of recorded crow distress calls and regular patrols by tame falcons.[44]

Animals may also play with objects, and this can be seen in animals that are not known to play with other animals. A captive Komodo dragon played with a shovel, pushing it noisily about the enclosure.[45] A metre-long wild alligator in Georgia spent forty-five minutes playing with the drops of water falling from a pipe into a pond, stalking the pipe, snapping at the drops, letting them fall on his snout and then snapping at them in mid-air.[46]

In other animals object play quickly becomes social play. A captive dolphin at an oceanarium played with a feather, carrying it to an intake pipe, letting it be swept off by the current and then chasing it. Another dolphin joined in and they are said to have taken turns. In another game three or four dolphins vied for possession of a feather,[47] and wild dolphins play similar keep-away games with various objects.[48] Beluga whales carry stones or seaweed on their heads and the other whales at once try to knock it off.[49] Lions, both adults and cubs, may try to wrest pieces of bark or twigs from each other.[50] Captive gorillas and chimpanzees enjoy playing with dolls and spend time in other imaginative play, as when the gorilla Koko pretends to brush her teeth with a toy banana,[51] or when the chimpanzee Loulis, playing alone, puts a board on his head, signing 'That's a hat.'[52]

Teasing is a form of play, at least for the one doing the teasing. Some animals tease conspecifics and they may also tease members of other species. A captive dolphin teased a turtle by tossing it out of the water and by rolling it along the bottom of the tank. Another dolphin teased a fish that lived in a rock crevice in the tank by putting bits of squid near the hole: when the fish came out to get the squid, the dolphin would snatch it away.[53]

Ravens tease peregrines by flying closer and closer past them, croaking, until the falcon lunges after them.[54] Swans, with their large dignity, are often the target of teasing. In the water, little grebes have been seen to tweak swans' tails and then dive. On land, carrion crows may pull their tails repeatedly, leaping back each time the swan turns on them.[55]

Foxes will tease less nimble hyenas by coming close, circling, then sprinting away until the hyena can no longer ignore it and lunges for the fox. Several cases of hyenas actually catching and killing such a fox have been reported.[56] Maybe the fox is gaining information about the hyena's powers, useful when the fox snatches bites from the hyena's kills. Maybe the fox is accustoming the hyena to its presence, also useful when pillaging kills. This gives a practical explanation for why such behaviour persists, but doesn't explain what the fox actually feels. Why shouldn't the fox feel the mischievousness that has been imputed to the species over the centuries?

Other forms of play seem to be enjoyable for all the parties involved. Young animals and sometimes adults commonly wrestle, mock-fight and chase one another. A favourite game of young animals of many species, from wolves to red deer, is King of the Castle, where one player occupies a high place and defends it against the onslaughts of the others.

To what extent animals playing games recognise implicit rules is not clear. In a few instances trainers have successfully taught formalised games to animals. A simplified version of cricket was taught to elephants of the Bertram Mills' Circus after several months of training. Elephants understand about throwing objects, but the tasks of batting and fielding took some time to convey. It is said that after some months the elephants began to 'enter into the spirit of the game' and subsequently played with great enthusiasm.[57]

At an oceanarium, several dolphins were trained in the skills of water polo. First they learned to put a ball through a goal, each team having a different goal. Then the trainers tried to teach them to compete, by keeping the other team from scoring. After three training sessions the dolphins caught on, all too well. Uninterested in strictures against foul play, the dolphins zestfully attacked one another in such an unsporting fashion that the training was discontinued and they were never again given competitive games.[58] There is no indication that the dolphins thereafter tried to play polo on their own.

Animals sometimes find playmates across the barrier of species. In captivity species which would be unlikely to meet in the wild are often brought together. Thus a leopard and dog may play together, or a cat and a gorilla. One family who kept red kangaroos in their back yard with their dogs found the animals quite friendly towards each other, although there were difficulties. The dogs liked to chase and be chased by their friends, barking. The kangaroos preferred to wrestle and box, pastimes the dogs didn't care for.[59] Somehow they managed to play together.

Interspecies play, while not routine, is also found in the wild. Dwarf mongooses in Kenya have been seen attempting to play with ground squirrels, lizards and birds. Here again, the different styles of play can form a barrier. M'Bili, a young mongoose rebuffed by her mongoose playmates, ran over to a large lizard, hopping and uttering play calls, and began tossing dead leaves about. When this produced no reaction, she danced around the lizard, tapping it and pretending to nibble at the lizard's back, forefoot and face. The lizard closed its eyes and did not respond, and M'Bili gave up.

Another mongoose, Moja, tried to play with an African ground squirrel as he would play with another mongoose. Moja was playing with another mongoose when the squirrel hopped into their midst and, standing on its hind legs, stopped to gnaw on a nut. Moja raced over giving the 'play call', rose on his hind legs, put his forepaws on the squirrel's shoulders and started to 'waltz' around with the squirrel. A playful mongoose follows this by pretending to snap at the other animal's head and neck, which Moja did, but the squirrel didn't respond, simply standing passively and letting itself be waltzed around. Then Moja pounced on the squirrel's tail and bit it, whereupon the squirrel hopped away and Moja attacked a twig instead.

Another young mongoose, Tatu, had better luck with a white-headed buffalo weaver bird. Tatu chased the bird, making jumps up into the air at it. Instead of departing, the bird flew no more than a foot off the ground, repeatedly skimmed over Tatu's head and landed on twigs close to her. Tatu was the first to tire of this game.[60]

In a still more successful match, wild river otter cubs and beaver kits have been seen playing together. Adult beavers and otters were present and paid no attention as two cubs and two kits nosed, nudged and chased each other, both on a stream bank and in the water. The play continued until the otter parents moved their family along.[61]

At the end of his book on play in animals, Robert Fagen wrote:

> In the play of animals we find a pure aesthetic that frankly defies science. Why kittens or puppies chase and vigorously paw at each other in reciprocal fashion without inflicting injury, repeating this behavior almost to the point of physical exhaustion, is not known. Yet this behavior fascinates, indeed enchants.[62]

There is something compelling in the recognition that other creatures require leisure much as we do. Jacques Cousteau speaks of whales as 'sociable, affectionate, devoted, gentle, captivating, high-spirited creatures. The entire ocean is their empire – and their playground. Theirs is a "leisure society" that predates ours by some forty million years. They spend less than a tenth of their lives looking for food and feeding. The rest of the time they spend swimming, frolicking in the waves, conversing with each other, wooing the opposite sex and rearing their young – an inoffensive agenda if ever there was one! Apart from the harpoons of man, they have little to fear on the vast, featureless sea.'[63]

Interspecies play, a commonality in nature, has a special charm for humans. If two species of animals can reach out joyfully across the gap between them, it seems that we too might reach across this gap and share their joy.

CHAPTER EIGHT

Compassion, Rescue and the Altruism Debate

ONE EVENING during the rainy season in Kenya, a black rhinoceros mother and her baby came to a clearing where salt had been left out to attract animals.[1] After licking up salt, the mother moved away, but the rhino calf got stuck in the deep mud. It called out, and its mother returned, sniffed it, examined it and headed back into the forest. The calf called again, the mother returned, and so on, until the calf was exhausted. Apparently the mother rhino either could not see the problem – the calf was uninjured – or did not know what to do about it.

A group of elephants arrived at the salt lick. The mother rhino charged the elephant in the lead, who side-stepped her and went to a different salt lick a hundred feet from the baby rhino. Appeased, the mother went to forage in the woods again. An adult elephant with large tusks approached the rhino calf and ran its trunk over it. Then the elephant knelt, put its tusks under the calf and began to lift. As it did so, the mother rhino came

charging out of the woods, and so the elephant dodged away and
went back to the other salt lick. Over several hours, whenever the
mother rhino returned to the forest, the elephant tried to lift the
young rhino out of the mud, but each time the mother rushed
out protectively and the elephant retreated. Finally the elephants
all moved on, leaving the rhino still mired. The next morning,
as humans prepared to prize it loose, the young rhino managed
to pull free from the drying mud on its own, and joined its
waiting mother.

The elephant who tried to rescue the young rhinoceros ran some
risk of being injured by one of the mother's attacks. Why did it
bother trying to help? Clearly it would gain no selective benefit
from the survival of the rhino. Though both are pachyderms,
there is no reason to imagine that elephants ever confuse rhinos
with their own species. Perhaps it recognised the youth of the
rhino and its predicament and felt a generous impulse to help.

Elephants can also be nasty to rhinos, even young ones. They
have been seen to tease a rhino by surrounding it and kicking
dust in its face. In Aberdare National Park in Kenya, a deadly
encounter between elephants and rhinos took place one night in
1979. Elephants arriving at a waterhole chased a male rhino away.
Presently a mother rhino arrived with her baby, who began to play
with one of the baby elephants. The mother elephant picked up the
young rhino, threw it into the forest and made as if to impale it
with her tusks. But the mother rhino charged, and both mother
and calf escaped. At this point the male rhino who had been chased
away before made a return appearance. The irate mother elephant
charged him, knocked him a distance of three metres, knelt on
him and stabbed him with one tusk, killing him.[2]

There should be no more difficulty reconciling these two incidents than there is reconciling equally different human behaviours.
Sometimes people behave generously towards a strange child, and
sometimes badly. However, while there has been no significant
movement to deny that animals can fight and kill each other, there
is much argument that they cannot behave altruistically towards
each other, and that they lack the capacity for compassion and
generosity. Yet observations of what actually happens in the real
world do not confirm this view.

Young animals are often defended by unrelated animals. Other
members of their group may defend them. Young white oryx will

be defended not only by their mother, but by any oryx in the group.[3] A mother Thomson's gazelle will defend her fawn from a hyena by running between them – but so will other female gazelle. Four female gazelle have been seen simultaneously 'distracting' a hyena from a single fawn.[4]

It may not be necessary for a young animal to be a member of a group to be defended by unrelated adults. Thus a researcher who was trying to mark rhino calves discovered to his dismay that the loud squeals of a young rhino bring to its aid not only its mother, but every rhino within earshot.[5] While studying hyenas in Africa's Ngorongoro Crater, Hans Kruuk saw a hyena trailing a young eland calf. The only other eland around was an old bull, and the calf stuck close to him. Another hyena suddenly ran up and bit the calf, who kicked the hyena in the face and ran to the bull's side. Eventually, with the first hyena only a few feet away, the calf was pressed against the bull's side, when the bull butted the calf. The calf ran away, with the hyena on its heels, and Kruuk felt sure it would be killed. More hyenas joined the chase, but then the calf dashed into the midst of a scattered herd of eland. A cow ran swiftly at the hyenas and attacked the one nearest the calf. More eland cows came running and began to chase the hyenas and within one minute the calf had huddled together with five other calves guarded by twelve cows. In a few more minutes the hyenas gave up the pursuit.[6]

When a group of chimpanzees were hunting bushpigs and adolescent Freud captured a piglet, a sow charged and bit him to the bone. The piglet ran away, but the sow hung on to the screaming Freud. Gigi, a childless female chimp, charged the sow, who wheeled to face her. Though badly injured, Freud managed to clamber into a tree, and Gigi leapt free, escaping the pig's teeth by only inches.[7]

Zebras energetically defend both young and grown zebras of their group from predators. Hugo van Lawick saw wild dogs attack a zebra mother and foal. The wild dogs chased a group of about twenty zebras, despite being attacked by a stallion, until they managed to separate a mare, foal and yearling (probably the mare's previous foal). As the rest of the herd vanished over a hill, the pack surrounded these three zebras. Their principal target was the foal, but the mother and yearling kept them back. After a while the wild dogs began jumping at the mare, grabbing for her upper lip, a hold which nearly immobilises a zebra. Van Lawick thought the dogs would soon succeed and was astonished when he felt the ground shaking and looked up to see ten zebras thundering towards the scene. This herd galloped up, engulfed the three embattled zebras within its ranks and galloped away again. The wild dogs followed for only a short distance before giving up.[8]

Neither are young animals the only ones to be defended. African buffalo sometimes defend other buffalo even when adult. A lion was struggling with an adult buffalo when several more buffalo ran up and chased away the lion and two other lions that had been waiting nearby.[9]

Another form of altruistic behaviour is to feed another animal or allow it to share one's food, thus giving up a very tangible asset. As lion-watchers have pointed out, old lionesses who no longer bear young and have worn or missing teeth can survive for years because the younger lions share their kills with them.

Although biologist and fox-watcher David Macdonald has written that 'Thou shalt not share thy food' appears to be one of the commandments of red fox behaviour, he has also seen foxes bringing food to adult foxes when they are injured. One fox, Wide Eyes, was injured by a mowing machine (Macdonald took her to a vet, who found that her injuries were fatal). The next day her sister Big Ears brought food to the spot where Wide Eyes had been injured, uttered the whimper that summons cubs to eat (though Big Ears had no cubs), and left the food on the bloody spot where her sister had lain.

In another instance a dog fox got a thorn in his paw, which became infected. The dominant vixen in his group brought him food, and he recovered.[10]

Cynthia Moss reported the case of a young female elephant with a badly crippled hind leg, broken when she was a small calf. This animal could not possibly have survived had her mother and other members of her group not made allowances for her, such as avoiding difficult terrain and always waiting for her to catch up.[11] Gorillas, too, travel slowly to allow injured companions to keep pace. It is hard to believe that this is not a deliberate, conscious decision.

Tatu, a dwarf mongoose whose accidental separation from her family is described later in this chapter, injured her forepaw badly

157

in a fight with another group of mongooses. She could no longer catch prey by pouncing with both paws. She favoured the paw and its nails grew long, making it even more unusable. She travelled slowly and lost weight. The other mongooses spent more time with Tatu, and they groomed her when she stopped grooming herself. They never brought her food. However, according to observer Anne Rasa, they began foraging next to Tatu at an increased rate. When they caught something, she would ask for it and they would often relinquish their food to her. As a younger, female mongoose, Tatu was 'higher-ranking', so it wasn't surprising that they gave food up to her, only that they chose to forage near her so that this happened. At first, Rasa notes, she thought it was coincidence, but she soon became convinced that it was a deliberate choice on the part of the other mongooses. Although Tatu was getting almost half her food in this way, it did not prevent her eventual death. When she died, in a termite mound, the group stopped travelling, and only moved on when her body began to decompose.[12]

In a case of compassion for less dramatic illness, a woman who was working with Koko, the signing gorilla, had indigestion one day, and asked Koko what she should do for a 'sick stomach'. Koko, who was given extra orange juice whenever she was ill, signed 'Stomach you orange'. When the woman burped, Koko signed 'Stomach you there drink orange', with 'there' apparently referring to the refrigerator where the orange juice was kept. The woman drank some juice, told Koko she felt better and offered her some juice. Only then did Koko indicate interest in juice for herself. Ten days later, when the same woman visited again, and gave Koko some juice, Koko offered it to her and had to be assured that the visitor felt fine before she would drink the juice herself.[13]

Sick or injured animals may be helped in other ways besides feeding. As noted below, dolphins and whales often support a conspecific and carry it to the surface if it is having trouble breathing. This is exactly what a mother dolphin does with her newborn, and what 'midwife' dolphins do with a dolphin giving birth.

An adult pilot whale was shot and instantly killed by people on a ship. Its body was drifting towards the ship when two more pilot whales appeared, one on each side of the dead whale, pressed their noses on top of its head and dived with it. They managed to get it far enough away so that they were not seen again. This is particularly noteworthy because pressing down in this manner is not known to be a stereotyped cetacean behaviour.[14] Dolphins and whales have also been seen helping injured companions away from human attackers, and pushing and biting against lines fastened to nets or harpoons when others are captured.

Lions shot with darts containing anaesthetic react in a variety of interesting ways. Sometimes they attack neighbouring lions as if they suspect them of having caused the pain. Sometimes they look up into a tree above them as if something has fallen on them from the tree. Sometimes they charge the car in which the person firing is seated. Sometimes they run away for a short distance, and sometimes they climb a tree. Often they pull the dart out with their teeth, but on other occasions, other lions pull the darts out for them. (And sometimes, when the darted animals pass out, other lions attack them.)[15]

Ralph Dennard has spent nearly twenty years training hearing dogs to assist deaf people. These energetic signal dogs run to alert their owners when they hear a doorbell, telephone, timer, alarm clock or smoke alarm. Dennard believes that dogs feel some emotions, such as fear, love, grief and curiosity, but doubts that they feel compassion.[16]

One family received a signal dog from Dennard to assist the father of the family. Gilly, a Border collie, joined them a few months before the birth of their second child, and they worried that she might be jealous and hostile towards the new baby. On the baby's first night home, Gilly woke the mother from a deep sleep and ran urgently back and forth between the bed and the baby's cot. The mother went to the cot and found that the one-day-old baby was silent and blue. He had choked on mucus and stopped breathing. His mother was able to clear his airway and start his breathing again. Afterwards Gilly developed the habit of notifying the mother whenever the baby cried.[17]

In another incident, a hearing dog woke a woman when a visiting cat jumped on the stove, accidentally filling the kitchen with gas. 'Why did the dog respond to that? We don't know,' said Dennard, pointing out that there was no sound – no ring or buzzer – to signal the dog to respond. Clearly, a dog might object to the smell of gas and want a human to do something about it. But in the case of the baby, what troubled the dog? The baby may have made choking sounds, but the dog had not been trained to do anything with regard to the baby. It seems clear that the dog knew the baby needed help and wanted to summon that help. In humans, this is what it is to feel compassion.

Another signal dog, Chelsea, also showed concern for infants. Travelling with her owners on an airplane, Chelsea repeatedly tried to get them to go to the aid of a crying baby. Eventually, after a number of flights, they managed to convince Chelsea to leave crying infants to their parents' care.[18]

An affecting older account of sympathetic behaviour tells of Toto, a captive chimpanzee whose owner, Cherry Kearton, fell ill with malaria. According to Kearton's account, Toto sat by him all day. When instructed, he would bring quinine and a glass. When Kearton asked for a book, Toto would put his finger on one book after another (there were fewer than a dozen) until Kearton indicated that Toto was touching the desired book, whereupon Toto would bring it to him. Several times during convalescence, Kearton fell asleep on his bed fully dressed, and Toto removed his boots. 'It may be that some who read this book will say that friendship between an ape and a man is absurd, and that Toto, being "only an animal", cannot really have felt the feelings that I attribute to him,' Kearton wrote. 'They would not say it if they had felt his tenderness and seen his care as I felt and saw it at that time.'[19]

An ill, injured or unhappy animal may also be offered comfort, as in the grooming of the injured Tatu described earlier in this chapter. An adult wild chimpanzee, Little Bee, was seen to climb down from a tree to bring mabungo fruit to her mother, who was too old and tired to climb the tree herself.[20] It has already been noted that Nim, a chimp who was taught sign language, was very tender with people who wept. He was also responsive to other signs of grief. Indeed, his foster mother declared that during a time when her father was in the hospital, dying of cancer, Nim was more direct and more comforting in his response to her sorrow than was any other member of her family.[21] Nim's 36th word was 'sorry', which he used when a companion was upset.[22]

Compassion can occur by omission as well. In one grim and inexcusable experiment on fifteen rhesus monkeys, they were trained to pull either of two chains to get food. After a while a new aspect was introduced: if they pulled one of the chains a monkey in an adjacent compartment would receive a powerful electric shock. Two thirds of the monkeys preferred to pull the chain that gave them food without shocking the other monkey. Two other monkeys, after seeing shock administered, refused to pull either chain. Monkeys were less likely to shock other monkeys if they knew those monkeys, and were less likely to shock other monkeys if they had been shocked themselves.[23]

This contrasts with the experiment described earlier, in which rhesus monkeys who had been reared in isolation were taped to a cruciform restraining device and put in a cage with 'normal' cage-bred rhesus. The unrestrained monkeys eventually began performing various sadistic operations on the restrained monkeys. While they did touch and bite the tape, the experimenter concluded that they were not trying to free the restrained monkey, because they manipulated the tape less often than they did when there was no monkey in the restraining device. While one could argue about the restrained monkeys' lack of ability to solicit compassion or the ability of a monkey to understand the concept of untaping another monkey, lack of compassion in one situation does not invalidate the presence of compassion in another.

Altruism in animals has been passionately debated, with a sizable school holding that its existence is impossible. This altruism is not the same as altruism in everyday life. It means behaviour that benefits another but reduces the altruist's ability to survive. For example, Richard Dawkins has written, 'Altruism, for our purposes, may be defined as self-destructive behaviour performed for the benefit of others'.[24] How could natural selection ever favour an animal that wasted its energy or risked its life committing unselfish acts? It is argued that this could only benefit the animal – or rather, the animal's genes – if the one it helps is a relative. Extensive mathematical calculations have been made to show just how closely related an animal must be for it to be genetically worthwhile to help it. Altruism towards a close relative does not count as altruism under these rules.

An example of chimpanzee compassion for a person who was not suffering so very terribly occurred when a group of the Gombe chimps were being followed by researcher Geza Teleki. He discovered that he had forgotten his lunch, and tried to knock some fruit down with a stick while the chimpanzees fed in some trees near by. After ten minutes of unsuccessful efforts, an adolescent male chimpanzee, Sniff, collected some fruit, climbed down from the tree and gave it to Teleki.[25] This is altruistic by any definition, since the human and the chimp were not related.

Sniff's mother died some years later, and Sniff adopted his fourteen-month-old sister, sharing food with her, taking her into his sleeping nest and carrying her everywhere he went. Still unweaned, she could not survive without mother's milk, however, and she died after three weeks.[26] A sociobiologist would not count Sniff's behaviour as disinterested altruism, since the sister shared some of Sniff's genes. Yet in the usual sense of the word, a similar compassion, differing in its strength, may be said to have motivated his adoption of his sister and his gift of fruit to a hungry human.

Altruism in either people or animals is accompanied and arguably guided by emotions, which accordingly must be examined along with it. Some acts that may appear altruistic to the ordinary person – running risks to protect one's offspring, for example – are not considered altruism in science. Reproductive success guarantees the replication of genes; if an animal does not protect its offspring, it is less likely to pass its genes along. Altruism is also discounted if aid is directed towards kin other than children. It has been shown that some animals who do not get a chance to reproduce can still ensure that their genes will be passed along by helping siblings, nieces, nephews, parents and so on, since they share some genes with those relatives. The more genes one has in common, the more advantageous it is, in evolutionary terms, to help a relative. This kin selection has been used to explain the existence of alloparenting, in which an animal helps to raise children not its own. A wolf who remains with its parents and helps raise their next litter is an alloparent. Perhaps there is no territory available for this young wolf to start its own family, so its best chance of passing its genes along lies in helping to raise its siblings, with whom it has an average of fifty per cent of its genes in common.

Richard Dawkins, in his influential book *The Selfish Gene*, includes some examples of calculations which might be thought to predict whether altruism towards kin will take place. Thus he describes a hypothetical animal finding a clump of mushrooms and debating whether to give a food call that will attract its brother, its cousin and an unrelated member of its own species to share the food. If it does so it gets fewer mushrooms for itself, but also benefits the brother and cousin, who share some of its genes.

Dawkins' equation for the advantage to be gained from summoning the animal's relatives entails an elaborate cost-benefit calculation. It comes as no surprise to find that Dawkins does not suggest any animal actually makes such a cost-benefit computation. What he does suggest is that 'the gene pool becomes filled with genes which influence bodies in such a way that they behave as if they had made such calculations'.[27]

In another example, he discusses whether a male elephant seal should attack another male who has access to many female elephant seals, or whether he should wait for a more favourable chance. After imagining the elephant seal's internal debate on this subject, Dawkins says:

> This subjective soliloquy is just a way of pointing out that the decision whether or not to fight should ideally be preceded by a complex, if unconscious, 'cost-benefit' calculation . . . It is important to realise that we are not thinking of the strategy as being consciously worked out by the individual. Remember that we are picturing the animal as a robot survival machine with a pre-programmed computer controlling the muscles. To write the strategy out as a set of simple instructions in English is just a convenient way for us to think about it. By some unspecified mechanism the animal behaves as if he were following these instructions.[28]

But picturing the animal as a 'robot survival machine' seems perverse. Clearly it is a living, feeling creature.

Surely, this 'unspecified mechanism' includes emotions. In the case of altruistic behaviour, it includes the altruistic emotions of compassion, empathy and generosity. These emotions, even if they serve 'selfish genes', may also bring into being genuine altruism in the usual sense.

When discussing altruism, a hypothetical situation theorists frequently use is that of saving others from drowning. In a discussion of how a gene for saving relatives from drowning might spread, biologist J.B.S. Haldane noted that he had twice saved (possibly) drowning people without ever pausing to consider whether doing so was genetically beneficial.[29] Richard Dawkins notes: 'Just as we may use a slide rule without appreciating that we are, in effect, using logarithms, so an animal may be pre-programmed in such a way that it behaves *as if* it had made a complicated calculation.'

In real life, do animals save unrelated others from drowning? There are ancient tales of dolphins saving humans from drowning, but although some of these are plausible, none are documented. They seem plausible, though, because dolphins and whales not only support other cetaceans, but carry inanimate objects on their heads from time to time. When they do so, they act like a dolphin mother with a baby. When a calf dies, mother cetaceans may support its body at the surface for as long as several days. Scientists who have seen female belugas supporting logs or other driftwood on their heads in this way believe that these are mothers whose calves have recently died.[30] An Atlantic bottlenose dolphin carried a dead leopard shark on her snout for eight days.[31] Perhaps it is species vanity, but it seems possible that humans are at least as winsome as logs or dead sharks. Biologists Richard Norris and Kenneth Connor remark, 'If . . . stories of dolphins pushing humans ashore are true, they must be viewed in the same context as humans pushing stranded dolphins back to sea.'[32]

Washoe, the famous chimpanzee who was the first to be taught sign language, lived for a time in later years on a 'chimp island' at a research institute. When she was seven or eight years old, a chimpanzee who had just arrived at the institute was placed on the island, but became panicky, jumped over an electric fence and fell into the moat with a tremendous splash. As researcher Roger Fouts ran to the scene, intending to dive in and rescue her (a risky endeavour, considering how much stronger chimps are than humans), he saw Washoe run to the fence, leap over, land on a narrow strip of bank at its base, edge out into the mud and, clinging to the grass with one hand, pull the chimpanzee to safety with the other. Fouts notes that the two chimpanzees were not acquainted.[33]

Asked whether he was surprised at Washoe's actions, Fouts paused, bemused. 'Only later, when that theory came out and people said that there's no such thing as altruism. But prior to that . . . You know, I was about to do the same thing. I didn't know the chimp that well either, and I was headed down into the water too, taking my wallet out of my pants and getting ready to go in after her. Washoe beat me to it. So I guess I was responding to the same stimuli Washoe was – [an] individual in trouble.' Unfortunately, how the other chimpanzee behaved towards Washoe after being rescued is unknown. Fouts also cited a case in which an adult chimpanzee at the Detroit Zoo fell into a moat. The keepers were afraid to go in after him because adult chimpanzees are so strong, but a zoo visitor leapt in and saved the ape.[34]

Early in *The Selfish Gene*, Dawkins specifies that he uses the term altruism to refer to behaviour rather than 'the psychology of motives'.[35] Yet behaviour and motivation are not so easily separated, and to do so is to dodge an important issue. The sociobiological debate about altruism is deeply confused by the redefinition of this everyday word. If compassion for kin exists as an emotion, rather than exclusively as an adaptive behaviour, then compassion for non-kin also becomes possible.

In the evolutionary approach, an animal is more likely to receive compassion from a parent than a more distant relative; from a relative than from a non-relative; from an acquaintance than from a stranger; from a conspecific than from a member of another species. One would expect even less sympathy from an animal that does not guard its eggs. Even if this is true, compassion could be an overarching emotion that can and does produce altruism, even in the sociobiological sense.

Humans are usually excluded from these calculations, or are only discussed after a seemingly water-tight case has been built for universal selfishness, whereupon the sociobiologist might suddenly announce that human behaviour also is dictated by such rules, or that humans are a unique exception to these rules.

To help another, usually you must be able to realise that they need help. This recognition might be instinctive, cognitive or both. One night in an Arctic bay where beluga whales gather, three belugas got trapped near land by low tide. A gravel bar that they had swum over at high tide now barred their way. The three belugas, one adult and two juveniles, 'screamed and groaned and trilled'. The other belugas, free, swam back and forth on their side of the gravel bar and answered. A biologist waded out to the gravel bar, which would ordinarily have caused the whales to flee. This time they paid no attention.[36]

The whales were unable to help their fellows, but whale watchers kept the stranded belugas wet and they swam away on the next high tide. This is a story of raw emotion. The trapped whales were frightened and called for help. The other whales were concerned and came to help or possibly to show their concern. Whales are able to ask for aid from each other and to receive it in some situations. Here, the whales seemed to feel fear and empathy, even though the free whales could not actually help the trapped ones. There is speculation that the reason for the otherwise inexplicable beachings of whole pods may be the refusal to abandon a suffering colleague.

Animals have a capacity for dispassion which tends to dismay people. They regularly do things that shock us, such as eat their dead infants or allow their offspring to eat one another. A lion who has lost all but one of her litter will often abandon her remaining cub. A parent who has been vigorously defending its young from a predator may, if the predator finally succeeds in catching the young one, walk away with apparent indifference – although it could be despair.

Yet just as kindness and cruelty can coexist, so can compassion and dispassion. Incidents that suggest one do not cancel out incidents that suggest the other. As with any social emotion, a creature is most likely to display compassion towards a member of its own species. Some animals seem to recognise relationships broader than 'member of my species', such as 'fellow cat', 'fellow bird' or 'fellow cetacean'. For many humans, the greatest thrill an animal can give is to treat us as a conspecific or fellow of some kind.

A remarkable instance of fellow-feeling is displayed by orcas, also called killer whales. There is no known incident of an orca attacking fatally a human in the wild, though these carnivores eat anything in the sea from large fish to giant whales, to dolphins, seals and birds, and even occasionally a polar bear. Though they could easily prey on people, they have consistently refrained from doing so. Is this restraint compassion? Does it entail recognition of commonality? If so, our species has not reciprocated in kind.

Despite our differences, dolphins often treat humans as peers on some level. Even wild dolphins are sometimes interested in playing with humans. The famous wild dolphins of Australia's Monkey Mia beach have been coming for years to play with people. While it is traditional to offer them fish, the dolphins often do not accept the fish, or accept but do not eat them. It seems logical enough that a creature which can easily catch fresh fish might not be tempted by an hours-dead specimen.

What goes through the mind of a dolphin when it accepts a dead fish and then lets it drift away? Two reporters who visited Monkey Mia saw a dolphin receive a fish from a tourist, then push it towards them. Confused, they accepted it. As the dolphin watched them, they felt socially awkward and wondered whether they were supposed to eat the thing, give it back or do something else. As they dithered, the dolphin swam close, grabbed the fish back and dived away, leaving them feeling they had committed an unknown faux pas.[37]

Another way in which an animal might treat a human as a conspecific would be to ask it for help. The act of asking for help – soliciting compassion – may itself be said to indicate a capacity for compassion in that species. How could it ask for help from another if it did not know what help from another was? How could it ask for compassion to be shown if it did not know what compassion was? Mike Tomkies tells of rescuing a wounded badger: 'It explained her living alone in the sett, and perhaps why, after getting our scent and somehow sensing we were friendly, she had come close to us. It was odd how many sick wild creatures, including dying red deer in winter, came close to us, as if knowing they would be protected.'[38]

In Hope Ryden's *Lily Pond*, she recounts how an elderly female beaver she had been observing for several years, worn down and with a paw injury, unexpectedly approached her. As Ryden sat on the banks of the pond with her binoculars, the old beaver Lily swam over, hauled herself out of the water, clambered up the bank, looked Ryden in the eye and uttered the wheedling sounds of a beaver kit. Ryden's response was to begin bringing aspen branches (much appreciated by beavers) to the pond to supplement Lily's diet. The aspen was accepted. Though Ryden had brought branches to the pond before, she had done so surreptitiously, intending that the beavers not know she was the source.[39] Lily's grown son Huckleberry was perhaps less compassionate, frequently trying to steal aspen branches from his mother's grasp.

Cynthia Moss has written about a very ill wild elephant

who walked up to the window of her Land Rover and stood there, 'lifting her eyelids from time to time and looking in at me. I do not know what she was doing, but I sensed that she was somehow trying to communicate her distress to me and I was very touched and disturbed.'[40]

Barry Lopez, author of *Of Wolves and Men*, tells of a hunter who caught a large black wolf in a leghold trap. When he came up to the trap, the hunter reported, the wolf extended his trapped foot to the hunter and whined.[41]

At times the appearance of a bid for compassion may be deceiving. A rabbit in extremis, as in the jaws of a coyote, utters a surprisingly loud fear scream. Other rabbits ignore the scream, neither speeding to see what is the matter nor taking cover themselves. The benefit of the scream, it is believed, lies in attracting other predators to the scene, and rabbit fear screams do attract predators. Apparently, in the ensuing fracas between predators, rabbits sometimes escape.[42]

An aspect of empathy which is not considered genetically objectionable is that which results in cooperation, a situation in which both parties win. Thus if a lion understands that another lion is hunting a group of wildebeest, and joins in or helps, and shares in the resulting kill, this is considered cooperation, not altruism. In fact, it seems that when lions hunt cooperatively, they catch substantially more prey than they do when they hunt singly.[43] If the lion helped another lion hunt, and then did not share in the kill, and the other lion was not its offspring or close relative, that would be considered altruism.

Unfortunately for the study of altruism towards kin and kin selection, observers usually have a frustrating time figuring out who is related to whom. Most scientists, when they see one wild animal aid another, have no way of knowing if the two are related or how closely. Long-term studies, like those initiated by Jane Goodall at Gombe, throw some light on these matters. Most ethology studies do not have access to as much history. Even at Gombe, observers may know who a chimp's mother is, but only be able to guess who is its father. When they do know how the animals are related, they often don't know whether the animals themselves are aware that the other is, for example, their sister or uncle.

A handful of studies have shown that some animals sometimes

seem to favour their kin in surprising situations. Infant pigtail macaques preferred to play with other macaques who were their half-siblings, rather than unrelated macaques, even though they had never seen them before. Whether this is connected with altruistic behaviour, incest avoidance or some other function is unknown.[44]

Assumptions about which animals are kin can be mistaken. Among mountain goats, young animals may be seen following nanny goats with younger kids, as many animals follow their mothers for a year or two. Thus the observer seeing a goat group comprising a nanny, a kid, a yearling and a two-year-old might reasonably assume this to be a family group. In fact, that assumption has often been made. The yearling and two-year-old could be unrelated, however, since it has been discovered that young mountain goats often follow nannies other than their own mothers.[45]

Altruism towards kin has scientific respectability, since it can contribute to the survival of a creature's genes. Also respectable is reciprocal altruism, in which animals do favours for others in the expectation of receiving favours in return. That this does occur in animals as well as humans has been shown. Yet people often help those who are unlikely to help them in return. Indeed, society expects minor acts of this kind to be performed on a daily basis, and when they are not, there is much indignation.

In the theoretical model of reciprocal altruism, each of the two animals trading favours derives an overall advantage. An animal who does not return favours is detected by the other, and ceases to receive them. It has been suggested that the necessity for social animals to monitor their indebtedness to one another has contributed to the development of intelligence.[46]

Experimenters taped calls of vervet monkeys – the calls they use when threatening another vervet and at the same time soliciting assistance from other vervets – and later hid in the bushes, playing the calls of different individuals and noting how vervets responded to these solicitations. They found that vervets were most apt to respond to the calls of unrelated monkeys if they had recently groomed each other or shared other affinitive behaviour. In contrast, they responded to the calls of close relatives whether or not they had recently done favours for each other.[47]

While an animal might be keeping an unemotional tally of

who owes whom, such behaviour might also be mediated more emotionally, which would involve not only love, but gratitude and grudge-holding. Unfortunately, gratitude is one of the most slippery emotions to pin down, so much so that cynics sometimes claim it does not exist in people. If A does something for B, and B is subsequently very nice to A, it can be argued that B is grateful. Some will argue, however, that B hopes for more favours from A, or that B has just come to enjoy A's company, or that B is just acting the way society expects. If B is a dog, the same arguments could be applied. Yet most people believe that gratitude exists because they have felt grateful themselves. Why should animals not be able to feel gratitude also?

The human history of objectivity on this subject is not impressive. Perhaps because of guilty consciences, this is one of the emotions we would most like animals to feel – towards us. Joseph Wood Krutch has told of a letter written to a British quarterly, *The Countryman*, with news of a thankful butterfly. The reader had seen a parasitic mite clinging to a butterfly's eye and had delicately removed it. The butterfly uncoiled its tongue and licked his hand. The reader thought this was a caress of thanks. As other readers pointed out, butterflies often lick human skin, presumably for the salt.[48] It seems unlikely that a butterfly would interpret a lick as a grateful gesture: they do not lick each other as dogs do. The chance that an insect would thank a primate with this gesture seems rather small. Ornithologists are sometimes told stories of wild birds indicating their gratitude for favours humans have done them by singing. This too seems improbable, since there is no reason to suppose that birds know that people enjoy bird song.

In the Negev desert, Salim, a Bedouin stone carver, trapped a caracal, a lynx-like desert cat, who had been raiding his chicken house.[49] He intended to kill it, but relented, and after three days he let it go. It ran off, and by the next day had killed another chicken. In the ensuing months, the caracal would often come near Salim's house in the evenings, lie on the branch of an acacia tree, and stare at Salim, who would sit on a rock and look back. Even after the cat had killed the last of the chickens, it would come and stare at Salim. Perhaps the caracal was curious, or perhaps it was hostile towards the person who had trapped and held it captive. Perhaps it even felt some gratitude.

Parrot trainers sometimes try to modify the attitude of a hostile parrot by arranging for the person it dislikes to rescue the parrot from a frightening situation. Mattie Sue Athan, a parrot behaviour consultant, has written about a situation in which this occurred accidentally. The parrot, a very hostile African grey living in a pet store, had rebuffed the advances of several trainers. When Athan released it from its cage, the parrot bolted down the aisle to a ferret cage. The ferret grabbed the parrot's toe in a bloody bite and hung on fiercely. The parrot shrieked in pain and terror until Athan prized the ferret off. The bird at once became tame and friendly with her.[50] The rescue method of winning a parrot's good will works fairly reliably and is sometimes exploited by unscrupulous trainers in cruel ways. As for whether the rescued parrot feels gratitude toward its rescuer, or merely trust and admiration, this is the same question asked about humans who have been rescued.

Gratitude from one animal towards another, rather than towards humans, may be seen. In the Kenya bush one evening, Tatu, a young dwarf mongoose, became separated from her family after an antelope, frightened by a dust devil, hurtled through the group.[51] At dusk, mongooses retire into a termite mound, but Tatu was on a mound fifty yards from her family, afraid to cross the intervening ground. She uttered 'Where are you?' calls and trotted back and forth on her mound. Her family called back repeatedly with louder and louder 'Here I am' calls, but she dared not cross. By the time it was almost dark, Tatu was hoarse, and huddled on top of the mound. Her parents and another mongoose (probably her sister) finally set off towards her, keeping under cover as much as possible, while the rest of the band watched, scanning the earth and the sky for predators. When the three arrived, Tatu flung herself upon them, licking and grooming them. When she had groomed all three (first her mother, then her father, then the third mongoose) they went back to the group.

Was Tatu grateful, or merely glad to see her family? Her father did something unusual when she started to groom him, rubbing his cheek glands on her, which dwarf mongooses more typically do when preparing to fight one another. Conceivably

171

this indicated anger, and Tatu wanted to appease them.

The converse of gratitude is surely revenge. Parrots are notorious for holding grudges. It is certain that an animal can take a strong dislike to a human individual and treat it unusually aggressively. To stay on good terms with a parrot, it is best not to be the one who clips its nails or trims its beak. If one emotion is possible, why should the other not be?

Ola, a young false killer whale in an oceanarium, was accustomed to a staff of human divers working in his tank. One diver took to teasing Ola surreptitiously. Oceanarium management had their first inkling of this one day when Ola placed his snout on the man's back, pushed him to the floor of the tank and held him there. (He was wearing diving gear, so he didn't drown.) Seeking to free the diver, trainers gave Ola commands, tried to startle him with loud noises and offered fish, to no avail. After five minutes Ola released the diver, and subsequent investigation brought out the teasing.[52]

Gratitude and vengefulness, the tit-for-tat emotions, might prove to be mediators of reciprocal altruism. That reciprocal altruism exists does not suggest that all altruism is reciprocal, however: it is arguable from the evidence that animals may possess the capacity for compassionate and generous feelings, hence altruistic behaviour in the usual sense, such that even if this feeling evolved for genetic advantage, it produces behaviour which need not always be advantageous. Some theorists of animal behaviour have occasionally acknowledged this possibility. Thus Richard Dawkins, in discussing the phenomenon of monkeys adopting unrelated babies, remarks: 'In most cases we should probably regard adoption, however touching it may seem, as a misfiring of a built-in rule. This is because the generous female is doing her own genes no good by caring for the orphan. She is wasting time and energy which she could be investing in the lives of her own kin, particularly future children of her own. It is presumably a mistake which happens too seldom for natural selection to have "bothered" to change the rule by making the maternal instinct more selective.'[53] Consider the reaction to this quotation if one did not know it referred to animals.

A generous female 'making a mistake' hardly proves that generosity – and altruism – do not exist. Yet it usually disappears from explanations, so that in the final pages of *The Selfish Gene*, Dawkins asserts:

> It is possible that yet another unique quality of man is a capacity for genuine, disinterested altruism . . . We can even discuss ways of deliberately cultivating and nurturing pure, disinterested altruism – something that has no place in nature, something that has never existed before in the history of the world.[54]

Is pure altruism a human error? A recent scientific report on food-sharing in vampire bats noted that 'true altruism has never been documented in non-human animals, presumably because such a one-way system is not evolutionarily stable'. Yet the results of the study are a little different. Vampire bats share food (the blood of other animals, usually horses) with other bats in their sleeping areas. This is vital to bat survival, since they starve to death very quickly. A small captive colony of bats was set up to see whether they shared with kin, with friends (as in reciprocal altruism) and with strangers. Bats that had hunted successfully did indeed share with relatives and with certain friends. 'Only once did it occur between strangers,' the report noted. Rather than showing that vampire bats never behave altruistically, this shows that they can be altruistic, even if rarely. The researcher's interpretation is that the bat made a mistake.[55]

Altruistic acts, when recorded, are treated as rare exceptions unworthy of note. There seems to be a powerful allure to the proclamation that all the world is ruled by self-interest, proving to the naive that kindness, self-sacrifice and generosity cannot exist. This may be one of the more major projections of human values on to animals. There is the scientific hegemony involved in proclaiming that something everybody believes in from their experiences, such as animal compassion, is dead wrong. There is the additional pleasure of proving that all behaviour is selfish to the bone. Robert Frank, author of *Passions Within Reason*, has pointed out that 'The flint-eyed researcher fears no greater humiliation than to have called some action altruistic, only to have a more sophisticated colleague later demonstrate that it was self-serving. This fear surely helps account for the extraordinary volume of ink behavioral scientists have spent trying to unearth selfish motives for seemingly self-sacrificing acts.'[56] There can be no question that, for want of a better term, the 'politics' of what one selects to study plays a constricting role in ethology.

Not all scientists fall into this snare, and some have discussed the possibility of a generalised capacity for altruism. Richard Connor and Kenneth Norris queried whether reciprocal altruism is found among dolphins and concluded that it is, but also that the concept is insufficient to explain altruistic dolphin behaviour.[57] They postulate the existence of generalised altruistic tendencies in dolphins: '. . . altruistic acts are dispensed freely and not necessarily to animals that can or will reciprocate. They need not necessarily even be confined to the species of the altruistic individual.'

Connor and Norris point out that in dolphin society, individuals may be aware of the favour-granting status of other individuals not only with regard to themselves, but with regard to other dolphins in general. They concur with biologist Robert Trivers that such 'multi-party situations' can reward generalised altruistic behaviour, since individuals may become regarded by others as cheaters (or as generous):[58] 'In this case selection may favour an individual, A, dispensing altruism to another individual, B, even when A knows that B will not recompense him fully, or at all, in the future. The eventual increase in A's inclusive fitness will come from an increased tendency of those individuals who learned of A's altruism to act altruistically toward him.' Once having argued that generosity is theoretically possible in animals, it can also be argued that it is a real phenomenon in some species. Even ants exhibit what looks very much like compassion for one another. Leaf-cutting ants, when buried by accident, will stridulate, that is, make a vibrating sound, heard to a depth of 3 centimetres. Their fellow ants will come to their rescue and dig them out. It appears that these ants identify and rescue all other leaf-cutting ants, not only those in their own gene pool, but this is not definitely known.[59]

It can be wrong to attribute altruism to animals, such as in one interpretation of the notorious dolphin slaughter at Iki Island, Japan, where fishermen killed hundreds of dolphins to stop them competing for fish. This killing took place each year for five years, during which the fishermen had no difficulty in rounding up the dolphins for slaughter. This was puzzling to many observers who were trying to stop the killing, for it was widely believed that dolphins were extremely intelligent – perhaps more intelligent than humans. One theory to explain this held that the dolphins were being altruistic, allowing themselves to be trapped and killed in the hope that worldwide horror at the spectacle (which received international media coverage) would cause a revulsion of feeling and lead to the protection of wild animals.[60] They were martyrs. After five years, a group of the bottlenose dolphins, instead of allowing themselves to be rounded up, darted under the boats surrounding them and got away. Perhaps they tired of martyrdom.

How far will an animal go to help another? How much will it risk? How far will a person go? Yad Va Shem in Israel has an Avenue of the Righteous for those non-Jews who risked their lives to save Jews from extermination. Trees in honour of the saviours are added as new deeds of bravery are discovered. What would such an orchard for animals look like? Perhaps whales sing sagas of great acts of sacrifice by whale cows of days gone by.

CHAPTER NINE

Shame, Blushing and
Hidden Secrets

D ARWIN argued that only humans blush. Since then, the self-aware social emotions like shame, shyness, guilt, embarrassment and self-consciousness – all feelings of the self being perceived by others – are usually asserted to be exclusively human. Yet there is evidence that many animals feel them too. Shame may prove to be a surprisingly basic emotion. It is one of the most vividly remembered emotions.[1] When we recall being happy or frightened or angry, we do not usually experience that emotion again at the time of recalling it. Remembering an incident of embarrassment or shame can often bring a flood of shame sweeping back. Those who blush may blush again at a memory. In human psychology (and psychotherapy), shame received little attention for years; recently it has begun to be considered important. It has been called 'the master emotion', which societies use to enforce their norms.[2] The emotion of guilt is considered to refer to a particular event, and shame, which is more global, refers to the individual's entire state of being.

Some argue, not especially vigorously, as they have met little opposition, that only humans have self-conscious emotions. Animals, it is said, are incapable of self-consciousness. This argument is generally used to show the low level of animal cognition rather than an absence of emotion.

Charles Darwin, who investigated blushing at great length, seems to have been surrounded by people who blushed at the least provocation. He noted that it was usually accompanied by averting the eyes, the face or the whole body. He had difficulty explaining the value of this phenomenon, and gave a rather Lamarckian explanation for it. Humans, he said, care about their personal appearance and the opinion of others. When people feel attention, especially critical attention, being directed at them, this 'excite[s] into activity that part of the sensorium which receives the sensory nerves of the face; and this will react through the vaso-motor system on the facial capillaries. By frequent reiteration through numberless generations, the process will have become so habitual . . . that even a suspicion of . . . depreciation suffices to relax the capillaries, without any conscious thought about our faces.'[3]

After questioning British missionaries stationed around the world on this subject, Darwin concluded that people of all races blush, and that it is not learned, since people who have been born blind also blush. (His data contradicted those defenders of slavery who alleged that Negroes did not blush because they were incapable of shame and hence not fully human).[4] He called blushing 'the most peculiar and the most human of all expressions. Monkeys redden from passion, but it would require an overwhelming amount of evidence to make us believe that any animal could blush.'[5]

It would have interested Darwin to know that animals other than monkeys also exhibit reddening skin. The ears of a Tasmanian devil (a small carnivorous marsupial) in the Frankfurt Zoo turned red 'during a state of excitement'.[6] Some birds blush, as can be seen on featherless areas of skin. Like the turkey, the spangled honeyeater and the smoky honeyeater have unfeathered wattles which blush 'when the bird is excited'.[7] Macaws that have bare skin on their cheeks can be seen to blush. They do so when excited or enraged, and, according to parrot behaviourist Mattie

Sue Athan, they have also been seen to do so if they fall accidentally while clambering down from a perch. This certainly looks
like embarrassment.[8] On the other hand the macaw might just
be angry that it has fallen. Perhaps it will turn out to be true that
humans are the only animals to blush self-consciously. Humans
are unusually devoid of fur, feathers and other coverings, after
all and so provide a large canvas for this effect.

It may be that the function of blushing is not, or not wholly,
a visual one. The phenomenon of blushing need not be visible.
Many people feel tingling skin – and shame – without visibly
reddening. If people flushed, paled and turned green with the
frequency found in fiction, society would be a much more col-
ourful place. Perhaps many species of animals blush unnoticed.
No one has checked to see if, under the fur, a raccoon tingles
with mortification or flushes with pride. Whether macaws also
blush on the parts of their bodies covered by feathers or whether
other parrots flush beneath their feathers is unknown. But even
if they do not, it does not necessarily follow that if animals don't
blush they don't feel shame.

It might seem that shame involves more self-consciousness,
more intellectual comprehension of how other creatures view
one, than is compatible with the intellect of some or all animals.
But this need not be the case. There is no reason to suppose
that an animal couldn't feel shame without understanding why.
As Darwin noted, mental confusion is a prominent symptom of
shame. 'I can't think clearly in the moment of embarrassment,
and I don't know anybody else who can,' psychiatrist Donald
Nathanson has written.[9]

Emotion can exist either with or without understanding the
reasons for it. One animal might be ashamed or embarrassed
without being entirely conscious of the reason; another might
be ashamed or embarrassed and understand the reason perfectly.

Self-consciousness denotes both emotional and intellectual
states. Emotionally, it is an uncomfortable feeling of being
observed, a form of embarrassment. Intellectually, it is the
knowledge of one's own existence and acts, a contentious field
of study.

A chimpanzee allowed to become familiar with mirrors appears
to figure out that the image is its own. If such apes are anaesthetised, dabbed on the face with a dot of paint, and given a mirror

178

upon awakening, they will see the paint in their reflection, touch their face with their fingers, examine their fingers, and then try to remove the paint.[10] Orangutans also learn that the image in the mirror is of themselves; so far, monkeys have not done so. To some, this is evidence of self-consciousness. Others have sought to prove that it is nothing of the sort. J.S. Kennedy follows other critics in arguing that it is more parsimonious to assume that the chimpanzee merely 'forms a point-to-point association between the movements of the mirror image and his own movements.'[11]

The chimpanzees Sherman and Austin are monitored by video cameras and have learned to use these in a variety of ways. After several months of exposure to their own images on the video monitors, each ape appeared to suddenly realise that the image was his own. They use the monitor to watch themselves make faces, eat, or swirl water around in their mouths. Both have learned to distinguish between a live image and a taped image of themselves, by testing to see if their actions were duplicated on the screen. Sherman was using a hand mirror to guide his application of crayola make up one day, tired of the mirror, and gestured to have the video camera aimed at his face instead. He used the image to apply the make-up and to locate and remove any that had stained his teeth. Austin made valiant attempts one day to use the monitor to look down his throat while simultaneously shining a flashlight into it.[12]

Chimpanzees have been seen to save face. This implies self-conciousness. At the zoo in Arnhem, the chimpanzee Yeroen was slightly injured in a fight with another chimp, Nikkie. To the astonishment of researchers, Yeroen spent the next week limping dramatically – but only when he was in Nikkie's view.[13] A chimpanzee wishing to make peace with another sometimes will not approach directly, but will affect to discover a non-existent object and use the resulting gathering to make contact with the other, a strategy Frans de Waal thinks is used to save face.[14]

When a male baboon yawns, his impressive canine teeth are ostentatiously displayed. Observing wild baboons, the biologist Craig Packer found that males with worn or broken teeth yawn less than males with teeth in good condition – unless there are no other males around, in which case they yawn just as often.[15] Chimpanzees have been known to avoid glancing at a food source which they know about but that other chimps do not. On several occasions, lions in the Serengeti who had caught prey in high grass broke with the usual lion habit of beginning to eat at once. Instead the lion sat down and glanced around for as much as five minutes, as if it had caught nothing. When other nearby lions departed, the lion began to eat.[16] A mountain goat who sees a predator will often walk away calmly and slowly and then, the moment it is out of the predator's line of sight, take off, running at full speed.[17] These animals act as if they were conscious of others perceiving their behaviour. This level of self-consciousness might not permit a goat to look into a mirror and think 'That's me, but might be self-consciousness nonetheless. Self-awareness need not be all or nothing.

Embarrassment and shyness, also considered self-aware emotions, seem to be not only about appearing badly, but about being seen or regarded when one doesn't wish to be seen. Koko, the signing gorilla, has shown a rather touching form of embarrassment. Among her toys are a number of puppets and dolls. She was once seen signing 'kiss' to her alligator puppet. On another occasion Koko signed 'kiss' to her blue gorilla doll and 'bad bad' to her pink gorilla doll. Then she signed 'chase tickle', slammed the dolls together, made them wrestle and signed 'good gorilla good good'. On each occasion, and on other similar occasions, the moment she saw that she was being watched, she stopped playing.[18]

Animals do not wear clothing to conceal parts of their bodies that humans in many cultures consider vital for adults to conceal. They do not hide many actions that correspond to actions people often prefer to hide. This does not necessarily mean that there is nothing they prefer to hide.

It is not clear whether animals ever feel romantic or sexual embarrassment. Alex, the verbally accomplished African grey parrot, may be imprinted on human beings. According to Irene Pepperberg, he attempts to court certain of her male students. When courting, Alex may regurgitate food and do a little ritualised dance. 'If he is courting one of my students and I walk in, he immediately stops,' says Pepperberg. Perhaps Alex is embarrassed. If he merely wants a little privacy, why does he want it? Perhaps he is trying to avoid competition. Alex does not like to be seen courting. Is he shy? Shyness is an emotion that seems to shade into fear, the fear of being seen. It may be that shame is also related to fear.

The essence of shame is the unpleasant feeling that one appears badly – weak, stupid, helpless or inadequate in some way. At first sight this need have no connection with fear. At one oceanarium a bottlenose porpoise, Wela, was trained to jump out of the water and take a fish from a person's hand. One day when this stunt was being photographed, the trainer was distracted and forgot to drop the fish as she usually did. As a result, when Wela grabbed the fish, she inadvertently bit the trainer's hand. Wela, appearing 'hideously embarrassed', went to the bottom of the tank, put her snout in a corner and wouldn't come out until the trainer got in with her, petted her and coaxed her into calmness.[19]

Wela's behaviour is comparable to that of a dog who barks and threatens someone coming into the house – and suddenly realises that the someone is its owner. It has been argued that the comic reversal of behaviour in such a dog doesn't mean it's embarrassed, only that it seeks to appease a dominant animal – its owner – by showing submission. Whether this is accurate or not, it doesn't seem to describe Wela's behaviour. It sounds like embarrassment, a form of shame. The chimpanzee Washoe was seen to make a similar mistake, threatening an old friend (who had grown four or five inches since they had last met) before she recognised who it was and reacted with what would be called embarrassment if Washoe were human.[20] One might say that such behaviour is merely ritual submission, but then the same description could apply to a human apology.

Asked whether wild chimpanzees ever appear ashamed or embarrassed, Jane Goodall laughed. 'They do, actually. In the wild you don't see that very often. The best story I know of clear embarrassment was young Freud when he was about six years old. He was showing off – really, you could only describe it as showing off – in front of Uncle Figan, who was alpha male. Figan was trying to groom Fifi, the new baby was there, and Freud was just prancing around and shaking branches and making a real big nuisance of himself. He went up into a tall plantain tree: they have a rather weak trunk like a banana. He was swaying it to and fro, to and fro, and suddenly it snapped! – and he *crashed* on

181

to the ground. He just happened to land very close to me. I was able to see his face, and the first thing he did when he emerged from the grass was to take a quick little glance at Figan and then he crept quietly away and began feeding. That was quite clearly a big come-down for him.'[21]

If shame proves to be widespread in the animal kingdom, the evolutionary approach would predict that it should confer some advantage. Just what might be adaptive about global self-accusation is not immediately apparent.

The other self-conscious emotions seem to appear early in the lives of humans. In one series of experiments, researchers gave small children toys cunningly designed to fall apart, and then videotaped their play. When a toy broke, some children cried; some looked for another toy; some appeared ashamed or guilty. Some children looked away, their bodies 'collapsed' in what is considered a typical shame response. A child who appeared tense and averted his or her gaze, but then tried to fix the toy, was thought to be showing a guilt response.[22]

Helen Block Lewis, an early theorist in this field who focused on humans, viewed shame and guilt as regulators of social interactions, which combat narcissism and punish transgressions of group mores. Blushing signals to other group members that the blusher recognises such transgression and, therefore, recognises the group rules.[23]

Donald Nathanson does not consider shame a social emotion. He cites an experiment in which three- to four-month-old infants could control a display of flashing coloured lights by turning their heads. The babies apparently loved doing this and squealed with pleasure when the lights went on. When the experimenters changed the apparatus so that the babies' efforts were unsuccessful, the infants' heads and necks slumped, their breathing quickened, blood flow to their skin increased and they turned their faces away. Nathanson and other theorists interpret this as a primitive shame response which was independent of whether or not other people were present, and hence argue that shame is not necessarily a social emotion (it is not clear how we can exclude disappointment and frustration).[24] In Nathanson's analysis, shame is 'a biological system by which the organism controls its affective output so that it will not remain interested or content when it may not be safe to do so, or so that it will not remain in affective resonance with an organism that fails to match patterns stored in memory'. He believes that it evolved comparatively recently.[25]

As for the advantages of global self-accusation, Nathanson argues: 'If you were going to design a system capable of learning from experience and educating itself, you might as well build in the capacity to magnify failure. Shame augments our memory of failure and protects us from whatever danger might occur, when, in a moment of need, we might try something well beyond our capacity.'[26]

Another possibility is that shame might keep animals from attracting the attention of predators. Humans feel ashamed not only of their actual or perceived faults, but often of differences, even when those differences are neutral or even positive. To be stared at can be unnerving, even when the stare is an admiring one. Often people are uncomfortable when praised. To be singled out in any way can be acutely embarrassing.

Predators single out prey. Some predators select prey on the basis of physical condition, thus culling out sick and injured animals (and young animals). They may study herds of prey animals, chase some of them, and make an all-out effort to catch only a few. An examination of the bone marrow of wildebeest killed by lions revealed that a large percentage was in poor condition.[27] Hyenas hunting make random passes at herds, or zigzag through, then stop and watch them run, switching their attention from animal to animal, apparently looking for potential weakness. One experimenter who was shooting wildebeest with anaesthetic darts in order to measure and tag them found that, if he wasn't careful, these same animals would at once be killed by hyenas when he released them. Although the wildebeest looked normal to humans, and seemed to be able to run as fast as ever, the hyenas noted some difference. He had to herd the hyenas away with his vehicle until the wildebeest had more time to recover.[28]

But predators do not only look for signs of weakness. They also notice differences. A researcher once marked some wildebeest by painting their horns white. Within a few months, almost all of these animals had been killed by hyenas. Hans Kruuk has noted instances in which hyenas pursued animals who were presumably in good physical condition, but were acting oddly and were then singled out by hyenas. At night, when dazzled by the headlights of a car, wildebeest ran in an odd way – and were instantly pursued by hyenas. Away from the headlights, the wildebeest quickly got their bearings and escaped.

Kruuk also saw a herd of several hundred wildebeest in which only one was rolling and showing territorial behaviour. These actions, unremarkable in another context, instantly attracted a hyena's pursuit. The wildebeest escaped easily.[29] That the wildebeest escaped in these instances supports the idea that the hyenas were detecting difference rather than weakness.

Schooling or flocking behaviour can baffle some predators in a very simple way: by preventing them from focusing on individual prey. When a few members of a school of small silver fish were dyed blue, not only were they more frequently attacked by predators, but so were the normal, silver fish next to them. Faced by a cloud of identical fish, the predator could not pick out an individual, but it was able to pick out the blue one or the one next to the blue one.[30]

Prey animals often seem aware of the assessment of predators. In Zaire, Paul Leyhausen saw two uneasy-looking male kobs (large antelope) near a river. Presently he saw two lions lurking near the kobs, moving from behind one bush to another. The kob closest to the lions appeared to grow calmer and began grazing, but the other began to run back and forth in alarm. It soon became clear from their movements, Leyhausen says, that the lions were stalking the further kob – and that both kobs knew this well before the human observer figured out that the lions weren't going for the closest prey.[31]

Prey animals also seem able to tell when predators are hunting and when they are bent on other business entirely, and adjust their flight distance accordingly. A wish to conceal weakness and difference – behaviour evidencing negative affect at being scrutinized – could lead animals to take actions to avoid predation. They could pretend not to be weak, minimise their difference, or hide from the view of predators.

Predators are not the only creatures who might take advantage of an animal's display of vulnerability or weakness. Conspecifics are all too likely to be alert to signs of such weakness and to take advantage of them. When lions in the Serengeti were shot with anaesthetic darts, some of the other lions took advantage of their condition to attack them (and were driven off by the researchers). Thus, shame might well motivate animals to hide weakness from members of their herd or pack. If a caribou appears visibly weak or lame, it will be the first in its herd to be attacked by wolves, but the wolf who appears weak or sick may lose status in the pack. This could have serious consequences in terms of having offspring.

To survive, an animal must not only be fit, it must look fit. The sense of shame, painful to experience, may provide an emotional reason to hide infirmity.

Sickness and injury are often concealed. To the despair of animal breeders and veterinarians, many captive animals will diligently conceal all signs of sickness until they are too far gone to be saved. Birds are particularly adept at this, sometimes hiding all symptoms and enduring secretly until the moment when they literally topple from their perches.

Scottish red deer leave the herd when they become sick or are injured.[32] At one time it was suggested that they did this for the good of the herd, but it seems probable that a lone deer is less likely to be spotted by a predator than a herd of deer – and if a herd of deer is spotted, then the sick or injured one is most likely to be the first animal attacked. If the deer recovers, it returns to the herd. If predators zero in on difference, not merely weakness, animals might feel vulnerable or ashamed of things that attract the gaze of others.

It might seem odd that shame could lead to blushing. At first glance it seems counterproductive for an animal to blush visibly or physically show embarrassment: that doesn't look good, and isn't the objective to look good? Conceivably the tingle of the blush could tell the blusher to hide (or give them something to hide), which serves the purpose of hiding the weakness that the blusher was embarrassed about in the first place. Most animals don't blush visibly, if at all, so it may be that humans do have a small claim to distinction in being (some of us) such visible blushers, even if it is no longer possible to say that we are unique in feeling shame.

Pet owners often say that their cat or dog hates to be laughed at. Elephant keepers have reported that elephants who are laughed at have responded by filling their trunks with water and spraying those who are mocking them.[33] It seems curious that animals that do not laugh would recognise and resent laughter. Perhaps laughter should be considered the equivalent expression of something they do feel themselves.

Guilt – feeling remorse for a particular act – is more difficult to pin down than shame. An action which carries overtones of guilt usually does so because our culture has informed us that it is wrong. The guilt is easily confounded with fear of discovery and subsequent disapproval or punishment. The chimpanzee Nim Chimpsky, as we saw, was taught the sign 'sorry', and used it when he had 'misbehaved'. The examples of Nim's misdeeds that are cited – breaking a toy or jumping around too much – do not seem to be things that a chimpanzee would naturally regard as bad. He knew it was misbehaviour only because he had been taught that it was, like human children. Sometimes, it is reported, Nim signed 'sorry' before his teachers noticed what he had done. Whether Nim felt something other than the desire to avert possible wrath is unclear.[34] On the other hand, this is often unclear in humans, too.

Washoe's adopted son Loulis was teasing Roger Fouts one day, 'just being a pill', and poked him harder than usual, cutting Fouts with his nail. 'I made a big deal of it, crying and so on. Later, whenever I showed him that, to make him feel guilty, if you will, to use it to exploit that, he would squeeze his eyes tight and turn away. He would refuse to look at me whenever I tried to show him or talk about this old, old scratch that he had given me.' There are a variety of interpretations that can be given to this extraordinarily familiar behaviour, but guilt is very strongly suggested.

As for dogs, the most familiar guilty animal for many people, Desmond Morris has argued persuasively that dogs do at times feel remorse for their actions. When a dog that has committed some misdeed greets a human with an unusually submissive manner before the person has any reason to guess what has happened, Morris says it cannot be getting cues from human behaviour. 'It has an understanding that it has done something "wrong".'[35]

Human shame has only recently been deemed a respectable field of study. Donald Nathanson recounts how, early in his career, he organised a symposium on shame. When it was over a friend took him aside, complimented him on the success of the symposium, and urged him not to do any more work on shame, lest he get a reputation for it. 'It was in that moment that I learned that the very idea of shame is embarrassing to most people,' Nathanson says.[36] These are emotions to be hidden. Perhaps animals have been successful in hiding them from our gaze.

CHAPTER TEN

Beauty, the Bears and
the Setting Sun

T HE SENSE of beauty is not usually defined as an emotion.[1]
Yet it does not seem to be a wholly intellectual experience.
Sometimes beauty makes people happy, sometimes sad; perhaps
the experience is partly cognitive and partly emotional. We have
certainly always preferred to reserve it exclusively for our own
species.

Some who have observed bears in the wild often speak of them
sitting on their haunches at sunset, gazing at it, seemingly lost in
meditation. From all appearances it would seem that the bears are
enjoying the sunset, that they are taking pleasure in the aesthetic
experience. Scientists laugh at the naivety of this interpretation.
How could a bear be capable of such a contemplative state? Some
people also believe other people are incapable of such an emotion,
and most nineteenth-century scientists claimed that 'lower' races
could not enjoy the same aesthetic emotions that they could.

One can doubtless go too far with this, listening, for example,

188

to a bear exhaling and claim that he is sighing with melancholy awareness of the transience of things, observing his world and thinking that one day he will no longer be present to witness such beauty. An ursine Rilke. Momentary awareness of his own mortality is almost impossible to prove; a sense of beauty is easier.

Why do we have a sense of beauty? Some have claimed that human artistic creativity is rooted in exploratory play. Perhaps a sense of beauty rewards us for making our way through the world and for turning our senses upon it. It is valuable that we find our children and other loved ones beautiful. In a broader sense we may have evolved to find the world around us beautiful, to enjoy gazing on it, listening to it, breathing it in, moving through it, feeling and tasting it.

However, before an animal can find beauty in some set of sensations, sounds or images, it must be possible for the animal to detect these things physically, to sense them and to perceive them. Animal senses are poorly understood but seem to be tremendously variable. It is widely believed that bats are blind, but many bats have quite good vision.

Popular belief also holds that animals, or some of them, are colour-blind. This strangely counter-intuitive assertion has been widely repeated as scientific fact for decades and has made its way into some textbooks. Despite numerous articles in the scientific and popular press reporting colour vision in animals (including dogs), the idea that animals can see in colour is still being described as a 'myth'.[2]

Humans do have excellent colour vision. Along with many other primates, we are classified by optical scientists as trichromats, which means that we construct the range of colours we see from three basic colours. A person and an ape may see just the same colours when looking at a setting sun, and Adriaan Kortlandt once observed a wild chimpanzee gaze at a particularly spectacular sunset until darkness fell for a full fifteen minutes.[3] Many mammals, including cats and dogs, are dichromats, using two basic colours. They see in colour, though not as diversely as people. A few nocturnal animals, like rats, may be colour-blind. Some birds use four or five basic colours; perhaps their colour vision is better than ours. It has been known for decades that some insects can see ultraviolet light; recently it has been discovered that some birds, fish and mammals can, too.[4]

189

If animals were without colour vision, of what benefit would be a baboon's brightly coloured face and rump, or a peacock's tail? Yet even among those who concede the peafowl's capacity to detect plumage colours, there are some who argue that it is unlikely to *appreciate* those colours. A recent natural history book for popular audiences has it:

> . . . what is it about the peacock's fan that puts the female in the mood for mating: The iridescence? The graceful shape? The spots that look like eyes? The truth is, what wows humans may not impress female peafowl at all. Instead, the sheer size of the fan may be the irresistible feature because of what it says about the bird that carried it. Namely, if a bird with a large fan has survived to breeding age despite his unwieldy handicap, he must be both strong and wily. In the same way, females may value colorful plumage not for its beauty, but because the sheen shows that the bird is free from parasites. Females that can spot these superior traits are rewarded by passing on their genes to offspring that, like their 'handicapped' father, are more likely to survive and reproduce.[5]

How seriously should this be taken? The view that the peahen *cannot*, on the one hand, be drawn to beauty, but *can*, on the other, think 'Shiny feathers mean low parasite load – I'll mate with this one so my chicks can benefit from his genes', is untenable. If any such claim for a peahen's ability to draw intellectual conclusions were explicitly made, it would promptly be rejected. Yet the assertion that the peahen does not sense beauty is in line with assertions routinely made in the field of animal behaviour, and is unlikely to be questioned.

If the peahen is not thought of as a calculating gene-shopper, what can an evolutionary approach suggest is going on? If, proximately, she admires the peacock's tail because she finds it beautiful – and in humans, it takes no giant brain or aesthetic training to do this – then she may mate with him, which has the *ultimate* result of selecting the male with the best genes. While human beings are occasionally heard to refer to others in terms of their genetic potential, this is not what typically goes through the mind of a person smitten with either lust or love.

To return to the question of animal senses, acute hearing is usually conceded to animals. Lately it has been discovered that the hearing of an unknown number of species goes far beyond our own; that elephants communicate extensively in sounds too low for us to hear; and that shrews, like bats, practise echolocation by means of sounds too high for our ears. In the case of birds, the implications of this are not always realised. When people argue about bird song, we are usually arguing about something we understand poorly. Birds are about ten times better than humans at temporally discriminating sounds. Thus, over a time interval in which we hear one note, a bird can hear ten notes. When recordings of bird songs are played at reduced speed, it is found that they make use of this ability – that their songs often contain sequences of notes which pass by too quickly for the human ear. A blackbird's song that sounds like a rusty hinge to us may sound quite different to the blackbird.[6]

Pet birds often appear to enjoy human music. They may prefer certain kinds of music, or react differently depending on what music is played. Gerald Durrell has written of a pet pigeon who listened quietly to most music and snuggled against the gramophone. When marches were played, he would stamp back and forth, cooing loudly, and when waltzes played, he would twist and bow, cooing softly.[7] Grey parrots sometimes flap their wings in delight when they hear favourite songs.[8] Given the difference in auditory acuity, one wonders whether much human music might not sound slow and sepulchral to birds.

Numerous species of animals utter lengthy and complicated calls which humans enjoy hearing. It would be odd if humpback whales did not appreciate their own songs or if wolves did not like the sound of their howling. Canid howling is not a random procedure and, as anyone who has howled with a pet dog knows, dogs adjust their howling according to the other sounds they hear. Hope Ryden observed a pair of howling coyotes who demonstrated this: they never howled on the same note. When the male's howl hit a note the female was on, she at once dropped her pitch, and when she howled on his note, the male instantly switched to falsetto.[9] Such duets are thought to convey the information to other coyotes that there are two coyotes howling, not just one, thus indicating that a territorial pair is present. This seems likely, but does not mean that the coyotes do not feel that the howling sounds better that way. There is no reason why the mechanism by which this advantageous behaviour is obtained could not be an aesthetic appreciation of song.

Similarly, the calls of gibbons seem to serve a territorial function, yet also might arise from an aesthetic sensibility. Gibbons sing together daily. In most but not all species, male and female calls are different. The duets of pairs, in which they exchange notes, may be sung spontaneously or in response to the songs of other gibbons. In most gibbon species, males sing long solos and females utter ringing 'great calls'. Juveniles often join in.[10]

Jim Nollman, whose avocation is playing music to and with wild animals, went to Panama in 1983 to try to make music with howler monkeys, who live in family groups and call extensively. Nollman writes that a zoologist (whose study of the howlers spanned a decade) predicted that they would not be interested in his playing, except perhaps to utter a few howls as a territorial claim. Finding a tree with howlers in it, Nollman sat beneath it and played his shakuhachi flute. The entire family at first responded with loud howls. Then one monkey began to howl between the notes of the flute, in apparent response. After an hour, darkness brought the interchange to an end. In following days, the family did not howl with the flautist's playing, but instead descended to low branches and watched him intently, despite their reputation for shyness.[11] Whatever the howlers thought of Nollman's flute music, it seems clear that they found it interesting although they were aware it was not produced by a conspecific. Perhaps they liked it. Even if they disliked it, that might represent an aesthetic opinion.

Michael, a gorilla in a sign-language programme, is fond of music, and enjoys the singing of tenor Luciano Pavarotti so much that he has been known to refuse an opportunity to go outdoors when a Pavarotti performance was on television. He likes to tap on pipes and strum on strings from burlap bags. Unfortunately, Michael is so strong that he would have a hard time not destroying a musical instrument.[12]

What role, if any, the pleasures of taste play in animal eating is almost wholly unknown. Siri, an Indian elephant confined in a small zoo exhibit, was often seen to step delicately on an apple or orange, split it open and then rub the pieces into her hay. Her keeper believed that Siri did this to flavour the hay.[13] A wild elephant eats a wide variety of plants, which presumably have differing tastes. The diet of captivity is far more monotonous.

Another sensory realm which humans apprehend little is that of smell. We possess this ancient sense, but not keenly, and make little conscious use of it. Hunters teach themselves to compensate for the superior sense of smell of many prey animals by approaching them from downwind or by disguising the human scent with others. Given the powerful olfactory sense of so many animals, it is not impossible for them to have aesthetic responses to stimuli people do not detect. An observer of coatimundis in Arizona reported that these animals frequently sit up or lean back and sniff the air intently, presumably gathering information. He commented that one old female, the Witch, would also sometimes arise during one of the group's intervals of relaxation on a cliff ledge, go to the edge and sit for five minutes or so, sniffing calmly, slowly and deeply. The thought that she might be appreciating and not just assessing the world around her occurred to observers, who could not resist comparing her to a concert-goer or gallery visitor.[14]

The frequent allegation that birds have no sense of smell is wrong. The olfactory bulbs in a bird's brain give them this sense. Its acuity varies widely: parrots and warblers seem to have a poor sense of smell, while albatrosses and kiwis have excellent ones. Not surprisingly, some vultures have been found to have an excellent sense of smell, which they use to locate carrion.[15]

There are other animal senses, such as the ability to sense magnetic fields, that science has only recently become aware of, and clearly there may be yet others. Any sense may be subject to preference. Most animals, like us, seem to dislike bitter flavours and enjoy sweet ones, a discrimination which has survival value. In such simple distinctions may lie the beginnings of aesthetics.

One scientist gathered data about the visual preferences of immature male rhesus monkeys in captivity. They liked short wavelength light: they preferred orange to red, yellow to orange, green to yellow, and they liked blue better still. They were more interested in the pictures of other animals than they were in pictures of monkeys, but preferred pictures of monkeys to pictures of people. They would rather look at flowers than at a Mondrian painting ('Composition', 1920), and pictures of bananas interested them least of all. They would rather watch a continuous cartoon than a cartoon film loop, but they preferred the loop to watching still pictures. They preferred their films to be in focus, and the worse the focus was on a film, the less they cared to watch it. These preferences were categorised as 'interest' and 'pleasure'.[16] The preference that seems the most likely to be aesthetic is the one for colours, since there is no reason to suppose that a plain blue wall is any more interesting than a plain yellow one. Nor are rhesus alone in their taste for blue.

Bernhard Rensch also examined colour and pattern preferences in primates and in other animals. The apes and monkeys generally preferred regular to irregular and symmetric to asymmetric designs. Nor were their tastes immutable: re-tested after an interval, some of them made different choices. When Rensch tested crows and jackdaws, they too selected regular designs, but fish seemed more attracted by irregular designs.[17]

Animals often select mates on the basis of their displays or songs. Sometimes the nature of the criteria they use can be simply quantified: they select the biggest or the loudest or the plumpest mate. Female widowbirds are attracted to male widowbirds with long tails, so that when an ornithologist glued extra tail feathers on to the end of the tails of some males, those males became more popular.[18] They also tend to favour animals with a symmetric appearance. Sometimes, however, more subtle aesthetic choices seem to be involved.

The bowerbirds and birds of paradise of New Guinea are favoured subjects of ornithological study.[19] The various species of bowerbirds do not form pairs. Instead the female visits the display sites, or bowers, of various males and the male performs courtship displays, which may or may not induce the female to mate with him. Some male bowerbirds – generally those that have the plainest plumage – construct very elaborate bowers resembling alleys, tunnels, maypoles, yards or tepees. They embellish these with coloured objects such as flowers, fruits, insect parts or human artefacts; and they may even paint parts of the bower with charcoal and crushed berries, using a bark 'brush'.

Different populations of a bowerbird species prefer different colours when choosing curios to decorate their bowers. They often visit one another's bowers and steal decorations. When selecting adornments, the satin bowerbird – a blue-eyed species – favours blue items.[20] When the male bowerbird dec-orates his bower, and when the female bowerbird mates with the male whose bower she likes best, they are exhibiting taste. (And when interfering biologists steal the adornments from certain bowers, those males are able to mate less often). The evolutionary approach suggests that the ultimate cause of their artistic preferences may be to enable the male to exhibit how fit he is, how much time he has to devote to collecting decorations (and defending them from theft), and for the female to assess this. The proximate cause, however, is unlikely to be anything like this. It is most unlikely that the female estimates how many bird-hours went into a bower like this, and whether that indicates good genes. The male does not decide to decorate with blue objects because, let us say, they are rare, or because he knows that will indicate to females that he ranges over a wide area due to his good genes. It is more parsimonious to postulate that both female and male bowerbirds like the way blue looks.

Naturalist Bruce Beehler observed the bowers of the streaked bowerbird. These birds are not born especially beautiful but must create their own beauty. Hence their bowers. These resemble tepees with centre poles, and on the base of the pole the bird constructs a tidy wall of moss adorned with coloured objects. Each type of decoration is on a different section of the wall and the effect is 'quite artistic and very beautiful'.[21] Beehler notes: 'Some biologists believe that the remarkable construction of the male bowerbirds is evidence of an esthetic sense. Others prefer to believe that this spin-off of mating behavior is the product of the remarkable sexual competition among males to mate with females – a process that Charles Darwin named "sexual selection".'

These two explanations are not opposed, but fully compatible. Yet something important is suggested by the comment that some 'prefer' to believe in competition. This is the stumbling-block of what people *like* to believe or think they ought to believe about animals.

The same issue arises with respect to birds of paradise, famous for the gorgeous plumage of the males. At a display site of the lesser bird of paradise, many males gather. All of the females who visit are seen to mate with just one male, and biologists have wondered why this should be. Bruce Beehler writes:

> Some researchers believe that it is the product of acute female discrimination and that the females are choosing the 'prettiest' or 'sexiest' male. I tend to believe that it is caused, in part, by a despotic control of the lek [communal breeding ground] mating hierarchy by the dominant bird. The alpha male, by periodic physical aggression and continual psychological intimidation, is able to keep control over the subordinate males in the lek. The females are able to perceive this hierarchy in the lek, just as humans can make the same perception about dominance and subordination in a social situation. Females will naturally tend to mate with the alpha male, because his genetic material will most likely give the female the best chance of producing offspring with his qualities – the qualities that may help her male offspring dominate a lek of the next generation.[22]

This analysis, with its focus on male aggression and its rewards, leaves unexplained the huge golden tail feathers which the males vibrate in their displays. Humans find these so beautiful that in the past the very existence of some species was threatened by hunting for export.

New Guinea tribes have differing styles of costume for ritual occasions, which almost invariably include feathers from various species of birds of paradise, usually on men's head-dresses. Bowerbirds often take human artefacts such as brightly coloured candy wrappers, cartridge cases or shiny keys to decorate their bowers. One can imagine birds creeping near human habitations to steal coloured objects and humans creeping near bird habitations to steal coloured feathers. When we do it, it is for the sake of art. When they do it, it is for the sake of competition. Both explanations are compatible, and both may be in part correct.[23] What is disturbing and irrational is the decision to explain human behaviour in spiritual terms of a sense of beauty, and animal behaviour in mechanistic terms of demonstrating fitness. Again, the object seems to be to define humans as higher and unique.

The issue of artistic creation in animals is a fascinating one but little work has been done in this area. This is one of the many activities that has been said to mark a boundary between humans and animals. Various apes, particularly chimpanzees, have drawn or painted in captivity, as have capuchin monkeys. Alpha, a chimp at the Yerkes laboratory, loved to draw and would beg visitors for paper and pencil – in preference to food – and then sit in a corner and draw. Once, lacking paper, she tried to draw on a dead leaf. By giving her paper that already had geometric designs on it, it was found that her drawing was influenced by what was already on the paper. She filled in some figures, scribbled in the missing parts of others, such as a circle with a wedge cut out, and added marks that 'balanced' other figures. Her drawings were promptly taken from her, because after she had drawn on both sides of a sheet of paper, she'd put it in her mouth.[24]

Following this work, Desmond Morris had no difficulty in persuading another chimpanzee, Congo, to draw and paint. When interrupted before he had finished a picture, Congo screamed with rage until he was allowed to complete it. Congo also changed his drawing depending on what was already on the paper. His favourite design was a fan of radiating lines, which he made in various different ways, and not by a single, stereotyped technique.[25]

Gorillas such as Koko and Michael have also made many drawings. In no case have apes produced incontrovertibly representational drawings. One chimp, Moja, produced an unusually simple drawing with parallel horizontal curves, and signed that it was a bird. Asked to draw a berry, she produced a compact drawing in one corner of her paper.[26] Either drawing is plausible but not irrefutable as a representation.

In a later experiment Moja and Washoe were asked to draw such items as a basketball, a boot, a banana, an apple, a cup and a brush, either from the actual objects or from colour slides. At later sessions they were asked to draw the same items and the drawings were examined for consistency. Drawings of the boot were inconsistent, but those of the cup and brush did show similarities. None of these were drawings that a human would be likely to identify as cups or brushes: requests to draw the cup always produced a centrally placed solid vertical fan of strokes, whereas the brush was denoted by vertical strokes crossing horizontal strokes. Drawings of flowers included radial patterns, and drawings of birds always included 'a pointed action', whether denoting a beak, the movement of flight or something else is unknown.

'The one that threw us with Moja was the basketball, in that it just was a scribble across the page,' Roger Fouts said.

But after Moja drew it in the same way – vertical zig-zags on the lower part of the paper – at intervals six weeks apart, researchers realised it might represent not the appearance of the ball, but its motion. Small children sometimes produce kinaesthetic drawings of this kind.

The boredom or leisure of captivity must be considered as a motivating factor for all such animals, yet it is interesting that they appear to find the act of drawing or painting rewarding in itself (bear in mind the fact of individualism: some captive chimps absolutely refuse to draw or paint).

In 1980, a young Indian elephant named Siri (the same who rubbed fruit into her hay) was assigned a new keeper, David Gucwa. Noticing Siri making scratches on the floor of her enclosure with a pebble – and then 'fingering' them with the tip of her trunk – Gucwa began providing Siri with a pencil and drawing pad (which he held in his lap). She responded by producing dozens of drawings. All could be classified as either 'abstract' or scribbles, but all are confined to the boundaries of the paper, and to many observers, they seem lyrical, energetic and beautiful. She was never rewarded with food for drawing, although she might have found Gucwa's attention a reward in itself.

Gucwa and journalist James Ehmann sent copies of Siri's drawings to scientists, most of whom declined to comment, and to artists, many of whom were enthusiastic. Artists Elaine and Willem de Kooning, in particular, looked at the drawings before reading the covering letter, and were struck by their 'flair and decisiveness and originality'. Learning the identity of the maker, Willem de Kooning remarked, 'That's a damned talented elephant'.[27] (In fact, Siri hardly deserves credit for the originality: given her circumstances, it is difficult to see how she could be derivative.)

Copies of her drawings were shown to other zoo keepers, who said that was nothing new: *their* elephants scribbled on the ground with sticks or stones all the time. Why, then, had nobody written about it before?

Siri's opportunity to draw on paper ended after two years due to differences between Gucwa and the zoo director, and to her transfer to another zoo during renovation. She was never given paper with predrawn designs on it to see how that would affect her drawing, but on several occasions she made two drawings on one sheet of paper, and apparently placed the second with reference to the first. It would have been nice to know whether Siri ever disliked any of her own work – did she ever tear anything up? Gucwa always removed her drawings promptly, so that she wouldn't smear them with her damp trunk when she 'fingered' them. And if other elephants also liked to draw, how would they react to one another's drawings?

Other elephants have made images on paper or canvas, but perhaps none with so little direction as Siri. For example, Carol, an Indian elephant at the San Diego Zoo, was taught to paint as a visitor attraction, and is given commands by her trainer, who tells her when to pick up the brush, supplies her with colours, rotates the canvas so the brush strokes go in different directions, and rewards her with apples.[28] But just as the existence of paint-by-numbers kits does not invalidate the existence of artistic originality, Carol's dutiful paintings do not negate Siri's apparent urge to draw.

More recently, Ruby, an Asian elephant in the zoo at Phoenix, Arizona, has been encouraged to paint. Selected because she was the most active – but not the only – doodler among the elephants, Ruby becomes excited when she hears the word paint. She loves to paint, but also continues to doodle in the dirt in her enclosure. A handler thinks the African elephants who share the yard with Ruby are jealous of the attention she gets, because they have begun making highly visible drawings on the walls, using the ends of logs.[29]

A different kind of creativity was seen in rough-toothed dolphins. Trainer Karen Pryor had run out of stunts for the dolphins to perform in shows and decided to reward one of them, Malia, only for performing new behaviours. The trainers waited until Malia did something new, then rewarded her by blowing a whistle and tossing her a fish. Malia quickly learned what was being reinforced that day – tail-slapping, backwards tail-walking – and performed that action. In a few weeks they had run out of new behaviours to reinforce. After a few frustrating days, Malia suddenly began performing a dramatic array of wholly new activities, some quite complex. She swam on her back with her tail in the air, or spun like a corkscrew, or jumped out of the water upside-down, or made lines on the floor of the tank with her dorsal fin. She had learned that her trainers were not looking for certain actions, but that they were looking for novelty. Sometimes she was very excited when training sessions were about to start, and her trainers could hardly stop themselves believing that Malia 'sat in her holding tank all night thinking up stuff and rushed into the first show with an air of: "Wait until you see *this* one!" '

Determined to make a scientific record of this remarkable behaviour, the trainers filmed the same process with a second dolphin, Hou. A less optimistic and excitable individual, Hou took longer to catch on, but at the sixteenth training session suddenly performed a burst of novel activities and continued to do new stunts in session after session. Pryor reports that this experience changed Hou lastingly, 'from a docile, inactive animal to an active observant animal full of initiative'. Hou also gave more anger signals – having apparently acquired an artistic temperament. Both dolphins began to produce novel behaviours outside training sessions, including opening gates between tanks, leaping over gates, and jumping out of the water and sliding around on the concrete in order to rap trainers on the ankles.

While some thought these results showed how intelligent dolphins are, Pryor disagreed: she replicated the experiment with pigeons and ended up with birds that spontaneously lay on their backs, stood with both feet on one wing or flew two inches into the air and hovered there. Such creativity is unexpected in a species usually deemed intellectually unimpressive.[30]

Human emotions occur in the context of culture, which is not to say that they exist only because of culture. Culture, in part, conditions our sense of what is beautiful. Thus an investigation of the sense of beauty in animals may lead to the question of animal culture.

Culture and its transmission include much that is cognitive, which is beyond the scope of this book, yet it should be noted that there are many examples of its existence. In Japanese monkey troops, different traditions between troops have been noticed: some troops eat shellfish and some don't; some eat the seed of the muku fruit and some throw it away; some babysit for each other and some don't. The most famous example of cultural transmission comes from the story of Imo, the 'monkey genius' who invented several feeding techniques, such as throwing handfuls of sandy grain into water so that the sand sank and the grain could be scooped off the surface of the water and eaten. Imo's methods were gradually copied by more and more of the monkeys in her troop, until they all practised these techniques.[31]

Elizabeth Marshall Thomas has written of prides of lions in the Kalahari desert in Southern Africa that had a tradition (later lost) of coexistence with humans, and of leopards in different areas that used different hunting methods for human prey.[32] George Schaller has described variant hunting techniques used by different groups of lions, and different traditions of resting in trees.[33] A group of olive baboons in Kenya was observed to switch from occasional meat-eating on the part of adult males, to the custom of hunting and eating prey in males, females and juveniles.[34] An amusing example comes from the chimpanzees at Arnhem Zoo, where a dominant male injured his hand in a fight and instead supported himself with his wrist while walking. The young chimpanzees copied him and began hobbling on their wrists, too.[35]

Culture has been described as yet another factor that makes humans unique. Examples of cultural transmission of behaviour like those just mentioned are dismissed as 'just interesting oddities'.[36] They may be more than that. Cultural transmission may be more widespread among animals than is commonly believed. No one is likely to argue that any animal species lives in a culture that approaches the complexity of the most 'primitive' of human cultures. However, the argument that if the sense of beauty is culture-bound, animals cannot possess it, does not match the evidence.

Just as two people do not find all the same things beautiful, a person and an animal might disagree. But to dismiss the possibility that an animal can sense beauty at all is narrow-minded. Discussing bird song, Joseph Wood Krutch wrote:

Suppose you had heard at the opera some justly famous prima donna singing 'Voi che sapete' . . . or even Mary Martin washing that man out of her hair. You have assumed that the one genuinely loves music and experiences some emotion related to that which Mozart's aria expresses, also that the other in some sense enjoys her performance. But a scientist of another kind – an economist – comes along and says, 'I have studied the evidence. I find that in both cases the performer really sings for so many thousand dollars per week. In fact she won't sing in public unless she is paid quite a large sum . . . You may sing in the bath because you are happy and you like to do it. But so far, at least, as professional singers are concerned, they sing for nothing but money.' The fallacy – and it is the fallacy in an appalling number of psychological, sociological and economic 'interpretations' of human behaviour – is, of course, the fallacy of the 'nothing but' . . . There is nothing in human experience or knowledge to make it seem unlikely that the cardinal announcing from the branch of a tree his claim on a certain territory is not also terribly glad to be doing it, very joyous in his realization of his own vigor and artistry . . . Whoever listens to a bird song and says, 'I do not believe there is any joy in it' has not proved anything about birds. But he has revealed a good deal about himself.[37]

Researchers studying elephants in Kenya camp in the middle of the East African bush. Sometimes at night the people sing and play guitars and the elephants draw near to listen. Perhaps they are merely curious, but perhaps they take pleasure in the music.[38] Human curiosity should permit asking whether elephants find beauty in music, just as the human sense of beauty allows appreciation of the image of the big animals moving silently through the darkness listening to the songs.

CHAPTER ELEVEN

Maternal Cannibalism, Justice and the Inexpressible

PEOPLE have immortal souls and animals do not, according to much of Western religion. Animal lovers resist this, citing animals' virtues and affirming that they must have souls, or saying that heaven would be a paltry place if there were no dogs in it. The existence of a soul is far more problematic than the existence of emotions. Science is of no help. Yet the theological view may point to a difference between the emotional lives of humans and those of other animals. Animals have not been observed to have religious practices, and people do.

Religion is not an emotionless affair of pure intellect. Awe, faith, self-righteousness, rectitude – all these have emotional components. Some theorists describe awe as a form of shame.[1] Are the religious emotions ones that animals do not feel? Or are they emotions that exist in other parts of life which come into play again in the human religious impulse? Further study of animal emotions may shed some light. Elizabeth Marshall

203

Thomas compares the behaviour of a person humbly kneeling to pray and a dog showing its belly – demonstrating submission – to a person. Her husband's dog, she notes, ritually shows his belly first thing in the morning, like a morning devotion. In the end, Thomas concludes that the parallel is not exact, that dogs probably do not think of humans as gods, yet, 'as we need God more than he needs us, dogs need us more than we need them, and they know it'.[2]

The sense of justice has been called uniquely human. Has it an emotional component? Emotions are certainly aroused when injustice is perceived, and examples of outraged animals exist. The stories of crow parliaments which hold trials and pass judgment on their members are fantasy, but less organised manifestations of what may be a sense of justice exist in many stories of righteously indignant chimps, for example. Nim Chimpsky learned when to expect praise and when to expect censure, and accepted these artificial standards. If he broke a toy, punishment did not surprise him, and he accepted it. But if one of his teachers punished him for something the others ignored, or if one failed to praise him for something the others rewarded, Nim became sulky.[3]

Perhaps Nim was merely upset because his world lacked predictability, because his settled expectations were violated. But this sense is a big part of legal justice among humans. Beyond this, the chimpanzees in the Arnhem colony seem to react to a sense of unjust treatment of others. In one instance the chimpanzee Puist 'kidnapped' one-year-old Tarzan from his mother, Tepel, and carried him up a tree, where he screamed with fright. After Tepel recovered her child, she attacked Puist, although Puist was larger and more dominant. The male Yeroen rushed up to them and stopped the fight by seizing Puist and flinging her away. This was unusual, because Yeroen and Puist were allies, and on all other occasions Yeroen had intervened on Puist's side. Frans de Waal concludes that Yeroen agreed with Tepel that she had cause for complaint.[4] Puist later showed what appeared to be grievance on her own behalf, backing up another chimpanzee, Luit, in a dispute with Nikkie. Nikkie made a threatening display at Puist, who stretched out her hand in appeal to Luit. Luit did not respond, and Puist instantly rushed at him, barking and even hitting him, apparently because he had violated the tradition of supporting one's supporters.[5] Solidarity is part of many human notions of primitive fairness.

Thomas gives an instance that may illustrate a sense of justice or perhaps a sense of propriety that underlies rectitude. Her husky, Maria, one day discovered that by rushing around a cage full of mice and parakeets, lunging at the occupants, she could send them into a hysterical frenzy. The pug dog Bingo ran in, slammed his body into the much bigger Maria, and, when she lunged at the cage again, uttered a loud bark and slammed against her once more. Maria left the room. Thomas was surprised because Bingo was smitten with Maria and usually did not oppose her in any way. Whether Bingo was motivated by compassion for the mice and parakeets, by vicarious ownership of the mice and parakeets or by disapproval of Maria's obstreperousness, it seems that he wanted to stop her aggression and make her behave better towards them.[6]

Observers of wild coatimundis in Arizona suggest that they have a system of entitlement expressed through a variety of squeals in cubs. When cuffed by an older animal for lagging behind the troop, a cub would crouch submissively and utter the 'don't beat me' squeal, which seemed to indicate no resistance. On several occasions, when a subadult animal committed the unusual act of trying to take food from a cub and cuffed it, the cub would utter a different squeal – and an adult female would come and drive the subadult away, apparently enforcing a tradition of tolerance towards cubs.[7] This may be merely different cub feelings being expressed in different situations of threat, but it is telling that there is a difference. Enforcing and cushioning hierarchy also plays a part in human justice systems.

Untangling the emotions associated with the sense of justice is difficult. Anger felt at injustice is obvious. Revenge and compassion are equally involved but more complex. Harder still is untangling the emotional and intellectual aspects of justice. Yet this only supports the view that emotional aspects are essential to fully understanding it.

The narrative urge is another very human characteristic. We like to tell each other stories, to relate events, to gossip, to analyse. We talk to animals; we may talk to ourselves. Does language create the narrative urge, or would we have this need even if we did not have language in the way we do?

Animals who have been taught sign language have been said to display little wish to narrate. Herbert Terrace, who arranged for the chimpanzee Nim Chimpsky to be taught sign, said that most of Nim's utterances were imitations or fragments of things his teachers had just signed, and argued that the same is true of other signing apes. He also argued that a large part of ape signing consists of requests for food, toys and affectionate gestures like tickling and hugging. This, with the scarcity of spontaneous verbal communication, would seem to indicate little narrative urge. On rare occasions, Nim would sign unasked the names of things he saw. Often he spontaneously signed the names of things he recognised in pictures when leafing through books and magazines. Perhaps these are rudiments of a narrative urge, which only await encouragement and opportunity.

Nim's language lessons (as in most such experiments) were structured to offer him the chance to earn food and other rewards, so it is not surprising that he made many such requests. It is also worth noting that Nim's early teachers were not fluent signers. Most of them could only improvise a few sentences on any given topic – they could not tell Nim a story, relate the events of their day, or pass on interesting gossip. Nim began learning sign at five months, but did not get a fluent teacher (and then not for long) until he was three and a half years old.[8] This is not unusual. Signing apes have all been raised and taught largely by humans who used rather rudimentary sign language. None have been raised in an environment of fluent sign.[9] Suppose a child were raised by people who spoke halting, recently learned pidgin. Suppose also that the child had no playmates or classmates with whom to speak. Such a child might fall linguistically behind children whose parents freely and naturally spoke to each other and to others, as well as to the children. This child might not tell stories.

Terrace mentions that on the occasions when Nim met fluent signers, he was transfixed. He would stare spellbound for up to fifteen minutes (a long time for a young chimpanzee) as they conversed. In contrast, spoken language interested him for only a few seconds. Terrace notes that when Nim finally got a teacher fluent in sign, at three and a half – apparently his fifty-fourth teacher – he was already passing into adolescence.[10] Terrace thinks Nim's signing might have progressed more quickly had

206

he had more exposure to fluent signers at an early age. Washoe, the first chimpanzee to be taught sign language, adopted a son, Loulis, who has learned sign language not from human tutoring, but from Washoe and the other chimps in her colony. Yet Washoe herself did not learn sign from fluent signers. It is possible that apes have not yet been adequately challenged to acquire sign fluency. If so, there has not yet been a full test of their possible desire to narrate.

Signing chimpanzees other than Nim have been seen to sign to a considerable extent in the rudiments of a narrative mode. They sign to each other even when no humans are around (as revealed in remote videotaping) and, like humans, 'talk' to themselves. Washoe has been filmed perched in a tree, hiding from her human companions, and signing 'Quiet quiet' to herself. They may describe their own activity to themselves, signing 'Me up' and then running up a wall. They have even been seen to use imaginative speech when playing alone. Moja, who knows the word 'purse' perfectly well, once put a purse on her foot and walked around signing 'That's a shoe'.[11]

There is a sense in which bees are entirely narrative, letting other hive members know where the best flowers are, and how to get there. The most revolutionary discovery of Karl von Frisch concerned the symbolic communication employed by honeybees: 'In the scientific climate of opinion prevailing forty years ago it was shocking and incredible to be told that a mere insect could communicate to its companions the direction, distance and desirability of something far away.'[12]

Chimpanzees Sherman and Austin were taught how to communicate by lighting symbols on a board. Researcher Sue Savage–Rumbaugh notes that they can use these symbols to make spontaneous comments about their impending actions and about events going on around them, but that they do so relatively seldom. 'Their behaviour suggests that it is difficult for them to understand that others do not have access to the same information that they do. In the various paradigms used to encourage communication between them, it was always necessary for them to experience the roles of speaker and listener a number of times before their behavior, as speaker, suggested that they knew that they had information which the listener did not have,' Rumbaugh writes.[13] While Sherman and Austin learned about the possible ignorance of the listener in individual situations, and do not seem to have generalised their observations, it is not impossible that they might do so. They were taught to share food with one another in a most un-chimpanzee-like manner and came to enjoy this greatly. Perhaps narration is something they might learn in a similar way.

Certainly it is possible that great apes will never show more language ability than they have so far, that they have reached their linguistic limits. It may well be that the urge to confide, to boast, to retell and to mythologize will remain all our own, but we know too little to be confident of this. Some of the most vocal animals are very little understood. Some species of whale are clamorous, incessantly uttering a wide variety of squeaks, grunts, trills, bellows, chirps, groans, yaps and whistles, as well as echolocatory clicks and pings. Perhaps this means only 'Here I am. Where are you?' Alternatively, the findings of whale scientist Dr Roger Payne were reported by Jim Nollman to indicate that humpback whales may repeat their entire song from one year to the next, 'with slight but clearly discernible differences. Here was a very clear instance of an oral tradition. It implies that humpbacks possess at least the rudiments of learned culture.'[14] Perhaps they are telling the history of the species.

The search for emotions which humans feel and other animals do not is an old one. While it violates the usual human assumption that humans are the perfected endpoint of evolution and the luckiest recipients of nature's gifts, we already know of many things some animals have which we do not. Some we are proud of not having: tails, fur, horns. Some we shrug off: a keen sense of smell. Others are undeniably impressive: wings.

Some animals have senses we do not possess. Bats and shrews have built-in technology it has taken humans centuries to imitate. They can navigate in darkness by listening to echoes of their own supersonic squeaks. Many snakes can sense heat. An increasing number of ocean creatures are found to have electromagnetic navigation senses. At least one species of bird, the Australian silvereye, can apparently 'see' – that is, detect with the eye – magnetic fields.[15] Humans have only recently discovered that animals have these capacities. It is unclear how widespread such senses are, or what other animal senses remain to be discovered. By extension, are there feelings animals have that humans do not? How would we know? It will take scientific humility and philosophical creativity to provide even the beginning of answers.

A mother lion observed by George Schaller had left her three small cubs under a fallen tree. While she was away, two lions from another pride killed the cubs. One male ate part of one of the cubs. The second carried a cub away, holding it as he would a food item, not as a cub. He stopped from time to time to lick it and later nestled it between his paws. Ten hours later, he still had not eaten it. When the mother returned and found what had happened, she sniffed the last dead cub, licked it, and then sat down and ate it, except for the head and front paws.[16]

This mother lion was acting like a lion, not like a person. But in understanding what lions do, what she felt is part of the picture. Maybe she felt closer to her dead offspring when it was part of her body once again. Maybe she hates waste. Maybe she cleans up all messes her cubs make, as part of her love. Maybe this is a lion funeral rite. Maybe it is something only a mother lion can feel.

After thirty years of working with chimpanzees, Roger Fouts doubts that they have emotions that humans do not also have. Indeed, if new and unknown emotions were to be discovered, they would most likely be found in animals less like us than the great apes.

One spring evening, George Schaller watched a female wild giant panda, Zhen-Zhen, eat and then, although she saw him watching her, lean back on some bamboo uttering 'bleating honks' and fall asleep. Her seeming indifference was a surprise to Schaller:

> On meeting a gorilla or a tiger, I can sense the relationship that binds us by the emotions they express, for curiosity, friendliness, annoyance, apprehension, anger, fear are all revealed by face and body. In contrast, Zhen and I are together, yet hopelessly separated by an immense space. Her feelings remain impenetrable, her behavior inscrutable. Intellectual insights enrich emotional experiences. But with Zhen I am in danger of coming away empty-handed from a mountain of treasure.[17]

This is not to say that pandas are unknowable. Schaller believes that he could learn to understand. 'To comprehend her, I would need to transform myself into a panda, unconscious of myself, concentrating on her actions and spirit for many years, until finally I might gain fresh insights.' His fear is that pandas may not last long enough as a species for humans to understand them.

Some people argue that even if animals have emotions, they do not feel them as human beings do because they cannot be aware that they have those emotions, bring them into consciousness and express them to themselves. Perhaps an elephant can be sad, the argument goes, but if it cannot say, even to itself, 'I am sad', then it cannot be *as* sad as a person – who can describe sadness, predict sadness, lose an argument with sadness. If this is true, then language has given humans a tremendous attachment and vulnerability to their feelings. It is rash, at this point in knowledge, to be at all certain that an emotion that cannot be expressed in language, far less in language we can recognise, cannot be felt as keenly.

Humans believe they suffer from emotions they are not consciously aware of and that are not articulated. This does not mean that these emotions have no significance or cannot really be felt. It could equally well be argued that language sets emotion at a distance, that the very act of saying 'I am sad', with all the connotations that the words have, pushes the feeling away a little, perhaps making it less searing and less personal. To the extent this is true, then the world of emotion, from which humans sometimes feel estranged, would be one some animals would live *more* fully.

Herbert Terrace describes what might be an actual example of language pushing feeling away in an animal:

> Certain usages of Nim's signs were quite unexpected. At least two of them (*bite* and *angry*) appeared to function as substitutes for the physical expression of those actions and emotions. Nim learned the signs *bite* and *angry* from a picture book showing Zero Mostel biting a hand and exhibiting an angry face. During September 1976, Amy began what she thought would be a normal transfer to Laura. For some reason, Nim didn't want to leave Amy and tried to drive Laura away. When Laura persisted in trying to pick him up, Nim acted as if he was about to bite. His mouth was pulled back over his bare teeth, and he approached Laura with his hair raised. Instead of biting, however, he repeatedly made the *bite* sign near her face with a fierce expression on his face. After making this sign, he

210

appeared to relax and showed no further interest in attacking Laura. A few minutes later he transferred to Laura without any sign of aggression. On other occasions, Nim was observed to sign both *bite* and *angry* as a warning.[18]

Whether animals feel emotions less or more intensely may depend on which emotion is involved. Animals doubtless feel pity for one another, sometimes even passing beyond the species barrier, but it seems unlikely, though not impossible, that they experience it as elaborately or as intensely as humans do. For example, it is doubtful that dolphins would care as much about humans slaughtering one another as some humans care about the slaughter of dolphins by other humans. But this may only be because they do not have the same information access that we do. Or perhaps they know and have rules of non-interference in human matters. Or perhaps they truly are indifferent, or take a longer view.

There are some emotions, on the other hand, which humans may experience less intensely than some animals. Many people have had the feeling, for example, that some animals seem more capable of joy. One of the explanations for the popularity of watching and listening to birds is the pleasure of hearing bird songs which seem to be joyful. Or as Julian Huxley, describing the courtship of herons winding their long necks together, wrote: 'Of this I can only say that it seemed to bring such a pitch of emotion that I could have wished to be a heron that I might experience it'.[19]

The intensity of emotion in other animals has been a perennial source of human envy. Joseph Wood Krutch writes: 'It is difficult to see how one can deny that the dog, apparently beside himself at the prospect of a walk with his master, is experiencing a joy the intensity of which it is beyond our power to imagine much less to share. In the same way his dejection can at least appear to be no less bottomless. Perhaps the kind of thought of which we are capable dims both at the same time that it makes us less victims of either. Was any man, one wonders, ever as dejected as a lost dog? Perhaps certain of the animals can be both more joyful and more utterly desolate than any man ever was.'[20]

To examine questions like these it is vital to treat animals as members of their own species. To treat them as either machines or people is to denigrate them. Acknowledgment of their emotional lives is a first step, and the understanding that their emotional lives are their own and not ours is the second.

If as cognitive beings and creatures of elaborate cultures humans have no peers, as emotional beings we are anything but alone. Why should we try to comprehend the world of animal emotions, which exist on some intangible plane between the measurable worlds of oxytocin levels in a cat's bloodstream and the cat's purring? Why not refrain from hypothesising the cat's happiness? Emotions are in a real sense where we live, what we care about. Human life cannot be understood without emotions. To leave questions of animal emotion as forever unapproachable and imponderable is arbitrary intellectual helplessness.

In March 1989 hikers in the Michigan woods came across a mother black bear with small cubs still in hibernation, curled up at the base of a tree. Instead of heeding advice to stay away from mother bears, they began taking photographs. When the mother bear seemed insufficiently lively for their artistic purposes, they shouted and prodded her with sticks so she would look up. Instead of attacking, she finally ran away, leaving behind her two eight-week-old cubs. Rangers followed the mother bear's tracks and decided she wasn't coming back. Zoos had all the black bears they wanted. Although most bear researchers didn't want a strange cub corrupting their data, wildlife biologist Lynn Rogers, working in Minnesota's Superior National Forest, agreed to see if he could get the cubs adopted. When trying to find a home for the female cub, Gerry, Rogers was accompanied by a photographer who had asked to come along. They snowshoed out into the woods and located Terri, a wild bear with two cubs, who was used to human presence. Rogers produced the squalling cub. 'I tossed it to her and immediately she wanted it,' he recalls. The cub ran away from the strange bear, and back to the humans. To the photographer's horror, she climbed his leg like a tree. As he stood rooted to the spot, gazing pleadingly at Rogers, Terri walked over, took the cub in her mouth, peeled her off his leg, and carried her back to the den with the other two cubs.

The adoption of Gerry's brother by another bear was also successful. Terri was an excellent mother, and Gerry rambled the north woods, learning from Terri how to forage – breaking into ant-hills, traveling forty miles to a stand of hazelnut trees, grazing on aquatic vegetation – and curling up under a pine tree at night. She grew up to use part of Terri's territory and to have cubs of her own.

During a period when Rogers was at odds with government agencies, state officials announced that Gerry had been accused of attacking humans. To protect the public, Gerry was captured, along with one of her cubs. Caged, Gerry moaned constantly with distress. 'She just was crying all the time,' Rogers says. 'Then when we caught the other cubs and put them in the cage with her, she was fine from that moment.'

Official plans were to transfer Gerry to a game farm, where she would be used to produce cubs for sale, and where her toes would be clipped off for safety reasons. Appalled, Rogers managed to arrange for her to be sent to a small 'but good' zoo instead, where she lives to this day in an enclosure covering several acres. The next year, when her three cubs were old enough to be on their own, they were released in a North Carolina forest.

'That bear was so trustworthy, even with cubs,' Rogers mourns. 'I could scoop her up in my arms . . . and she'd just relax and look around.' As for Terri, she had ranged outside the protected part of the forest during the previous year and been shot by a hunter.[21] In this story the sources of tragedy have nothing to do with bears and everything to do with mistakes that only humans make.

Can it really be that the emotional lives of these bears are wholly inaccessible to us? To deny the terror of the abandoned bear cub, the welcoming affection of the adoptive mother Terri, Gerry's despair at being locked up away from two of her cubs, is to defy credibility.

Curiosity about the feelings of animals, which science so often tries to train out of its students, may be reciprocated by animals. When observing wild lions, Elizabeth Marshall Thomas discovered that the lions were returning human scrutiny. During the day the scientists watched the lions sleep. At night, tracks revealed that four lions came to the fence and peered at the sleeping scientists. As the people examined the scats of the lions, the lions dug up the human latrine and inspected its contents, sometimes adding their own.[22]

Wild chimpanzees who have overcome their fear of humans show considerable curiosity about human behaviour, although none seems to have gone so far as to make a career out of it.

Scientific humility tells us that we will probably never understand other animals completely. But if we do not begin by insisting that we already know what characteristics they do not have, we will understand a lot more. To learn about other animals, we must take them on their own terms, and these terms include their feelings.

CONCLUSION

Sharing the World with
Feeling Creatures

Jeffrey Moussaieff Masson

W HAT ARE the implications of finding that animals lead emotional lives comparable to our own? Must we change our relationships with them? Have we obligations to them? Is animal testing defensible? Is experimentation on animals ethical? Can we confine them for our edification? Can we kill them to cover, sustain and adorn ourselves? Should we cease eating animals who have complex social lives, passionate relations with one another, and desperately love their children?

Is something like us more worthy of respect than something not like us? Humans often behave as if this were the case with respect to other human beings. Racism can partly be described, if not explained, in this way. Men treat other men better than they treat women, based in part on their view that women are

215

not like them. Many of these so-called differences are disguises for whatever a dominant power can impose. Think, for a moment, of how human beings treat trees, the rationales used. As John Fowles put it: 'Unlike white sharks, trees do not even possess the ability to defend themselves when attacked; what arms they sometimes have, like thorns, are static and their size and immobility means they cannot hide, they are the most defenceless of creation in regard to man . . .'[1] Which is why they are destroyed in such large numbers.

The basic idea seems to be that if something does not feel pain in the way a human being feels pain, it is permissible to hurt it. Even though this is not necessarily true, the illusion of differences is maintained out of fear that seeing similarity will create an obligation to accord respect and perhaps even equality. This appears to be especially true when it comes to suffering, pain, sorrow, sadness. We do not want to cause these things in others because we know what it feels like to experience them ourselves. No one defends suffering as such. But animal experimentation? The arguments revolve around their utility, pitting the greater good against the lesser suffering. Implicit, usually, is the greater importance of those who stand to gain, compared with the lesser importance of those who are sacrificed to their benefit.

An animal experimenter, almost by definition, is going to deny that an animal suffers in the same way that a human does. If that were not so, then an admission of cruelty would be implicit. Experimental suffering is not randomly imposed without consent on human beings and defended as ethical on the grounds that it would bestow enormous benefit to others. Animals suffer. Can we, should we, measure it, compare it to our own? Why should the suffering have to be like ours? It has been argued that humans experience pain more acutely because we remember and anticipate it. It is not apparent that an animal cannot do both. But even if it could not, there is no reason to suppose that it suffers any less than a human, and some reason to suppose that some may suffer more. Brigid Brophy, for example, points out that 'pain is likely to fill the sheep's whole capacity for experience in a way it seldom does in us, whose intellect and imagination can create breaks for us in the immediacy of our sensations'.[2] But isn't the fact that they suffer at all enough?

It is often said that if slaughterhouses were made of glass,

216

most people would be vegetarians. If the general public knew what went on inside animal experimentation laboratories, they would be abolished. However, the parallel is not exact. Slaughterhouses are invisible because the public wants them that way. Everyone knows what goes on inside them; they simply do not want to be confronted with it. Most people do not know what goes on with animal experimentation. Slaughterhouses allow visits. Laboratories where animal experiments are performed are secretive. Perhaps those who conduct the experiments know they would be stopped if what they do were known even by other scientists. Perhaps they are ashamed.

One animal experimentation group ran a paid advertisement which they saw as amusing in a newspaper, appealing for donations. It said: 'Send a mouse to college.' The language disguises the purpose of mice in the university. The experimenters dare not say: 'Grow a tumour on a mouse.' They dare not say: 'Send a cat or a dog to college.' People do not like to think of their pets as the subjects of experiments. Rats and mice are not generally regarded as pets, but as pests; they have few defenders. Yet the pain a rat or a mouse feels is every bit as real as that of any pet. In laboratories, they suffer, as anybody who has heard them moan, cry, whimper and even scream knows. The experimenters dissimulate about this by insisting that they are merely vocalising. Descartes lives on.

Perhaps the sounds fail to reach these scientists because they are not immediately recognisable as a form of communication. One thing clear from examining the human view of differences between humans and animals is that humans assign primary significance to speech. Our glorious uniqueness, many philosophers have claimed, lies in our ability to speak to one another. It thus came as a shock to learn that a simple African grey parrot not only 'parroted' human speech, but spoke, communicated – the word meant something. When psychologist Irene Pepperberg turned to leave her parrot, Alex, in a veterinarian's office for lung surgery, Alex called out, 'Come here. I love you. I'm sorry. I want to go back.' He thought he had done something bad and was being abandoned as punishment.[3] Imagine what would happen if an animal addressed us on its imminent murder. In a slaughterhouse, a pig cried out: 'Please don't kill me.' As a hunter looked into the eyes of a deer, it suddenly broke into speech: 'I want to live, please don't shoot, my children need me.' Would the hunter pull

217

the trigger? Such speech did not stop concentration camp inmates from being murdered during the Holocaust – the victims, it was said, were lice and rats.

No one assumes the pig wants to die. It would avoid slaughter if it could. It *feels* the desire to live and the pain of its sorrow just as humans do; the only difference is that it cannot say so in words. The crying of the pigs being slaughtered is horrible. People report that they sound like human screams. The pigs are communicating. They are speaking of their terrible fear. Recently a steer on the way to the slaughterhouse was reported to have bolted when it was close enough to hear the anguished cries of the animals. It fled through the town like a prisoner condemned to death. Its sudden lunge for freedom gave everyone pause, even the driver of the death caravan. Was it right to send an animal to slaughter who so desperately wished to live? Perhaps just this one could be saved.[4] Then what about the others? Do they feel the same way? Does lack of resistance confer a right to kill?

We do know what the cow wants: the cow wants to live. The cow does not wish to sacrifice itself for any reason. That a cow will willingly offer itself as food is a fable.

When humans refuse to inflict pain on others, surely it is because they assume they *feel*. It is not because another person can think, nor because they can reason, nor even because they can speak that we respect their physical boundaries, but because they feel. They feel pain, humiliation, sorrow and other emotions, perhaps even some we do not yet recognise. We do not want to cause suffering. If, as I believe, animals feel pain and sorrow and all the other emotions, these feelings cannot be ignored in behaviour towards them. A bear is not going to compose Beethoven's Ninth Symphony, but then neither is our next-door neighbour. We do not for this reason conclude that we have the freedom to experiment upon him, hunt him for sport or eat him for food.

Modern philosophers seem somewhat more willing than biologists[5] to consider animal emotions, and they have also become engaged in issues of animal rights. Philosophers like Mary Midgley and Brigid Brophy in Britain, Peter Singer in Australia, Tom Regan and Bernard Rollin in the United States, have all argued forcefully that animals are capable of complex emotions. In an influential passage written in 1789 Jeremy

Bentham connected sentient feelings with rights in this way:

> The day *may come*, when the rest of the animal creation may acquire those rights which never could have been withholden from them but by the hand of tyranny. The French have already discovered that the blackness of the skin is no reason why a human being should be abandoned without redress to the caprice of a tormentor. It may come one day to be recognised, that the number of the legs, the villosity of the skin, or the termination of the *os sacrum*, are reasons equally insufficient for abandoning a sensitive being to the same fate. What else is it that should trace the insuperable line? Is it the faculty of reason, or, perhaps, the faculty of discourse? But a full-grown horse or dog is beyond comparison a more rational, as well as a more conversable animal, than an infant of a day, or a week, or even a month, old. But suppose the case were otherwise, what would it avail? the question is not, Can they reason? nor, Can they talk? but, Can they suffer?[6]

Peter Singer, in his book *Animal Liberation*, explicitly based on Bentham's eighteenth-century utilitarianism, held that creatures which could feel pain deserved to be shielded from that pain, especially from scientific experimentation and hurtful farming methods. The argument is that sentience – the capacity to have conscious experiences – demands that we give equal consideration to the interests of all creatures. However, although it lays a moral ground for them, this position does not explicitly accord animals rights.

In *The Case for Animal Rights*, Tom Regan argues for protecting the rights of animals who are 'capable of being the subject of a life'. Every animal used in every experiment in every laboratory has its own life story. It has felt strong emotions, has loved and hated, and has been devoted to others of its own kind. It is a subject and is therefore violated by being treated as an object. Have we the right to tear this being away from its fellows and all that gives life meaning, and put it in a sterile, hostile, aseptic environment to be tortured, maimed and ultimately destroyed in the name of anything, far less of service to our own species? Or do we have only the power to do such things?

Is what is learned from these experiments always of benefit

to humans? It was recently reported in a German psychiatric journal that a researcher gave largactil, a neuroleptic tranquilliser, to a spider, and succeeded either in diminishing the size and complexity of its web, or in stopping the spider from spinning a web at all. This so-called advance in both psychiatry and animal research led to the article being held up as evidence of the great value of animal research in psychology. It means, said the researcher, that anti-psychotic drugs can be given to 'schizophrenics' to stop them from spinning webs, that is, from creating fantasies in their heads.[7] But why should a spider or a human not spin webs if so inclined? Who bestowed upon us the right to intervene, interfere and ultimately destroy the delicate product of a creature's innermost being? Whether such practices ultimately enhance humanity is also questionable. The microbiologist Catherine Roberts condemns Harry Harlow's 'odious' experiments on rhesus monkeys, pointing out that they 'degrade the humanness of those who designed and perpetrated them'.[8]

It might be hard for us to imagine ourselves in the sensual universe of another species, but it is not impossible. We know, from watching our dog's intense sniffing, that she is picking up and responding to something far beyond our ken. We are impressed by her ability to take in information hidden from us; we honour the resulting sudden shifts of mood. We know we are in the presence of something *different* from us but worthy of our respect. Surely one of the most common emotions that we humans feel in the presence of another species is *awe*. We marvel at the ability of a hawk to soar, of a seal to race through the waves; we may be envious of them, but are more often simply humbled.

It is clear that animals form lasting friendships, are frightened of being hunted, have a horror of dismemberment, wish they were back in the safety of their den, despair for their mates, look out for and protect their children whom they love. Though animals do not write autobiographies, it is possible to write their biographies. They are individuals, and members of groups, with elaborate histories that take place in a concrete world and involve a large number of complex emotional states. They *feel* throughout their lives, just as we do.

Marc Bekoff recently provided me with the following account:

From 1977 to 1983 I and a large number of students studied the social behaviour and ecology of coyotes living outside Jackson, Wyoming. For four years we observed the same mated pair in a pack. In late 1980 the female began making solitary forays of increasing duration. She was not being forced out of the pack; perhaps she was ill. At first when she would leave, members of the group would observe her curiously. When she returned they would all run to greet her extensively, whining, tails wagging, and then they would all begin to play. After a couple of weeks, her journeys away from the pack got longer, sometimes six or seven hours. The pack would follow her part of the way, then stop. As her time away increased, the animals seemed to become edgy and concerned about her. Some of the pack members would travel in the direction in which she had gone and stop, look around and howl, to indicate their presence. Just as there could be no mistake that they were thrilled when she returned, greeting her effusively and licking her muzzle, there could be no mistake that they missed her when she was gone. One day she left the pack and never came back. The whole pack waited for her for days and days. They took long forays in the direction she had gone, sniffing where she had been, howling as if calling her home. For more than a week, some spark, something, seemed to have gone out of them. They missed her. I know that sounds anthropomorphic, and that's just fine. I also know, as sure as I know that I am attached to this world, that those coyotes have deep and complicated feelings.[9]

Jane Goodall points out that 'chimpanzees differ genetically from *homo sapiens* by only about one per cent, and that while they lack speech, they nevertheless behave similarly to humans, can feel pain, share our emotions and have sophisticated intellectual abilities'.[10] She pleads that we stop enslaving, imprisoning, incarcerating, torturing them, and instead protect them from exploitation.

Douglas Chadwick, in a recent book, writes:

If I learned anything from my time among the elephants, it is the extent to which we are kin. The warmth of their families makes me feel warm. Their capacity for delight gives me joy. Their ability to learn and understand things is a continuing revelation for me. If a person can't see these qualities

221

when looking at elephants, it can only be because he or she doesn't want to.[11]

Humans have long recognized that animals have the potential to connect emotionally with humans as well. Perhaps the most famous account testifying at least to the hope, and possibly the fact, of gratitude, friendship and compassion between a person and an animal is the ancient account of Androcles (called Androclus in Latin) and the lion. An early recorded Latin version appears in the *Attic Nights* of Aulus Gellius in the second century. The account is prefaced with a claim to authenticity: 'The account of Apion, a learned man who was surnamed Plistonices, of the mutual recognition, due to old acquaintance, that he had seen at Rome between a man and a lion . . . This incident, which he describes in the fifth book of his *Wonders of Egypt*, he declares that he neither heard nor read, but saw himself with his own eyes in the city of Rome.' Gellius then quotes Apion:

> In the Great Circus a battle with wild beasts on a grand scale was being exhibited to the people. Of that spectacle, since I chanced to be in Rome, I was an eye-witness. There were many savage wild beasts, brutes remarkable for their huge size, and all of uncommon appearance or unusual ferocity. But beyond all others did the vast size of the lions excite wonder, and one of these in particular surpassed all the rest because of the huge size of his body . . . There was brought in . . . the slave of an ex-consul; the slave's name was Androclus. When that lion saw him from a distance he stopped short as if in amazement, and then approached the man slowly and quietly, as if he recognized him. Then, wagging his tail in a mild and caressing way, after the manner and fashion of fawning dogs, he came close to the man, who was now half dead from fright, and gently licked his feet and hands . . . Then you might have seen man and lion exchange joyful greetings, as if they had recognized each other.[12]

The emperor, Gaius Caesar, known more popularly as Caligula, wanted to know why the lion had spared the man. Androclus related how he had run away from his master into the lonely desert and hidden in a remote cave. A lion came into the cave with a bleeding paw, groaning and moaning in pain. The lion,

Androcles is reported to have said, 'approached me mildy and gently, and lifting up his foot, was evidently showing it to me and holding it out as if to ask for help'. Androclus took out a huge splinter and cared for the foot. 'Relieved by that attention and treatment of mine, the lion, putting his paw in my hand, lay down and went to sleep.' For three years after that they shared the cave, the lion hunting for both of them. Then Androcles was recaptured, returned to Rome, and condemned to death in the arena. After hearing this story, Caligula, after a vote by the people, freed lion and man. They walked the streets together 'and everyone who met them anywhere exclaimed: "This is the lion that was a man's friend, this is the man who was physician to a lion." '[13]

Is this fiction, testimony to an ancient longing in the human heart to love and be loved by another animal as one longs to love and be loved by another person? It is not so far removed from Joy Adamson's account of the lioness Elsa, whom she raised and then released, returning from the wild to visit for years afterwards with her children and her mate.[14]

Reciprocity on the level of Androcles and the lion, this dream of equality, may be closed to us for now; whether or not it can be realised, we do owe animals something. Freedom from exploitation and abuse by humankind should be the inalienable right of every living being. Animals are not there for us to drill holes into, clamp down, dissect, pull apart, render helpless and subject to agonising experiments. They are, like us, endangered species on an endangered planet, and we are the ones who are endangering them, it and ourselves. They are innocent sufferers in a hell of our making. We owe it to them, at the very least, to refrain from harming them further. If no more, we could leave them be.

When animals are no longer colonised and appropriated by us, we can reach out to our evolutionary cousins. Perhaps then the ancient hope for a deeper emotional connection across the species barrier, for closeness and participation in a realm of feelings now beyond our imagination, will be realised.

NOTES AND REFERENCES

Preface, *Searching the Heart of the Other*

1. D. Griffin, *The Question of Animal Awareness: Evolutionary Continuity of Mental Experience* (Rockefeller University Press, New York, 1976). Griffin is the discoverer of bat sonar. In the bibliography are listed those of his books and articles which affected the thinking in this book.

2. P. Cavalieri and P. Singer, eds, *The Great Ape Project: Equality Beyond Humanity* (Fourth Estate, U.K., 1993), p. 12.

3. R. Jean Campbell, *Psychiatric Dictionary*, 5th ed. (Oxford University Press, 1981), p. 24.

4. Lame Deer, J. Fire and R. Erdoes, *Lame Deer: Seeker of Visions* (Simon & Schuster, N.Y., 1972), p. 123.

5. E. Bullard, 'The emergence of plate tectonics: a personal view', *Annual Review of Earth and Planetary Science* 3 (1975), 1–30, p. 5. As Bertrand Russell wrote in the *Outline of Philosophy* (1927), 'One may say broadly that all the animals that have been carefully observed have behaved so as to confirm the philosophy in which the observer believed before his observations began'.

6. C. Darwin, *The Expression of the Emotions in Man and Animals* (1872; reprinted University of Chicago Press, 1965).

7. C. Darwin, *The Descent of Man; and Selections in Relation to Sex* (1871; reprinted Princeton University Press, 1981), pp. 62, 76. Also see the discussion of animal emotions in J. Howard Moore, *The Universal Kinship* (1906; reprinted Centaur Press, U.K., 1992).

8. Thus the Journal of Comparative Psychology announces in each issue that it publishes 'research on the behavior and cognitive abilities of different species (including humans) as they relate to evolution, ecology, adaptation, and development. Manuscripts that focus primarily on issues of proximate causation where choice of specific species is not an important component of the research fall outside the scope of this journal.'

9. In a much discussed article in *Der Spiegel* (1980, no. 47, pp. 251–62) entitled 'Tiere sind Gefühlsmenschen' [Animals are Emotional People], Konrad Lorenz speaks of 'crimes against animals' and says that anybody who intimately knows any individual higher mammal such as a dog or an ape and does *not* believe that this creature has feelings similar to his own is crazy: *'Ein Mensch, der ein höheres Säugetier, etwa einen Hund oder*

225

einen Affen, wirklich genau kennt und nicht *davon überzeugt wird, dass dieses Wesen ähnliches erlebt wie er selbst, ist psychisch abnorm . . .'*

10. E. S. Savage-Rumbaugh, *Ape Language: From Conditioned Response to Symbol* (Columbia University Press, N.Y., 1986), p. 25.

Chapter 1, *In Defence of Emotions*

1. J. H. Williams, OBE, *Elephant Bill* (Doubleday, N.Y., 1950), pp. 82–4.
2. E. S. Savage-Rumbaugh, *Ape Language: From Conditioned Response to Symbol* (Columbia University Press, N.Y., 1986), p. 266.
3. J. Goodall, interview by S. McCarthy, 7 May 1994.
4. M. Midgley, 'The mixed community', in E. C. Hargrove, ed., *The Animal Rights/Environmental Ethics Debate* (State University of New York Press, 1992), p. 214.
5. G. Gebel-Williams and T. Reinhold, *Untamed: The Autobiography of the Circus's Greatest Animal Trainer* (William Morrow, N.Y., 1991), p. 28.
6. G. Schaller's foreword to S. Strum, *Almost Human: A Journey into the World of Baboons* (Random House, N.Y., 1987), p. xii.
7. A. Rasa, *Mongoose Watch: A Family Observed* (Anchor Press/Doubleday, N.Y., 1986).
8. T. Rowell, *The Social Behaviour of Monkeys* (Penguin Books, U.K., 1972), p. 79.
9. D. Keith Candland, *Feral Children & Clever Animals: Reflections on Human Nature* (Oxford University Press, 1993), pp. 250, 385. The experiments in question are reported in the *Journal of Comparative Psychology* (No. 101, 1987), pp. 345–8, but the learning by the female baboons is not, since 'the observation cited here is unique in frequency and thus not reportable'.
10. H. Ryden, *God's Dog* (Coward, McCann & Geoghegan, N.Y., 1975), pp. 87, 92–101.
11. J. Maynard Smith and M. G. Ridpath, 'Wife sharing in the Tasmanian native hen, *Tribonyx mortierii*: a case of kin selection?' *The American Naturalist* 106 (July–August 1972), pp. 447–52.
12. R. Cochrane, 'Working elephants at Rangoon', quoted in *The Animal Story Book*, Vol. IX, The Young Folks Library (Hall & Locke Co., Boston, 1901).
13. Quoted in P. Schullery, *The Bear Hunter's Century* (Dodd, Mead, N.Y., 1988), p. 142.
14. D. McFarland, ed., *The Oxford Companion to Animal Behaviour* (Oxford University Press, 1987), p. 151.
15. C. Izard and S. Buechler, 'Aspects of consciousness and personality in terms of differential emotions theory', in *Emotion: Theory, Research, and Experience, Vol. I: Theories of Emotion*, R. Plutchik and H. Kellerman, eds (Academic Press, N.Y., 1980), pp. 165–87.
16. J. de Rivera, *A Structural Theory of the Emotions* (International Universities Press, N.Y., 1977), pp. 156–64.
17. J. Callwood, *Emotions: What they are and how they affect us, from the basic hates & fears of childhood to more sophisticated feelings that later govern our adult lives: How we can deal with the way we feel* (Doubleday, N.Y., 1986), p. 33.
18. R. Thomson, 'The concept of fear', in *Fear in Animals and Man*, W. Sluckin, ed. (Van Nostrand Reinhold, N.Y, 1979), pp. 1–23, 20–21.
19. M. Lewis, *Shame: The Exposed Self* (The Free Press/Macmillan, N.Y., 1992), pp. 13–14.

20. C. E. Izard, *Human Emotions* (Plenum Press, N.Y./U.K., 1977).

21. A. Wierzbicka, 'Human emotions: universal or culture-specific?, *American Anthropologist* 88 (1986), pp. 584–94.

22. Ibid., p. 588. She refers to an article by Morice Rodney, 'Psychiatric diagnosis in a transcultural setting: the importance of lexical categories' in the *British Journal of Psychiatry* 132 (1977), pp. 87–95.

23. G. M. Burghardt, 'Animal awareness: current perceptions and historical perspective', *American Psychologist* 40 (August 1985), pp. 905–19.

24. F. de Waal, *Peacemaking Among Primates* (Harvard University Press, 1989), p. 25.

25. For an account of the problems with correlating testosterone levels and aggressiveness, for example, see A. Kohn, *The Brighter Side of Human Nature: Altruism and Empathy in Everyday Life* (Basic Books, N.Y., 1990), pp. 27–8.

26. See G. G. Gallup, Jr. and S. D. Suarez, 'Overcoming our resistance to animal research: man in comparative perspective', in *Comparing Behavior: Studying Man Studying Animals*, D. W. Rajecki, ed. (Lawrence Erlbaum Associates, Hillsdale, New Jersey, 1983), p. 10. They note that 'The basic biological principles governing the metabolic, endocrinological, neurological, and biochemical activities in man are basically the same in many other organisms. Behavior, therefore, has become the last stronghold for the Platonic paradigm . . . If we accept the proposition that, in the last analysis, behavior is nothing more than an expression of physiological processes, then to admit the biological but deny the psychological similarities between ourselves and other species seems logically inconsistent and indefensible.'

27. Quoted in T. Regan and P. Singer, eds, *Animal Rights and Human Obligations* (Prentice-Hall, New Jerksey, 1979), pp. 61–4. The original passage is from *Discours de la méthode*, 5, A. Bridoux, ed. *Oeuvres et lettres de Descartes*, pp. 165–6. (Gallimard, 1953).

28. Quoted in T. Regan, *The Case for Animal Rights* (University of California Press, 1983), p. 5.

29. F. A. de Voltaire, *Dictionnaire philosophique*, J. Benda and R. Naves, eds. (Garnier Frères, Paris, 1961), pp. 50–51. Trans. J. Masson.

30. F. A. de Voltaire, 'The beasts', Article 6 in *Le philosophe ignorant*, from *Les Oeuvres Complètes de Voltaire*, Vol. Mélanges, J. van den Heuvel, ed. (Gallimard, Paris,), p. 863. Trans J. Masson.

31. The French text is quoted in H. Hastings, *Man and Beast in French Thought of the Eighteenth Century*, vol. 27 (The Johns Hopkins Press, U.S., 1936), p. 183. Trans. J. Masson. See also T. H. Huxley, 'On the hypothesis that animals are automata, and its history', in *Method and Results: Essays* (1893; reprinted, Macmillan, U.K., 1901), pp. 199–250. He writes, 'I confess that, in view of the struggle for existence which goes on in the animal world, and of the frightful quantity of pain with which it must be accompanied, I should be glad if the probabilities were in favour of Descartes' hypothesis; but, on the other hand, considering the terrible practical consequences to domestic animals which might ensure from any error on our part, it is as well to err on the right side, if we err at all, and deal with them as weaker brethren, who are bound, like the rest of us, to pay their toll for living, and suffer what is needful for the general good. As Hartley finely says, "We seem to be in the place of God to them." ' (Ibid., p. 237). For a complete history of the Descartes debate, see L. Cohen

Rosenfield, *From Beast-Machine to Man-Machine: Animal Soul in French Letters from Descartes to La Mettrie* (1940; new ed. Octagon Books, New York, 1968); the introduction in F. Dagognet, 'L'animal selon Condillac' in *Traité des animaux* (Librairie Philosophique J. Vrin, Paris, 1987); and G. Boas, *The Happy Beast in French Thought of the Seventeenth Century: Contributions to the History of Primitivism* (The Johns Hopkins Press, U.S., 1933).

32. I. Pepperberg, interview by S. McCarthy, 22 February 1993.
33. E. M. Thomas, 'The old way', *The New Yorker* (15 October 1990), p. 91.
34. F. de Waal, *Peacemaking*, p. 220.
35. D. Macdonald, *Running with the Fox* (Unwin Hyman, U.K., 1987), p. 164.
36. Konrad Lorenz, *The Year of the Greylag Goose* (Eyre Methuen, London, 1975; Harcourt Brace Jovanovich, N.Y., 1978), p. 56.
37. Cf. Mary Midgley, *Beast and Man: The Roots of Human Nature* (Cornell University Press, 1978; Methuen, U.K., 1979) pp. 344–5

Chapter 2, *Unfeeling Brutes*

1. N. K. Humphrey, 'The social function of intellect', in *Growing Points in Ethology*, P. P. G. Bateson and R. A. Hinde, eds, (Cambridge University Press, 1976), pp. 303–17.
2. D. Symons, *The Evolution of Human Sexuality* (Oxford University Press, 1979), pp. 78–9.
3. D. Goldfoot *et al*, 'Behavioral and physiological evidence of sexual climax in the female stump-tailed macaque', *Science* 208 (1980), pp. 1477–9. Cited in de Waal, *Peacemaking*, pp. 151–3.
4. F. de Waal, *Peacemaking Among Primates* (Harvard University Press, 1989), pp. 151–3, 198–206.
5. This splendid example of benightedness is also quoted by Mary Midgley in her article 'The mixed community', in Hargrove, *Animal Rights/Environmental Ethics Debate*, p. 223. The article is a very long and learned one written by N. W. Thomas, in Vol. I of the *Encyclopaedia of Religion and Ethics*, J. Hastings, ed. (T. & T. Clark, Edinburgh), pp. 483–535. The article actually begins (p. 483) by citing the 'great gulf that exists between man . . . and the elephant and the anthropid ape'.
6. M. Cartmill, *A View to a Death in the Morning: Hunting and Nature Through History* (Harvard University Press, 1993), p. 222.
7. V. Arzt and I. Birmelin, *Haben Tieren ein Bewusstsein?: Wenn Affen lügen, wenn Katzen denken und Elefanten traurig sind* (C. Bertelsmann, Munich, 1993), p. 154. Trans. J. Masson.
8. 'Another assessment of pain in fish comes from a team of researchers under the direction of Professor John Verheijen at the University of Utrecht in the Netherlands [in 1988]. They concluded that fish do feel pain and experience fear.' R. B. Orleans, *In the Name of Science: Issues in Responsible Animal Experimentation* (Oxford University Press, 1992), p. 148. Can an ant feel pain? For years, the received wisdom was that insects did not feel pain, hence one could do anything one liked to them. But Wigglesworth in a 1980 article in the prestigious journal *Antenna* (4, pp. 8–9) entitled 'Do insects feel pain?' argued that they do. An even more recent article with the arresting title of 'The moral standing of insects and the ethics of extinction' published in the *Florida Entomologist* in 1987 (70, pp. 70–89) states that 'existing evidence indicates that insects qualify as sentient and their lives ought to be included in moral deliberations'. For

another positive response to the question, see C. H. Eisemann *et al*, 'Do insects feel pain? A biological review', published in *Experientia* in 1984 (40, pp. 164–7).

9.   J. Wood Krutch, *The Best of Two Worlds* (William Sloane Associates, New York, 1950), p. 95.

10. E. S. Turner recently commented about his 1964 book *All Heaven in a Rage*, one of the first books to challenge attitudes toward animals: 'In my original introduction I commented that in our attitude to animals we are hopelessly, perversely inconsistent. Reviewing this book in the *Observer*, Philip Toynbee followed up the point, remarking that the rage of English foxhunters knew no bounds when they learned that the Russians had shot a dog into space. He thought that a certain pattern could be traced in these bewildering inconsistencies. "We abominate the cruelties which we are not tempted to perform, and we abominate them all the more when they are practised by people who do not belong to our own group". He could have added "or when they are practised by people of another nation".' E. S. Turner, *All Heaven in a Rage* (Centaur Press, U.K., 1992), pp. 323–4.

11. This incredible practice is well attested in medical sources. See K. J. S. Anand and P. J. McGrath, eds, *Pain in Neonates* (Elsevier, Amsterdam, 1993); N. Schechter, C. B. Berde and M. Yaster, eds, *Pain in Infants, Children, and Adolescents* (Williams and Wilkins, Baltimore, 1993); 'Medicine and the Media' (editorial) *British Medical Journal* 295 (12 September 1987), pp. 659–60; I. S. Gauntlett, T. H. H. G. Koh and W. A. Silverman, 'Analgesia and anaesthesia in newborn babies and infants' (Letters), *Lancet* (9 May 1987); N. Hall, 'The Painful Truth', *Parenting* (June/July 1992).

12. R. N. Emde and K. L. Koenig, 'Neonatal smiling and rapid eye-movement states', *Journal of the American Academy of Child Psychiatry*, 8 (1969), pp. 57–67. Cited in C. Izard, *Human Emotions* (Plenum Press, U.S./U.K., 1977).

13   D. McFarland, ed., *The Oxford Companion to Animal Behaviour* (O.U.P. 1987), p. 17.

14. H. Davies and D. Balfour, eds, *The Inevitable Bond* (Cambridge University Press, 1992), p. 23.

15. J. S. Kennedy, *The New Anthropomorphism* (Cambridge University Press, 1992), pp. 3–5.

16. Ibid., p. 167.

17. J. A. Fisher, 'Disambiguating anthropomorphism: an interdisciplinary review', in *Perspectives in Ethology* 9 (1991), p. 49.

18. 'Male/female differences in attitudes and knowledge of animals were substantial and implied the need for better understanding and appreciation of female attitudes toward and interests in wildlife. Particularly provocative were variations in basic feelings and ethical concern for animals. The most outstanding result was the much greater humanistic concern for animals among females.' S. R. Kellert and J. K. Berry, *Phase III: Knowledge, Affection and Basic Attitudes Toward Animals in American Society* (U.S. Fish and Wildlife Service, 1980), p. 59. Phase Three gives the results of a U.S. Fish and Wildlife Service-funded study of 'American Attitudes, Knowledge and Behaviours Toward Wildlife and Natural Habitats'.

19. F. de Waal, *Chimpanzee Politics: Power and Sex among Apes* (Jonathan Cape, U.K., 1982), pp. 41–2.

20. J. Adamson, intro. Julian Huxley, *Living Free* (Collins & Harvill Press, U.K., 1961), p. xi.

21. This theme is also expressed in T. X. Barber, *The Human Nature of Birds: A Scientific Discovery with Startling Implications* (St Martin's Press, N.Y., 1993).
22. S. Montgomery, *Walking with the Great Apes* (Houghton Mifflin, Boston, 1991), p. 143.
23. C. Moss, *Elephant Memories: Thirteen years in the Life of an Elephant Family* (William Morrow, N.Y., 1988), p. 37.
24. E. M. Thomas, 'The old way', *The New Yorker* (15 October 1990), p. 99.
25. P. Tyack, 'Whistle repertoires of two bottlenosed dolphins, *Tursiops truncatus*: mimicry of signature whistles?' *Behavioral Ecology and Sociobiology* 18 (1989), pp. 251–7.
26. M. Tomkies, *Last Wild Years* (Jonathan Cape, U.K., 1992), p. 172.
27. M. Midgley, 'The concept of beastliness: philosophy, ethics and animal behavior', *Philosophy* 48 (1973), pp. 111–35.
28. Kennedy, *The New Anthropomorphism*, p. 87.
29. A fuller exposition is given as follows: 'If consciousness has evolved as a biological adaptation for doing introspective psychology, then the presence or absence of consciousness in animals of different species will depend on whether or not they need to be able to understand the behaviour of other animals in a social group. Wolves and chimpanzees and elephants, which all go in for complex social interactions, are probably all conscious; frogs and snails and codfish are probably not . . . The advantage to an animal of being conscious lies in the purely private use it makes of conscious experience as a means of developing an ideology which helps it to model another animal's behaviour. It need make no difference at all whether the other animal is actually experiencing the feelings with which it is being credited; all that matters is that its behaviour should be understandable on the assumption that such feelings provide the reasons for its actions. Thus for all I know no man other than myself has ever experienced a feeling corresponding to my own feeling of hunger; the fact remains that the concept of hunger, derived from my own experience, helps me to understand other men's eating behaviour.' N. K. Humphrey, 'Nature's psychologists', in *Consciousness and the Physical World*, B. D. Josephson and V. S. Ramachandran, eds (Pergamon Press, Oxford, 1980), pp. 57–80
30. M. Midgley, *Beast and Man: The Roots of Human Nature* (Cornell University Press, N.Y., 1978), pp. 41, 344–57. Also see M. Midgley, *Animals and Why They Matter* (University of Georgia Press, 1983).
31. J. Ortega y Gasset, *Meditations on Hunting*, trans. H. B. Wescott (Scribner, N.Y., 1972), pp. 136–8. Cited from M. Cartmill, ibid, p. 240.
32. K. Pryor, *Lads Before the Wind: Adventures in Porpoise Training* (Harper & Row, N.Y., 1975), p. 240. Reference is to K. Pryor, R. Haag, and J. O'Reilly 'The creative porpoise: training for novel behavior', *Journal of the Experimental Analysis of Behavior* 12 (1969), pp. 653–61.
33. M. Tomkies, *On Wing and Wild Water* (Jonathan Cape, U.K., 1987), pp. 136–7.
34. J. E. R. Staddon, 'Animal psychology: the tyranny of anthropocentrism', in *Whither Ethology? Perspectives in Ethology*, P. P. G. Bateson and P. H. Klopfer, eds (Plenum Press, New York, 1989), p. 123.
35. R. W. Mitchell and N. S. Thompson, eds, *Deception: Perspectives on Human and Nonhuman Deceit* (State University of New York Press, 1986), p. 177–81

36. J. Goodall, *In the Shadow of Man* (Collins, U.K., 1971), p. 202.

37. D. E. H. Russell, *The Politics of Rape: The Victim's Perspective* (Stein & Day, N.Y., 1977); D. E. H. Russell, *Rape in Marriage* (Macmillan, N.Y., 1982); and D. E. H. Russell and N. Howell, 'The prevalence of rape in the United States revisited', *Signs: Journal of Women in Culture and Society* 8 (Summer 1983), pp. 668–95.

38. D. E. H. Russell, 'The incidence and prevalence of intrafamilial and extrafamilial sexual abuse of female children', *Child Abuse and Neglect: The International Journal* 7 (1983), pp. 133–46; and D. E. H. Russell, *The Secret Trauma: Incestuous Abuse of Women and Girls* (Basic Books, N.Y., 1986).

39. E. M. Thomas, *The Hidden Life of Dogs* (Houghton Mifflin, Boston, 1993).

Chapter 3, *Fear, Hope and the Terror of Dreams*

1. A. Conover, 'He's just one of the bears', *National Wildlife*, vol. 30 (June–July 1992), pp. 30–6.

2. L. Rogers, interview by S. McCarthy, 15 July 1993.

3. A. Mayes, 'The physiology of fear and anxiety', in *Fear in Animals and Man*, W. Sluckin, ed., 24–55 (Van Nostrand Reinhold Co., New York and London, 1979), pp. 32–3.

4. D. McFarland, ed., *The Oxford Companion to Animal Behaviour* (Oxford University Press, 1987), p. 180.

5. M. Konner, *The Tangled Wing: Biological Constraints on the Human Spirit* (Holt, Rinehart and Winston, New York, 1982), p. 215.

6. M. Barinaga, 'How scary things get that way', *Science*, vol. 258 (6 November 1992), pp. 887–8.

7. R. Thomson, 'The concept of fear', in *Fear in Animals and Man*, W. Sluckin, ed., 1–23 (Van Nostrand Reinhold Co., New York and London, 1979), p. 3.

8. K. Pryor, *Lads Before the Wind: Adventures in Porpoise Training* (Harper & Row, New York, 1975), p. 178.

9. *Gorilla: Journal of the Gorilla Foundation* 15, no. 2 (Woodside, California, June 1992), p. 5.

10. Konner, p. 235.

11. D. H. Chadwick, *A Beast the Color of Winter: The Mountain Goat Observed* (Sierra Club Books, San Francisco, 1983), pp. 57–8.

12. W. de Grahl, *The Grey Parrot*, trans. W. Charlton (T.F.H. Publications, N.Y., 1987), pp. 44–5.

13. D. H. Chadwick, *The Fate of the Elephant* (Viking, London, 1993; Sierra Club Books, U.S., 1992), pp. 129, 327.

14. Chadwick, *Beast the Color of Winter*, p. 89.

15. P. A. Russell, 'Fear-evoking stimuli', in *Fear in Animals and Man*, W. Sluckin, ed., 86–124 (Van Nostrand Reinhold Co., New York and London, 1979), pp. 97–8.

16. T. Bledsoe, *Brown Bear Summer: My Life among Alaska's Grizzlies* (Dutton, N.Y., 1987), p. 129.

17. Pryor, *Lads Before the Wind*, p. 178.

18. J. Adams, *Wild Elephants in Captivity* (Center for the Study of Elephants, Dominguez Hills, California, 1981), p. 146.

19. De Grahl, *Grey Parrot*, pp. 210–12.

20. B. Arjan Singh, *Tiger! Tiger!* (Jonathan Cape, U.K., 1984), pp. 75, 90.

21. K. Laidler, *The Talking Ape* (Stein and Day, N.Y., 1980). Laidler was

shocked by Cody's terror of his own species and arranged for Cody to meet and eventually be caged with another young orangutan. The two apes became friendly and would walk about hand in hand.

22. J. Crumley, *Waters of the Wild Swan* (Jonathan Cape, U.K., 1992), pp. 85–6.
23. E. M. Thomas, *The Hidden Life of Dogs* (Houghton Mifflin, Boston, 1993), p. 71.
24. Chadwick, *Beast the Color of Winter*, p. 115.
25. C. Moss, *Elephant Memories: Thirteen Years in the Life of an Elephant Family* (William Morrow, N.Y., 1988), pp. 315–16.
26. M. Ventura, 'The zoo where you're fed to God', *L.A. Weekly*, 11–17 December 1992, p. 18.
27. E. P. Walker, *Mammals of the World*, 2nd ed. (Johns Hopkins Press, U.S., 1986), p. 1460.
28. Bledsoe, *Brown Bear Summer*, pp. 171–6.
29. Ibid., p. 132.
30. L. Rogers, interview by S. McCarthy, 15 July 1993.
31. P. Leyhausen, *Cat Behavior: The Predatory and Social Behavior of Domestic and Wild Cats*, trans. B. A. Tonkin (Garland STPM Press, New York and London, 1979), pp. 286–7.
32. Chadwick, *Beast the Color of Winter*, p. 19.
33. M. Cottrell Houle, *Wings for my Flight: The Peregrine Falcons of Chimney Rock* (Addison–Wesley, U.S., 1991), p. 105.
34. H. A. Hornstein, *Cruelty and Kindness: A New Look at Oppression and Altruism* (Prentice–Hall, Englewood Cliffs, New Jersey, 1976), p. 81. Citing experiments by Prof. D. O. Hebb.
35. H. S. Terrace, *Nim: A Chimpanzee who Learned Sign Language* (Washington Square Press, N.Y., 1979), p. 44. The mother chimpanzee's apprehensions were justified: she was tranquillised and the infant was taken away, named Nim Chimpsky, and taught 125 words of American sign language. Years later Nim was returned to the Institute.
36. H. Kruuk, *The Spotted Hyena: A Study of Predation and Social Behavior* (University of Chicago Press, 1972), p. 161.
37. Chadwick, *Beast the Color of Winter*, p. 26
38. G. B. Schaller, *The Serengeti Lion: A Study of Predator–Prey Relations* (University of Chicago Press, 1972), p. 266.
39. Kruuk, *Spotted Hyena*, p. 161.
40. 'Cheetahs in the Land of Lions', an episode of *Nature: with George Page*, 1992.
41. C. Moss, *Elephant Memories*, p. 162.
42. F. Patterson and E. Linden, *The Education of Koko* (Holt, Rinehart and Winston, N.Y., 1981), pp. 135–6. Also Wendy Gordon, interview by S. McCarthy, 29 April 1994.
43. R. A. Gardner and B. T. Gardner, 'A cross-fostering laboratory', in *Teaching Sign Language to Chimpanzees*, R. Allen Gardner, B. T. Gardner and T. E. Van Cantfort, eds., 1–28 (State University of New York Press, 1989), p. 8.
44. B. T. Gardner, R. Allen Gardner and S. G. Nichols, 'The shapes and uses of signs in a cross-fostering laboratory', in *Teaching Sign Language to Chimpanzees*, p. 65.
45. R. S. Fouts, D. H. Fouts, and T. E. Van Cantfort, 'The infant Loulis learns signs from cross-fostered chimpanzees', in *Teaching Sign Language to Chimpanzees*, pp. 280–92. Before being given to Washoe, Loulis had

been reared by his mother and another female. His mother could not take care of Loulis by herself because she suffered from the after-effects of brain research (R. Fouts, personal communication).

46. L. Wittgenstein, *Philosophical Investigations*, 3rd ed., trans. G. E. M. Anscombe (Macmillan, N.Y., 1968), p. 174.

Chapter 4, *Hope, Dominance and Cruelty in Peace and War*

1. A. I. Dagg and J. B. Foster, *The Giraffe: Its Biology, Behavior and Ecology* (Van Nostrand Reinhold, N.Y., 1976), p. 3.
2. See, for example, H. Ryden's *God's Dog* (Coward, McCann & Geoghegan, New York, 1975), p. 223, where she complains '. . . my animals got along so well that I was unable to determine their relative ranks'.
3. P. Leyhausen, *Cat Behavior: The Predatory and Social Behavior of Domestic and Wild Cats*, trans. B. A. Tonkin (Garland STPM Press, N.Y., 1979), pp. 174–9.
4. B. Clark, *High Hills and Wild Goats* (Little, Brown, Boston, 1990), p. 116.
5. M. G. Hornocker, 'Winter territoriality in mountain lions', *Journal of Wildlife Management* 33 (July 1969), pp. 457–64.
6. B. Arjan Singh, *Tiger! Tiger!* (Jonathan Cape, London, 1984), p. 71.
7. D. H. Chadwick, *A Beast the Color of Winter* (Sierra Club Books, U.S., 1983), pp. 126–8, 140.
8. M. S. Athan, *Guide to a Well-behaved Parrot* (Barron's Educational Series, N.Y., 1993), p. 138.
9. N. R. Chalmers, 'Dominance as part of a relationship', *Behavioral and Brain Sciences* 4 (1981), pp. 437–8.
10. I. S. Bernstein, 'Dominance: the baby and the bathwater', *Behavioral and Brain Sciences* 4 (1981), pp. 419–29. (Followed by peer commentary.)
11. T. Rowell, *The Social Behaviour of Monkeys* (Penguin Books, U.K., 1972), pp. 162–3.
12. B. Smuts, 'Dominance: an alternative view', *Behavioral and Brain Sciences* 4 (1981), pp. 448–9.
13. C. Bachmann and H. Kummer, 'Male Assessment of Female Choice in Hamadryas Baboons', *Behavioral Ecology and Sociobiology* 6 (1980) p. 315–21. This paper continues a tradition of referring to male hamadryas baboons as 'owners' of females.
14. S. C. Strum, *Almost Human* (Random House, N.Y., 1987), pp. 118–20.
15. Leyhausen, *Cat Behavior*, pp. 256–7.
16. T. Bledsoe, *Brown Bear Summer* (Dutton, N.Y., 1987), pp. 68–69, 126–8.
17. F. de Waal, *Chimpanzee Politics* (Jonathan Cape, U.K., 1982), pp. 88–90, 186.
18. A. F. Richard, 'Malagasy prosimians: female dominance', in *Primate Societies*, B. B. Smuts et al., eds, (University of Chicago Press, 1986), pp. 25–33.
19. President Theodore Roosevelt, 'an enthusiastic imperialist and a staunch believer in the superiority of the Anglo-Saxon race, was also a renowned Great White Hunter who devoted much of his life to killing large animals throughout the world and writing books recounting his adventures'. The early Canadian conservationists John Muir (founder of the Sierra Club) and William J. Long engaged the president in a much followed debate in the popular press. When Roosevelt contended that they lacked manliness and did not know 'the heart of the wild thing', Long snapped back with a famous counterattack:

Who is he to write, 'I don't believe for a minute that some of these nature writers know the heart of a wild thing'. As to that, I find after carefully reading two of his big books that every time Mr Roosevelt gets near the heart of a wild thing he invariably puts a bullet through it.

This quote and the earlier one about Roosevelt come from M. Cartmill's *A View to a Death in the Morning* (Harvard University Press, 1993), pp. 153–4.

20. Clark, pp. 67–8.
21. De Waal, p. 188.
22. B. Gilbert, *Chulo* (Knopf, N.Y., 1973), pp. 230–31.
23. S. T. Emlen and P. H. Wrege, 'Forced copulations and intraspecific parasitism: two costs of social living in the white-fronted bee-eater', *Ethology* 71 (1986), pp. 2–29.
24. R. O. Bailey, N. R. Seymour and G. R. Stewart, 'Rape behavior in blue-winged teal', *Auk* 95 (1978), pp. 188–90. Also, D. P. Barash, 'Sociobiology of rape in mallards (*Anas platyrhynchos*): responses of the mated male', *Science* 197 (19 August 1977), pp. 788–9.
25. D. P. Barash, ibid., p. 139.
26. Pryor, *Lads Before the Wind*, pp. 78–9.
27. N. Angier, 'Dolphin courtship: brutal, cunning and complex', *New York Times*, 18 February 1992.
28. H. Kruuk, *The Spotted Hyena* (University of Chicago Press, 1972), p. 232.
29. J. Goodall, *The Chimpanzees of Gombe; Patterns of Behavior* (Harvard University Press, 1986), p. 502.
30. A. Rasa, *Mongoose Watch* (The Anchor Press/Doubleday, N.Y., 1986), pp. 230–31.
31. Kruuk, pp. 254–6.
32. J. Alcock, *Animal Behavior: An Evolutionary Approach*, 4th ed. (Sinauer Associates, Sunderland, Mass., 1989), pp. 372–3.
33. Dagg and Foster, *Giraffe*, pp. 36–7.
34. Pryor, *Lads Before the Wind*, p. 123.
35. Ibid., p. 214.
36. Quoted in T. M. French, *The Integration of Behavior, Volume 1: Basic Postulates* (University of Chicago Press, 1952), pp. 156–7.
37. *What Everyone Who Enjoys Wildlife Should Know*, pamphlet from Abundant Wildlife Society of North America, Gillette, Wyoming. Also *Abundant Wildlife*, Special Wolf Issue, 1992.
38. M. W. Fox, *The Whistling Hunters: Field Studies of the Asiatic Wild Dog (Cuon Alpinus)* (State University of New York Press, 1984), p. 63.
39. C. Moss, *Portraits in the Wild: Behavior Studies of East African Mammals* (Houghton Mifflin, Boston, 1975), p. 296.
40. Leyhausen, *Cat Behavior*, pp. 128–30.
41. Ibid., pp. 136–7.
42. E. M. Thomas, 'The old way', *The New Yorker* (15 October 1990), p. 93.
43. Leyhausen, p. 137.
44. Bledsoe, *Brown Bear Summer*, p. 67.
45. Kruuk, *Spotted Hyena*, p. 89.
46. See, for example, T. R. Mader, 'Wolves and Hunting', *Abundant Wildlife*, Special Wolf Issue (1992), 3. Accounts of wolves surplus-killing deer in Minnesota, caribou calves in Canada and Dall sheep in Alaska are used to argue that wolf numbers must be limited. Also photo caption, p. 1.

47. Kruuk, p. 119. Also S. E. Glickman, personal communication, 5 November 1992.
48. Ibid., pp. 165, 204.
49. G. Gormley, *Orcas of the Gulf* (Sierra Club Books, U.S., 1990), p. 85.
50. G. B. Schaller, *The Serengeti Lion: A Study of Predator-Prey Relations* (University of Chicago Press, 1972), p. 383. He adds that lions tend to treat humans as fellow predators rather than as prey.
51. D. Morris, *Animal Days* (Jonathan Cape, London, 1980), pp. 222–3.
52. Leyhausen, *Cat Behavior*, pp. 234–5.
53. G. Gebel-Williams and T. Reinhold, *Untamed: The Autobiography of the Circus's Greatest Animal Trainer* (William Morrow, N.Y., 1991), p. 61.
54. W. Jordan, *Divorce Among the Gulls: An Uncommon Look at Human Nature* (North Point Press, California, 1991), p. 30.
55. S. Berggren, *Berggren's Beasts*, trans. from Swedish by I. Rodger (Paul S. Eriksson, N.Y., 1970), p. 76.
56. H. S. Terrace, *Nim: A Chimpanzee who Learned Sign Language* (Washington Square Press, N.Y., 1979), pp. 51–2.
57. Ibid., pp. 174–5.
58. J. Y. Henderson, *Circus Doctor*, as told to R. Taplinger (Little, Brown, Boston, 1951), p. 152.
59. This is an example of observational learning, and animals have frequently been said to be unable to do this. However, observational learning has been experimentally demonstrated in animals as diverse as cats and octopuses.
60. I. Pepperberg, interview by S. McCarthy, 22 February 1993.
61. W. de Grahl, *The Grey Parrot*, trans. W. Charlton (T.F.H. Publications, N.Y., 1987), p. 46.
62. Athan, *Guide to a Well-behaved Parrot*, p. 11.
63. D. C. Reed, *Notes from an Underwater Zoo* (Dial Press, N.Y., 1981), pp. 248–51. Kianu was separated from the other orcas, became visibly depressed and was sold to a Japanese oceanarium. Nepo died in 1980. Yaka is still at the original oceanarium.
64. De Waal, *Chimpanzee Politics*, p. 168.
65. Leyhausen, *Cat Behavior*, pp. 265–8.
66. For an overview see N. Angier, 'Mating for life? It's not for the birds or the bees', *New York Times*, 21 August 1990, C1, C8.
67. J. T. Winslow, N. Hastings, C. S. Carter, C. R. Harbaugh and T. R. Insel, 'A role for central vasopressin in pair bonding in monogamous prairie voles', *Nature* 365 (7 October 1993) pp. 545–8.
68. C. Moss, *Elephant Memories: Thirteen Years in the Life of an Elephant Family* (William Morrow, N.Y., 1988), pp. 100–101.
69. Moss, *Portraits in the Wild*, p. 49.
70. E. M. Thomas, *The Hidden Life of Dogs* (Houghton Mifflin, Boston, 1993), p. 55.
71. De Waal, *Chimpanzee Politics*, p. 116. Also De Waal, *Peacemaking Among Primates* (Harvard University Press, 1989).
72. De Waal, *Peacemaking among Primates*, p. 5.
73. Ibid., p. 22.

Chapter 5, *Family, Friends and Lovers*

1. J. H. Williams, *Elephant Bill* (Hart-Davis, U.K.; Doubleday, N.Y., 1950), pp. 82–4.

2. C. Roberts, *The Scientific Conscience: Reflections on the Modern Biologist and Humanism* (George Braziller, N.Y., 1967).
3. J. Goodall, *In the Shadow of Man*, revised ed. (Houghton Mifflin, Boston, 1988), p. 194.
4. J. Benyus, *Beastly Behaviors: A Zoo Lover's Companion: What Makes Whales Whistle, Cranes Dance, Pandas Turn Somersaults, and Crocodiles Roar: A Watcher's Guide to How Animals Act and Why* (Addison-Wesley, Reading, Mass., 1992), p. 52.
5. E. M. Thomas, *The Hidden Life of Dogs* (Houghton Mifflin, Boston, 1993).
6. P. Holt, 'Puppy love isn't just for people: author says dogs, like humans, can bond', *San Francisco Chronicle*, 9 December 1993.
7. For example, C. E. Izard, *Human Emotions* (Plenum Press, U.S./U.K., 1977) does not include love on his list of the eight basic emotions.
8. I owe this description to Prof. R. I. Vane-Wright. It originally derives from M. Rothschild, 'Female butterfly guarding eggs', in *Antenna* (London) 3 (1979), p. 94.
9. J. Traherne Moggridge, *Harvesting Ants and Trap-door Spiders: Notes and Observations on their Habits and Dwellings* (L. Reeve & Co., London, 1873), pp. 113–14.
10. B. P. Wiesner and N. M. Sheard, *Maternal Behaviour in the Rat* (Oliver & Boyd, Edinburgh, 1933), pp. 121–2.
11. B. Clark, *High Hills and Wild Goats* (Little, Brown, Boston, 1990), p. 34.
12. B. Kevles, *Females of the Species: Sex and Survival in the Animal Kingdom* (Harvard University Press, 1986), p. 154.
13. A. I. Dagg and J. B. Foster, *The Giraffe: Its Biology, Behavior and Ecology* (Van Nostrand Reinhold, N.Y., 1976), pp. 38–9.
14. F. McNulty, *The Whooping Crane: The Bird that Defies Extinction* (E. P. Dutton, N.Y., 1966), p. 37.
15. S. P. Young, *The Wolves of North America: Their History, Life Habits, Economic Status, and Control*, Part II: Classification of Wolves by Edward A. Goldman (American Wildlife Institute, 1944), pp. 109–10, citing a 1935 article by Peter Freuchen.
16. D. G. Kleiman and J. R. Malcolm, 'The evolution of male parental investment in mammals', in *Parental Care in Mammals*, ed. D. J. Gubernick and P. H. Klopfer (Plenum Press, N.Y., 1981).
17. G. Durrell, *Menagerie Manor* (Hart-Davis, London; Avon, N.Y., 1964), pp. 127–9.
18. D. Macdonald, *Running with the Fox* (Unwin Hyman, U.K., 1987), pp. 140–42.
19. C. Moss, *Portraits in the Wild: Behavior Studies of East African Mammals* (Houghton Mifflin, Boston, 1975), pp. 104–105.
20. G. B. Schaller, *The Serengeti Lion: A Study of Predator-Prey Relations* (University of Chicago Press, 1972), p. 332.
21. S. C. Strum, *Almost Human: A Journey into the World of Baboons* (Random House, N.Y., 1987), p. 40.
22. T. Rowell, *The Social Behaviour of Monkeys* (Penguin Books, U.K., 1972), p. 76.
23. S. Montgomery, *Walking with the Great Apes* (Houghton Mifflin, Boston, 1991), p. 43.
24. C. Moss, *Elephant Memories* (William Morrow, N.Y., 1988), p. 267.
25. F. Patenaude, 'Care of the young in a family of wild beavers, Castor canadensis', *Acta Zool. Fennica* 174 (1983), pp. 121–2.

26. Rowell, *Social Behaviour*, p. 110.
27. Moss, *Portraits in the Wild*, pp. 16–17.
28. B. Arjan Singh, *Tiger! Tiger!* (Jonathan Cape, U.K., 1984), p. 207.
29. J. J. Teal, Jr., 'Domesticating the wild and woolly musk ox' *National Geographic* (June 1970).
30. P. Leyhausen, *Cat Behavior* (Garland STPM Press, N.Y., 1979), pp. 242–3.
31. H. Ryden, *Lily Pond: Four Years with a Family of Beavers* (William Morrow, New York, 1989).
32. F. Colmenares and H. Rivero, 'Male–male tolerance, mate sharing and social bonds among adult male brown bears living under group conditions in captivity', *Acta Zool. Fennica* 174 (1983), pp. 149–51.
33. E. S. Savage, J. Temerlin and W. B. Lemmon, 'The appearance of mothering behavior toward a kitten by a human-reared chimpanzee', paper delivered at the Fifth Congress of Primatology, Nagoya, Japan, 1974.
34. D. H. Chadwick, *The Fate of the Elephant* (Viking, London, 1993; Sierra Club Books, U.S., 1992), pp. 270–71.
35. Prof. W. Jankowiak, interview by S. McCarthy, 15 December 1992. Also see D. Goleman, 'Anthropology goes looking for love in all the old places', *New York Times*, 24 November 1992, B1.
36. Prof. C. Lindholm, interview by S. McCarthy, 12 January 1993.
37. Prof. L. Plotnicov, interview by S. McCarthy, 14 December 1992. Also L. Plotnicov, 'Love, lust, and found in Nigeria', paper presented at the 1992 American Anthropological Association annual meeting, San Francisco, 2 December 1992.
38. A. J. Magoun & P. Valkenburg, 'Breeding behavior of free-ranging wolverines (*Gulo*)', *Acta Zool. Fennica* 174 (1983), pp. 175–7.
39. E. St. Vincent Millay, 'Passer mortuus est', in *Collected Lyrics* (Washington Square Press, N.Y., 1959), p. 56.
40. K. Pryor, *Lads Before the Wind* (Harper & Row, N.Y., 1975), p. 171.
41. M. S. Athan, *Guide to a Well-behaved Parrot* (Barron's Educational Series, Hauppauge, N.Y., 1993), p. 138.
42. M. S. Athan, interview by S. McCarthy, 23 August 1993.
43. H. Ryden, *God's Dog* (Coward, McCann & Geoghegan, N.Y., 1975), pp. 60–62.
44. L. Rogers, interview by S. McCarthy, 15 July 1993.
45. H. Kummer, *Social Organization of Hamadryas Baboons; A Field Study* (University of Chicago Press, 1968), p. 63. This study refers to such caretaking by male baboons as mothering and as 'maternal' behaviour.
46. B. P. Wiesner and N. M. Sheard, *Maternal Behavior*, p. 148.
47. R. Cochrane, 'Some parrots I have known', in *The Animal Story Book*, The Young Folks Library, vol. IX (Hall & Locke, Boston, 1901), pp. 208–209.
48. H. Kruuk, *The Spotted Hyena* (University of Chicago Press, 1972), p. 171.
49. G. Archibald, 'Gee whiz! ICF hatches a whooper', *The ICF Bugle* (July 1982).
50. G. Maxwell, *Raven Seek Thy Brother* (Penguin Books, U.K., 1968), pp. 59–61.

Chapter 6, *Grief, Sadness and the Bones of Elephants*

1. Quoted in H. C. Bernhard Grzimek, ed., *Grzimek's Animal Life Encyclopedia*, vol. 12 (Van Nostrand Reinhold, N.Y., 1975).

2. M. C. Houle, *Wings for my Flight: The Peregrine Falcons of Chimney Rock* (Addison-Wesley, Reading, Mass., 1991), pp. 75–87. The female peregrine had reportedly been shot. The two surviving nestlings fledged successfully.

3. E. M. Thomas, *The Hidden Life of Dogs* (Houghton Mifflin, Boston, 1993).

4. J. Y. Henderson, *Circus Doctor*, as told to R. Taplinger (Little Brown, Boston, 1951), p. 78

5. K. Pryor, *Lads Before the Wind* (Harper & Row, N.Y., 1975), pp. 276–7.

6. A. Alpers, *Dolphins: The Myth and the Mammal* (Houghton Mifflin, Boston, 1960), pp. 104–5.

7. E. M. Thomas, 'The old way', *The New Yorker* (15 October 1990), p. 91.

8. C. Moss, *Elephant Memories* (William Morrow, N.Y., 1988), pp. 269–71.

9. C. Moss, *Portraits in the Wild: Behavior Studies of East African Mammals* (Houghton Mifflin, Boston, 1975), p. 34.

10. Moss, *Elephant Memories*, pp. 272–3.

11. F. de Waal, *Chimpanzee Politics* (Harper & Row, N.Y., 1982), pp. 67–70.

12. A. Rasa, *Mongoose Watch* (Anchor Press/Doubleday & Co., Garden City, N.Y., 1986), p. 226.

13. L. Wilsson, *My Beaver Colony*, trans. J. Bulman (Doubleday, N.Y., 1968), pp. 61–2.

14. F. Colmenares and H. Rivero, 'Male–male tolerance, mate sharing and social bonds among adult male brown bears living under group conditions in captivity', *Acta Zool. Fennica* 174 (1983), pp. 149–51.

15. Moss, *Elephant Memories*, p. 112.

16. P. Leyhausen, *Cat Behavior* (Garland STPM Press, London/N.Y., 1979), pp. 287–8.

17. J. Goodall, *Through a Window: My Thirty Years with the Chimpanzees of Gombe* (Houghton Mifflin, Boston, 1990), p. 230.

18. Cited in R. M. Yerkes and A. W. Yerkes, *The Great Apes: A Study of Anthropoid Life* (Yale University Press, 1929), p. 472.

19. Pryor, *Lads Before the Wind*, pp. 82–3.

20. R. Reinhold, 'At Sea World, stress tests whale and man', *New York Times*, 4 April 1988, A9.

21. Pryor, p. 132.

22. D. McFarland, ed., *The Oxford Companion to Animal Behaviour* (Oxford University Press, 1987), p. 599.

23. L. E. Hinsie and R. J. Campbell, eds, *Psychiatric Dictionary*, 4th ed. (Oxford University Press, 1970).

24. Harlow said that his 'device was designed on an intuitive basis to reproduce such a well [of despair] both physically and psychologically for monkey subjects'. See the trenchant criticism by James Rachels in 'Do animals have a right to liberty?' in *Animal Rights and Human Obligations*, ed. T. Regan and P. Singer (Prentice Hall, Englewood Cliffs, 1976), p. 211. See also P. Singer's criticism in Chapter 2 of his *Animal Liberation* (London: Jonathan Cape, 1976, 1992).

25. 'Do animals have a right to liberty?', ibid. p. 211. See also the fine criticism of Harlow's work in Chapter 2 of P. Singer's influential *Animal Liberation*, ibid.; the original article by Harlow is written with S. J. Suomi: 'Depressive behavior in young monkeys subjected to vertical chamber confinement', *Journal of Comparative and Physiological Psychology* 80 (1972), pp. 11–18. Harlow published his articles in prestigious journals. For example, see his 'Love in infant monkeys', *Scientific American*

200 (1959), pp. 68–74; and 'The nature of love', *American Psychologist* 13 (1958), pp. 673–85. Cf. D. Haraway, *Primate Visions* (Routledge, N.Y., 1989)

26. M. E. P. Seligman, *Helplessness: On Depression, Development, and Death* (W. H. Freeman, San Francisco, 1975), pp. 23–5. While restrained, each dog was given 64 shocks of 6.0 milliamperes, lasting for five seconds.

27. Ibid., p. 54.

28. J. B. Sidowski, 'Psychopathological consequences of induced social helplessness during infancy', in *Experimental Psychopathology: Recent research and theory*, ed. H. D. Kimmel (Academic Press, N. Y., 1971), pp. 231–48.

29. R. J. Rutter and D. H. Pimlott, *The World of the Wolf* (J. B. Lippincott, N.Y., 1968), p. 138; Lois Crisler, *Captive Wild* (Harper & Row, N.Y., 1968), p. 210.

30. I. Redmond, 'The Death of Digit', *International Primate Protection League Newsletter* 15, no. 3, December 1988, p. 7.

31. R. M. Yerkes and A. W. Yerkes, *The Great Apes: A Study of Anthropoid Life* (Yale University Press, 1929), p. 161.

32. W. Frey, II, with M. Langseth, *Crying: The Mystery of Tears* (Winston Press, Minneapolis, 1985).

33. R. L. Sadoff, 'The nature of crying and weeping', in *The World of Emotion: Clinical Studies of Affects and their Expression*, ed. C. W. Socarides (International Universities Press, N.Y., 1977), p. 388.

34. S. B. Ortner, 'Shera purity', *American Anthropologist* 75 (1973), pp. 49–63. Quoted in Paul Rozin and April Fallon, 'A perspective on disgust', *Psychological Review* 94 (1987), pp. 23–41.

35. H. S. Terrace, *Nim: A Chimpanzee who Learned Sign Language* (Washington Square Press, N.Y., 1979), p. 56.

36. W. de Grahl, *The Grey Parrot* (T.F.H. Publications, N.Y., 1987), p. 189.

37. V. B. Scheffer, *Seals, Sea Lions, and Walruses: A Review of the Pinnipedia* (Stanford University Press, 1958), p. 22. See also Frey, *Crying*.

38. *Macacus maurus*, the Celebes macaque, is now denoted *Cynomacaca maurus*. The passage from Darwin that was cited at the beginning of the Preface to this book continues: 'Sir E. Tennent, in describing those which he saw captured and bound in Ceylon, says some "lay motionless on the ground, with no other indication of suffering than the tears which suffused their eyes and flowed incessantly". Speaking of another elephant, he says, "When overpowered and made fast, his grief was most affecting; his violence sank to utter prostration, and he lay on the ground, uttering choking cries, with tears trickling down his cheeks". In the Zoological Gardens the keeper of the Indian elephants positively asserts that he has several times seen tears rolling down the face of the old female, when distressed by the removal of the young one.' See Heathcote Williams, *Sacred Elephant* (Jonathan Cape, U.K., 1989), p. 93 for other examples. An influential German book in its time, Karl Friedrich Burdach's *Blicke ins Leben* (3 vols., Leopold Woss, Leipzig, 1842), vol. 2, p. 130, cites examples of female seals who 'shed copious tears when they were abused', giraffes who cried when they were removed from their companions, and tears in fur seals when their young were stolen (*geraubt*) and in an elephant seal when it was treated roughly.

39. Frey, *Crying*, p. 141.

40. Ibid., p. 141.

41. V. Arzt and I. Birmelin, *Haben Tieren ein Bewusstsein?: Wenn Affen lügen,*

wenn Katzen denken und Elefanten traurig sind (C. Bertelsmann, Munich, 1993), p. 154.

42. R. Gordon Cummings, *Five Years of a Hunter's Life in the Far Interior of South Africa* (1850), quoted in R. Carrington, *Elephants: A Short Account of their Natural History, Evolution and Influence on Mankind* (Chatto & Windus, U.K., 1958), pp. 154–5.

43. G. Lewis, as told to B. Fish, *Elephant Tramp* (Little, Brown, Boston, 1955), pp. 52, 188–9.

44. Victor Hugo, *Carnet intime*, 1870–1. Publié et presenté par Henri Guillemin (Gallimard, 7th edn, Paris, 1953), p. 88.

45. D. H. Chadwick, *The Fate of the Elephant* (Viking, London, 1993; Sierra Club Books, U.S., 1992), p. 327.

46. This suggestion was proposed by Dr W. Frey.

47. L. S. Lavrov, 'Evolutionary development of the genus *Castor* and taxonomy of the contemporary beavers of Eurasia', *Acta Zool. Fennica* 174 (1983), pp. 87–90.

48. Dian Fossey, *Gorillas in the Mist* (Hodder & Stoughton, U.K.; Houghton Mifflin, Boston, 1983), p. 110.

49. D. M. Frame, trans., *The Complete Works of Montaigne*, Vol. 2 (Anchor Books, N.Y., 1960), pp. 105–9.

Chapter 7, *A Capacity for Happiness*

1. E. Izard, *Human Emotions* (Plenum Press, N.Y. and London, 1977), pp. 239–45.

2. M. E. P. Seligman, *Helplessness: on Depression, development, and Death* (W. H. Freeman, San Francisco, 1975), p. 98.

3. G. B. Schaller, *The Serengeti Lion* (University of Chicago Press, 1972), pp. 104, 304.

4. Reported in S. Montgomery, *Walking with the Great Apes* (Houghton Mifflin, Boston, 1991), p. 146.

5. E. M. Thomas, *The Hidden Life of Dogs* (Houghton Mifflin, Boston, 1993), p. 40.

6. L. Rogers, interview by S. McCarthy, 15 July 1993.

7. Darwin to Susan Darwin, 1838, *The Correspondence of Charles Darwin Volume 2; 1837–1843* (Cambridge University Press, 1986).

8. K. S. Norris, *Dolphin Days: The Life and Times of the Spinner Dolphin* (W. W. Norton, N.Y., 1991), pp. 42–3.

9. H. Ryden, *Lily Pond: Four Years with a Family of Beavers* (William Morrow, N.Y., 1989), p. 104.

10. H. S. Terrace, *Nim: A Chimpanzee who Learned Sign Language* (Washington Square Press, N.Y., 1979), p. 412.

11. F. Patterson and E. Linden, *The Education of Koko* (Holt, Rinehart & Winston, N.Y., 1981), p. 185.

12. R. Fouts, interview by S. McCarthy, 10 December 1993.

13. D. H. Chadwick, *A Beast the Color of Winter* (Sierra Club Books, U.S., 1983), pp. 150–51.

14. J. Goodall and D. A. Hamburg, 'Chimpanzee behavior as a model for the behavior of early man', in S. Arieti, ed., *American Handbook of Psychiatry*, 2nd ed. (Basic Books, N.Y., 1975), pp. 20–27. Cited here from C. N. Degler, *In Search of Human Nature: The Decline and Revival of Darwinism in American Social Thought*, (Oxford University Press, 1991), p. 336.

15. Terrace, *Nim*, pp. 140–42.

16. A. Alpers, *Dolphins: The Myth and the Mammal* (Houghton Mifflin, Boston, 1960), p. 102.
17. C. Moss, *Elephant Memories* (William Morrow, N.Y., 1988), pp. 124–5.
18. R. Monastersky, 'Boom in "cute" baby dinosaur discoveries', *Science News* 134 (22 October 1988), p. 261.
19. V. Arzt and I. Birmelin, *Haben Tieren ein Bewusstsein? Wenn Affen lügen, wenn Katzen denken und Elefanten traurig sind* (C. Bertelsmann, Munich, 1993), p. 173.
20. L. Wilsson, *My Beaver Colony*, trans. J. Bulman (Doubleday, N.Y., 1968), pp. 92–3.
21. Ibid., p. 131.
22. Ryden, *Lily Pond*, 185–7.
23. G. Gebel-Williams with T. Reinhold, *Untamed: The Autobiography of the Circus's Greatest Animal Trainer* (William Morrow, N.Y., 1991), p. 310.
24. K. Pryor and K. S. Norris, eds, *Dolphin Societies: Discoveries and Puzzles* (University of California Press, 1991), p. 346.
25. H. Hale Broun, 'Ever indomitable, Secretariat thunders across the ages', *New York Times*, 30 May 1993, p. 23.
26. R. Fouts, interviewed by S. McCarthy, 10 December 1993.
27. F. de Waal, *Chimpanzee Politics* (Jonathan Cape, London, 1982), p. 26.
28. J. Lee Kavanau, 'Behavior of captive white-footed mice', *Science* 155 (31 March 1967), pp. 1623–39.
29. P. B. Dews, 'Some observations on an operant in the octopus', *Journal of the Experimental Analysis of Behavior* 2 (1959), pp. 57–63. Reprinted in T. E. McGill, ed., *Readings in Animal Behavior* (Holt, Rinehart and Winston, N.Y., 1965).
30. F. Fraser Darling, *A Herd of Red Deer: A Study in Animal Behaviour* (Oxford University Press, 1937), p. 35.
31. 'Orangutan escapes exhibit, mingles with zoo visitors', *San Francisco Chronicle*, 19 June 1993 (Associated Press story).
32. G. B. Schaller, *The Last Panda* (University of Chicago Press, 1993), p. 66.
33. R. Fagen, *Animal Play Behaviour* (Oxford University Press, 1981), pp. 3–4.
34. Ibid., pp. 17–18. Fagen notes that whenever he lectured on animal play, 'Afterwards, to my discomfort and embarrassment, I would chiefly be asked "people questions".'
35. R. A. Hinde, *Animal Behavior* (McGraw-Hill, N.Y., 1966).
36. Fagen, *Animal Play*, pp. 20–21.
37. Moss, *Elephant Memories*, pp. 85, 142–3, 171.
38. H. Kruuk, *The Spotted Hyena* (University of Chicago Press, 1972), pp. 249–50.
39. G. Lewis, as told to B. Fish, *Elephant Tramp* (Little Brown, Boston, 1955), pp. 128–9.
40. Terrace, *Nim*, pp. 228–9.
41. Chadwick, *Beast the Color of Winter*, p. 70.
42. B. Arjan Singh, *Tiger! Tiger!* (Jonathan Cape, 1984), pp. 72–3.
43. F. de Waal, *Peacemaking Among Primates* (Harvard University Press, 1989), p. 195.
44. J. Boswall, 'Russia is for the birds', *Discover* (March 1987), p. 78.
45. C. Hill, 'Playtime at the Zoo', *Zoo-Life* 1, pp. 24–6.
46. J. D. Lazell, Jr., and N. C. Spitzer, 'Apparent play behavior in an American alligator', *Copeia* (1977), p. 188.
47. Alpers, *Dolphins*, pp. 90–93.

48. Norris, *Dolphin Days*, pp. 259–60.
49. F. Bruemmer, 'White whales on holiday', *Natural History* (January 1986), pp. 40–49.
50. Schaller, *Serengeti Lion*, pp. 163–4.
51. Patterson and Linden, picture caption.
52. R. Fouts interview, 10 December 1993.
53. Alpers, p. 90.
54. M. C. Houle, *Wings for my Flight: The Peregrine Falcons of Chimney Rock* (Addison-Wesley, Reading, Mass., 1991), p. 23.
55. J. Crumley, *Waters of the Wild Swan* (Jonathan Cape, U.K., 1992), pp. 53–4.
56. D. Macdonald, *Running with the Fox* (Unwin Hyman, U.K., 1987), pp. 78–9.
57. R. Carrington, *Elephants: A Short Account of their Natural History, Evolution and Influence on Mankind* (Chatto & Windus, U.K., 1958), pp. 216–7.
58. K. Pryor, *Lads before the Wind* (Harper & Row, N.Y., 1975), pp. 66–7.
59. G. Morey, *The Lincoln Kangaroos* (Chilton Books, Philadelphia, 1963), pp. 53–60.
60. A. Rasa, *Mongoose Watch* (Anchor Press/Doubleday, New York, 1986), pp. 44–5, 142–4.
61. H. Sawyer Buyukmihci, *The Hour of the Beaver* (Rand McNally, Chicago, 1971), pp. 97–8.
62. R. Fagen, *Animal Play Behaviour* (Oxford University Press, 1981), p. 494.
63. J. Cousteau and Y. Paccalet, *Whales*. Trans. I. M. Paris (Harry N. Abrams, N.Y., 1988), p. 217.

Chapter 8, *Compassion, Rescue and the Altruism Debate*

1. R. Helfer, *The Beauty of the Beasts: Tales of Hollywood's Animal Stars*, (Jeremy P. Tarcher, Los Angeles, 1990), pp. 109–10. Also interview by S. McCarthy, 11 November 1993.
2. E. and C. Bradley Martin, *Run Rhino Run* (Chatto and Windus, U.K., 1982), p. 28.
3. B. Clark, *High Hills and Wild Goats* (Little, Brown, Boston, 1990), p. 198.
4. H. Kruuk, *The Spotted Hyena: A Study of Predation and Social Behavior* (University of Chicago Press, 1972), pp. 197–8.
5. C. Moss, *Portraits in the Wild*, p. 72.
6. H. Kruuk, *Spotted Hyena*, p. 193.
7. J. Goodall, *With Love* (Jane Goodall Institute, Ridgefield, Connecticut, 1994).
8. Moss, pp. 111–12.
9. Cited in G. B. Schaller, *The Serengeti Lion* (University of Chicago Press, 1972), p. 262.
10. D. Macdonald, *Running with the Fox* (Unwin Hyman, U.K., 1987), p. 220.
11. Moss, p. 16.
12. A. Rasa, *Mongoose Watch* (Anchor Press/Doubleday, New York, 1986), pp. 257–8.
13. *Gorilla: Journal of the Gorilla Foundation* 15 (June 1992), no. 2, p. 8.
14. R. C. Connor and K. S. Norris, 'Are dolphins reciprocal altruists?', *The American Naturalist* 199, no. 3 (March 1982), p. 363.
15. Schaller, *Serengeti Lion*, pp. 25–6.
16. R. Dennard, interview by J. Masson and S. McCarthy, 24 September 1993.
17. C. Ott-Bales, interview by S. McCarthy, 30 September 1993. The baby suffered no ill effects from his single choking episode. Gilly, a

Border Collie, is trained to notify Ms Ott-Bales' husband of doorbells and so on.

18. P. Ogden, *Chelsea: The Story of a Signal Dog* (Little, Brown, Boston, 1992), p. 145.
19. C. Kearton, 1925, cited in R. M. Yerkes and A. W. Yerkes, *The Great Apes* (Yale University Press, 1929), p. 298.
20. Goodall, ibid.
21. H. S. Terrace, *Nim: A Chimpanzee who Learned Sign Language* (Washington Square Press, N.Y., 1979), pp. 56–7.
22. Ibid., p. 406.
23. J. H. Masserman, S. Wechkin, and W. Terris, ' "Altruistic" Behavior in Rhesus Monkeys', *American Journal of Psychiatry* 121 (1964), pp. 584–5.
24. D. McFarland, ed., *The Oxford Companion to Animal Behaviour* (Oxford University Press, 1987), p. 14.
25. S. Montgomery, *Walking with the Great Apes* (Houghton Mifflin, Boston, 1991), pp. 265–6.
26. J. Goodall, *Through a Window: My Thirty Years with the Chimpanzees of Gombe* (Houghton Mifflin, Boston, 1990), pp. 107–8.
27. R. Dawkins, *The Selfish Gene* (Oxford University Press, 1976) pp. 105–6.
28. Ibid., p. 74.
29. Ibid., p. 103.
30. F. Bruemmer, 'White whales on holiday', *Natural History* (January 1986), p. 48.
31. Connor and Norris, *American Naturalist*, p. 368.
32. Ibid., pp. 358–74.
33. Told in E. Linden, *Silent Partners: The Legacy of the Ape Language Experiments* (Times Books, New York, 1986), pp. 42–3. Also interview with R. Fouts by Susan McCarthy, 10 December 1993.
34. 'Ripples of controversy after a chimp drowns', *New York Times*, 16 October 1990. (The chimpanzee who drowned is not the same animal as the one saved.)
35. Dawkins, *The Selfish Gene*, p. 4.
36. Bruemmer, pp. 40–49.
37. M. Hutchins and K. Sullivan, 'Dolphin delight', *Animal Kingdom* (July/August 1989), pp. 47–53.
38. M. Tomkies, *Out of the Wild* (Jonathan Cape, 1985), p. 197.
39. H. Ryden, *Lily Pond: Four Years with a Family of Beavers* (William Morrow, N.Y., 1989), p. 217.
40. C. Moss, *Elephant Memories* (William Morrow, N.Y., 1988), p. 84.
41. B. H. Lopez, *Of Wolves and Men* (Dent, U.K., 1979; Scribner, N.Y., 1978), p. 198.
42. G. Högstedt, 'Adaptation unto death: function of fear screams', *American Naturalist* 121 (1983), pp. 562–70.
43. Schaller, *Serengeti Lion*, p. 254.
44. H. M. H. Wu, W. G. Holmes, S. R. Medina and G. P. Sackett, 'Kin preference in infant *Macaca nemestrina*', *Nature* 285 (1980), pp. 225–7.
45. D. H. Chadwick, *A Beast the Color of Winter* (Sierra Club Books, U.S., 1983), p. 15.
46. E. S. Morton and J. Page, *Animal Talk: Science and the Voices of Nature* (Random House, N.Y., 1992), pp. 138–9.
47. R. M. Seyfarth and D. L. Cheney, 'Grooming, alliances, and reciprocal altruism in vervet monkeys', *Nature* 308, no. 5 (April 1984), pp. 541–2.

48. J. W. Krutch, *The Best of Two Worlds* (William Sloane Associates, New World, 1950), p. 77.
49. Clark, *High Hills and Wild Goats*, p. 136.
50. M. S. Athan, interview by S. McCarthy, 23 August 1993.
51. Rasa, *Mongoose Watch*, pp. 83–4.
52. K. Pryor, *Lads before the Wind* (Harper & Row, N.Y., 1975), pp. 218–19.
53. R. Dawkins, *Selfish Gene*, p. 109.
54. Ibid., p. 215.
55. G. S. Wilkinson, 'Food sharing in vampire bats', *Scientific American* 262 (1990), pp. 76–82. Also G. Wilkinson, interview by Susan McCarthy, 4 March 1994.
56. Quoted in A. Kohn, *The Brighter Side of Human Nature: Altruism and Empathy in Everyday Life* (Basic Books, N.Y., 1990), p. 188.
57. Connor and Norris, 'Are dolphins reciprocal altruists?', pp. 358–74.
58. R. L. Trivers, 'The evolution of reciprocal altruism', *Quarterly Review of Biology* 46 (1971), pp. 35–57.
59. See Wilson & Hölldobler, *The Arts*, 1990, p. 257, The discovery was made by H. Markl. See his 'Stridulation in leaf-cutting ants' *Science*, 149 (1965), pp. 1329–93.
60. J. Nollman, *Animal Dreaming: The Art and Science of Interspecies Communication* (Bantam Books, N.Y., 1987), p. 59.

Chapter 9, *Shame, Blushing and Hidden Secrets*

1. I owe this observation to John McCarthy.
2. R. Karen, 'Shame', *Atlantic Monthly* 269 (February 1992), pp. 40–70.
3. C. Darwin, *The Expression of the Emotions in Man and the Animals* (1872; reprinted University of Chicago Press, 1965), p. 309.
4. D. Nathanson, *Shame and Pride: Affect, Sex and the Birth of the Self* (W. W. Norton, N.Y., 1992), p. 462.
5. Darwin, p. 344.
6. B. Grzimek, ed., *Grzimek's Animal Encyclopedia* (Van Nostrand Reinhold, N.Y., 1972), vol. 10, p. 82.
7. B. M. Beehler, *A Naturalist in New Guinea* (University of Texas Press, 1991), p. 57.
8. M. S. Athan, *Guide to a Well-behaved Parrot* (Barron's Educational Series, Hauppauge, N.Y., 1993), p. 13. Also M. S. Athan, interview by S. McCarthy, 23 August 1993.
9. Nathanson, *Shame and Pride*, p. 142.
10. G. Gallup, 'Self-recognition in primates: a comparative approach to the bidirectional properties of consciousness', *American Psychologist* 32 (1977), pp. 329–38. Gallup tested paint on himself before applying it to chimps.
11. J. A. Kennedy, *The New Anthropomorphism* (Cambridge University Press, 1992), pp. 107–8.
12. E. Savage-Rumbaugh, *Ape Language: From Conditioned Response to Symbol* (Columbia University Press, N.Y., 1986), pp. 308–14.
13. F. de Waal, *Chimpanzee Politics* (Jonathan Cape, U.K., 1982), pp. 47–8.
14. F. de Waal, *Peacemaking Among Primates* (Harvard University Press, 1989), pp. 238–9.
15. C. Packer, 'Male dominance and reproductive activity in Papio anubis' *Animal Behavior* 27 (1979), pp. 37–45.
16. G. B. Schaller, *The Serengeti Lion* (University of Chicago Press, 1972), p. 268.

17. D. H. Chadwick, *A Beast the Color of Winter* (Sierra Club Books, U.S., 1983), pp. 87–8.
18. F. Patterson and E. Linden, *The Education of Koko* (Holt, Rinehart and Winston, N.Y., 1981), pp. 136–7.
19. K. Pryor, *Lads Before the Wind* (Harper & Row, N.Y., 1975), p. 128.
20. R. Fouts, interview by S. McCarthy, 10 December 1993.
21. J. Goodall, interview by S. McCarthy, 7 May 1994.
22. Cited in M. Lewis, *Shame: The Exposed Self* (The Free Press/Macmillan, N.Y., 1992), pp. 5–26.
23. Nathanson, *Shame and Pride*, p. 218.
24. Ibid., pp. 169–70.
25. Ibid., p. 140.
26. Ibid., pp. 210–11.
27. Schaller, *Serengeti Lion*, p. 231.
28. H. Kruuk, *The Spotted Hyena* (University of Chicago Press, 1972), pp. 99–100, 150.
29. Ibid., pp. 153–5.
30. Cited in A. Alpers, *Dolphins: The Myth and the Mammal* (Houghton Mifflin, Boston, 1960), p. 188.
31. P. Leyhausen, *Cat Behavior* (Garland STPM Press, 1979), pp. 144–5.
32. F. F. Darling, *A Herd of Red Deer* (Oxford University Press, 1937), p. 81.
33. D. Gucwa and J. Ehmann, *To Whom It May Concern: An Investigation of the Art of Elephants* (W. W. Norton, New York, 1985), p. 200.
34. H. S. Terrace, *Nim: A Chimpanzee who Learned Sign Language* (Washington Square Press, N.Y., 1979), pp. 222–6.
35. D. Morris, *Dogwatching* (Jonathan Cape, U.K., 1986), p. 29.
36. Nathanson, *Shame and Pride*, p. 15.

Chapter 10, *Beauty, the Bears and the Setting Sun*

1. Izard, however, considers creativity part of an Interest–Excitement emotional complex, along with hope. C. E. Izard, *Human Emotions* (Plenum Press, New York and London, 1977), p. 42.
2. P. Dickson and J. C. Gould, *Myth-Informed: Legends, Credos, and Wrong-headed 'Facts' We All Believe* (Perigee/Putnam, 1993), p. 21. The authors write 'bulls, like many other animals, including dogs, see only shades of light and dark'. Also see J. Horgan, 'See Spot See Blue: Curb that dogma! Canines are not colorblind', *Scientific American* 262 (January 1990), p. 20. Horgan notes this assertion making its way into textbooks.
3. A. Kortlandt, 'Chimpanzees in the wild', *Scientific American* 206 (May 1962), pp. 128–38.
4. G. Jacobs, interview by Susan McCarthy, 30 September 1993.
5. J. M. Benyus, *Beastly Behaviors* (Addison-Wesley, Reading, Mass., 1992), p. 206.
6. J. C. Welty and L. Baptista, *The Life of Birds* (Saunders College Publishing, New York, 1988), pp. 82, 215. Among the functions of song, the authors note 'that some birds may sing from a sense of well-being, or simply "for the joy of it", should not arbitrarily be ruled out!'
7. G. Durrell, *My Family and Other Animals* (Allen & Unwin, U.K., 1963; Viking Press, N.Y., 1957), pp. 38–9.
8. W. de Grahl, *The Grey Parrot* (T.F.H. Publications, Neptune City, N.Y., 1987), p. 168.

9. H. Ryden, *God's Dog* (Coward, McCann & Geoghegan, New York, 1975), p. 70.

10. D. R. Leighton, 'Gibbons: territoriality and monogamy', in *Primate Societies*, ed. B. B. Smuts, D. L. Cheney, R. M. Seyfarth, R. W. Wrangham, and T. T. Struhsaker (University of Chicago Press, 1986), pp. 135–45.

11. J. Nollman, *Animal Dreaming: The Art and Science of Interspecies Communication* (Bantam Books, N.Y., 1987), pp. 94–7.

12. W. Gordon, (Gorilla Foundation, Woodside, California), interview by S. McCarthy, 29 April 1994.

13. D. Gucwa and J. Ehmann, *To Whom It May Concern: An Investigation of the Art of Elephants* (W. W. Norton, N.Y., 1985), p. 190.

14. B. Gilbert, *Chulo* (Knopf, N.Y., 1973), p. 202.

15. Welty and Baptista, *Life of Birds*, pp. 78–9.

16. N. K. Humphrey, ' "Interest" and "pleasure": two determinants of a monkey's visual preferences', *Perception* I (1972), pp. 395–416.

17. Cited in D. Morris, *The Biology of Art: A study of the picture-making behaviour of the great apes and its relationship to human art* (Methuen, London, 1966; Knopf, N.Y., 1962), pp. 32–4.

18. M. Anderson, 'Female choice selects for extreme tail length in a widowbird', *Nature* 299 (28 October 1982), pp. 818–820.

19. Both are members of the family Paradisaeidae.

20. Welty and Baptista, pp. 278–80.

21. B. M. Beehler, *A Naturalist in New Guinea* (University of Texas Press, 1991), p. 45.

22. Ibid., p. 147.

23. It is also worth keeping in mind that plumage may send a message to someone other than a potential mate or rival. Beehler and colleagues recently made the discovery that the hooded pitohui, also of New Guinea, has a powerful neurotoxin in its bright orange and black feathers, which is believed to protect it from predators. Here the plumage presumably has, at least in part, a warning message. See J. P. Dumbacher, B. M. Beehler, T. F. Spande, H. M. Garaffo, J. W. Daly, 'Homobatrachotoxin in the genus *Pitohui*: chemical defense in birds?' *Science* 258 (30 October 1992), pp. 799–801. Natives of New Guinea have long known that pitohuis have 'bitter' skin.

24. P. H. Schiller, 'Figural preferences in the drawings of a chimpanzee', *Journal of Comparative and Physiological Psychology* 44 (1951), pp. 101–11.

25. D. Morris, *Animal Days* (Jonathan Cape, U.K., 1979), pp. 197–8. Also D. Morris, *The Biology of Art* (Methuen, U.K., 1966).

26. K. Beach, R. S. Fouts and D. H. Fouts, 'Representational art in chimpanzees', *Friends of Washoe* 3 (Summer 1984), pp. 2–4; R. Fouts interview; also A. Gardner and B. Gardner, 'Comparative psychology and language acquisition', *Annals of the New York Academy of Sciences* 309 (1978), pp. 37–76. Cited in Gucwa and Ehmann.

27. Gucwa and Ehmann, *To Whom It May Concern*, pp. 119–20.

28. Ibid., pp. 93–7.

29. D. H. Chadwick, *The Fate of the Elephants* (Viking, U.K., 1993; Sierra Club Books, U.S., 1992), pp. 12–15.

30. K. Pryor, *Lads Before the Wind* (Harper & Row, N.Y., 1975), pp. 234–53; K. Pryor, R. Haag, and J. O'Reilly, 'The creative porpoise: training for novel behavior', *Journal of the Experimental Analysis of Behavior*

12 (1969), pp. 653–61. For the journal article all references to Hou as 'she' were changed to 'it'.

31. T. Nishida, 'Local traditions and cultural transmission', in *Primate Societies*, ed. B. B. Smuts, D. L. Cheney, R. M. Seyfarth, R. W. Wrangham and T. T. Struhsaker (University of Chicago Press, 1986), pp. 462–74; M. Harris, *Our Kind* (Harper & Row, N.Y., 1989), p. 63.

32. E. M. Thomas, 'The old way', *The New Yorker*, 15 October 1990.

33. G. B. Schaller, *The Serengeti Lion* (University of Chicago Press, 1972), p. 129.

34. S. C. Strum, *Almost Human: A Journey into the World of Baboons* (Random House, N.Y., 1987), pp. 128–33. This tradition of intensive hunting for meat later vanished.

35. F. de Waal, *Chimpanzee Politics* (Jonathan Cape, U.K., 1982), p. 135.

36. R. Dawkins, *Selfish Gene* (Oxford University Press, 1976), pp. 203–4.

37. J. W. Krutch, *The Best of Two Worlds* (William Sloane Associates, New World, 1950), pp. 92–4.

38. Chadwick, p. 63.

Chapter 11, *Maternal Cannibalism, Justice and the Inexpressible*

1. D. Nathanson, *Shame and Pride: Affect, Sex, and the Birth of the Self* (W. W. Norton, N.Y., 1992), p. 474.

2. E. M. Thomas, *The Hidden Life of Dogs* (Houghton Mifflin, Boston, 1993), pp. xvii–xviii.

3. H. S. Terrace, *Nim: A Chimpanzee who Learned Sign Language* (Washington Square Press, N.Y., 1979), p. 171.

4. F. de Waal, *Chimpanzee Politics* (Jonathan Cape, U.K., 1982), pp. 171–2.

5. Ibid., p. 207.

6. Thomas, *Dogs*, pp. 49–51.

7. B. Gilbert, *Chulo* (Knopf, N.Y., 1973), pp. 105–6.

8. Terrace, pp. 185–6.

9. The chimpanzees in the later sign language projects of the Gardners and the gorillas taught by Patterson did have some native signers among their teachers. In no case was the lead researcher a fluent signer, however.

10. Terrace, Appendix B., 'Recruiting Nim's Teachers', pp. 392–5.

11. R. Fouts, interview by S. McCarthy, 10 December 1993.

12. D. R. Griffin: 'The cognitive dimensions of animal communication', in *Fortschritte der Zoologie* 31 (1985), pp. 471–482.

13. E. Savage-Rumbaugh, *Ape Language: From Conditioned Response to Symbol* (Columbia University Press, N.Y., 1986), p. 337.

14. J. Nollman, *Animal Dreaming: The Art and Science of Interspecies Communication* (Bantam Books, New York, 1987), p. 105. Cf. the authoritative article in *The Encyclopedia of Mammals*: 'It is clear from its continuous nature and ordered sequence that the song potentially contains much information, but its precise function is not known', ed. D. Macdonald (Facts on File Publications, N.Y., 1984), p. 229.

15. W. Wiltschko, U. Munro, H. Ford and R. Wiltschko, 'Red light disrupts magnetic orientation of migratory birds', *Nature* 364 (5 August 1993), p. 525.

16. G. B. Schaller, *The Serengeti Lion* (University of Chicago Press, 1972), p. 50.

17. G. B. Schaller, *The Last Panda* (University of Chicago Press, 1993), pp. 79–80.

18. Terrace, pp. 222–26.
19. Quoted in J. W. Krutch, *The Best of Both Worlds* (William Sloane Associates, New World, 1950).
20. J. W. Krutch, *The Great Chain of Life* (Houghton Mifflin, Boston, 1956), p. 106.
21. L. Rogers, interviews by S. McCarthy, 15 July 1993 and 11 May 1994.
22. E. M. Thomas, 'The old way', *The New Yorker*, 15 October 1990, p. 100.

Conclusion, *Sharing the World with Feeling Creatures*

1. J. Fowles with F. Horvat, *The Tree* (Little, Brown, Boston, 1979).
2. Brigid Brophy: 'In Pursuit of a Fantasy', in *Animals, Men and Morals*, pp. 125–145, ed. S. and R. Godlovitch (Taplinger, N.Y., 1972), p. 129.
3. S. Begley and J. Cooper Ramo, 'Not just a pretty face', *Newsweek*, 1 November 1993, p. 67.
4. A German woman leaving a theatre performance of *The Diary of Anne Frank* was heard to say to her companion: 'That one, at least, should not have been killed.'
5. The new school of cognitive ethology, started by Donald R. Griffin, is an exception, and many of the biologists and animal behaviourists who work in this area, people such as Gordon Burghardt, Dorothy Cheney, Robert Seyfarth, Carolyn Ristau, Marc Bekoff, Alison Jolly and others would agree with the position that animals lead emotional lives, though they might not all agree on how complex and sophisticated they are.
6. This passage from *The Principles of Moral and Legislation* of 1789 (Chapter 18, sec., 1) as well as selections from his 'A utilitarian view' and John Stuart Mill's 'A defence of Bentham' can be found in the useful collection edited by Peter Singer and Tom Regan: *Animal Rights and Human Obligations* (Prentice-Hall, U.S., 1976).
7. Peter Nicholaus Witt. 'Die Wirkung einer einmaligen Gabe von Largactil auf den Netzbau der Spinne Zilla-x-notata', in *Monatschrift für Psychiatrie und Neurologie* 129 (1955), no. 1–3, pp. 123–128.
8. Catherine Roberts: *The Scientific Conscience: Reflections on the Modern Biologist and Humanism* (Braziller, N.Y., 1967), pp. 106–107.
9. M. Bekoff, Professor of Biology at the University of Colorado and a noted expert on canids, in a personal communication with Jeffrey Masson, 14 May 1994.
10. In *The Great Ape Project*, ed. P. Singer and P. Cavalieri (Fourth Estate, U.K., 1993), pp. 15–16.
11. D. H. Chadwick, *The Fate of the Elephant* (Viking, London, 1993). Quoted by E. M. Thomas in 'The Battle for the Elephants', *New York Review of Books*, 24 March 1994, p. 5.
12. *The Attic Nights of Aulus Gellius* with an English translation by C. Rolfe, 3 vols (Harvard University Press, 1984), vol. 1, pp. 421–7. Only fragments of the *Wonders of Egypt* exist. A very similar account, from the same source, was made famous in Europe in the 16th century by Michel Montaigne. See *The Complete Essays of Montaigne*, trans. Donald M. Frame (Stanford University Press, California, 1989), pp. 350–5.
13. Ibid.
14. Told in Joy Adamson's two books, *Born Free* and *Living Free* (Collins/Harvill Press, London, 1960 and 1961). See also Adrian House: *The Great Safari: The Lives of George and Joy Adamson: Famous for Born Free.* (Harper Collins, U.K., 1993).

BIBLIOGRAPHY

Adams, Jack. *Wild Elephants in Captivity*. Dominguez Hills, California: Center for the Study of Elephants, 1981

Adamson, Joy. *Born Free: A Lioness of Two Worlds*. London: Collins/Harvill Press, 1960

Adamson, Joy. *Living Free: The Story of Elsa and Her Cubs*. London: Collins/Harvill Press, 1961

Alcock, John. *Animal Behavior: An Evolutionary Approach,* 4th ed. Sunderland, Massachusetts: Sinauer Associates, 1989

Alpers, Antony. *Dolphins: The Myth and the Mammal*. London: John Murray, 1960

Anand, K. J. S., and McGrath, P. J., eds. *Pain in Neonates*. Amsterdam: Elsevier, 1993

Anderson, Malte. 'Female choice selects for extreme tail length in a widowbird.' *Nature* (U.K.) 299 (1982): pp. 818–20

Angier, Natalie. 'Dolphin courtship: brutal, cunning and complex.' *New York Times*, 18 February 1992

Archibald, George. 'Gee whiz! ICF hatches a whooper.' *The ICF Bugle* (July 1982): 1

Arzt, Volker, and Birmelin, Immanuel. *Haben Tieren ein Bewusstsein?: Wenn Affen lügen, wenn Katzen denken und Elefanten traurig sind*. Munich: C. Bertelsmann, 1993

Athan, Mattie Sue. *Guide to a Well-behaved Parrot*. Hauppauge, N.Y.: Barron's Educational Series, 1993

Bachmann, Christian, and Kummer, Hans. 'Male assessment of female choice in Hamadryas Baboons.' *Behavioral Ecology and Sociobiology* 6 (1980): pp. 315–21

Bailey, Robert O.; Seymour, Norman R.; and Stewart, Gary R. 'Rape behavior in blue-winged teal.' *Auk* 95 (1978): pp. 188–90

Barash, David P. 'Sociobiology of rape in mallards (*Anas platyrhynchos*): responses of the mated male.' *Science* 197 (19 August 1977): pp. 788–9

Barber, Theodore Xenophon. *The Human Nature of Birds: A Scientific Discovery with Startling Implications*. New York: St Martin's Press, 1993

Barinaga, Marcia. 'How scary things get that way.' *Science* 258 (6 November 1992): 887–8

Beach, Kathleen; Fouts, Roger. S.; and Fouts, Deborah H. 'Representational art in chimpanzees.' *Friends of Washoe* 3 (Summer 1984): pp. 2–4

Bibliography

Beehler, Bruce M. *A Naturalist in New Guinea*. Austin: University of Texas Press, 1991

Begley, Sharon, and Ramo, Joshua Cooper. 'Not just a pretty face.' *Newsweek* (1 November 1993): p. 67

Benyus, Janine M. *Beastly Behaviors: A zoo lover's companion: what makes whales whistle, cranes dance, pandas turn somersaults, and crocodiles roar: a watcher's guide to how animals act and why*. Reading, Mass.: Addison-Wesley, 1992

Berggren, Sigvard. *Berggren's Beasts*. Translated by Ian Rodger. New York: Paul S. Eriksson, 1970

Bernstein, Irwin S. 'Dominance: the baby and the bathwater.' *Behavioral and Brain Sciences* 4 (1981): pp. 419–29

Bledsoe, Thomas. *Brown Bear Summer: My Life among Alaska's Grizzlies*. New York: Dutton, 1987

Boas, George. *The Happy Beast in French Thought of the Seventeenth Century: Contributions to the History of Primitivism*. Baltimore: The Johns Hopkins Press, 1933

Boswall, Jeffrey. 'Russia is for the birds.' *Discover* (U.S.A.) (March 1987)

Broun, Heywood Hale. 'Ever indomitable, Secretariat thunders across the ages.' *New York Times* (30 May 1993): p. 23

Bruemmer, Fred. 'White whales on holiday.' *Natural History* (U.S.A.) (January 1986): pp. 41–9

Bullard, Edward. 'The emergence of plate tectonics: a personal view.' *Annual Review of Earth and Planetary Science* 3 (1975): pp. 1–30

Burghardt, Gordon M. 'Animal awareness: current perceptions and historical perspective.' *American Psychologist* 40 (August 1985): pp. 905–19

Buyukmihci, Hope Sawyer. *The Hour of the Beaver*. Chicago: Rand McNally, 1971

Callwood, June. *Emotions: What they are and how they affect us, from the basic hates & fears of childhood to more sophisticated feelings that later govern our adult lives: How we can deal with the way we feel*. Garden City, N.Y.: Doubleday, 1986

Campbell, Robert Jean. *Psychiatric Dictionary*, 5th Ed. Oxford University Press, 1981

Candland, Douglas Keith. *Feral Children & Clever Animals: Reflections on Human Nature*. Oxford University Press, 1993

Carrington, Richard. *Elephants: A Short Account of their Natural History, Evolution and Influence on Mankind*. London: Chatto and Windus, 1958

Carson, Gerald. *Men, Beasts, and Gods: A History of Cruelty and Kindness to Animals*. New York: Scribner, 1972

Cartmill, Matt. *A View to a Death in the Morning: Hunting and Nature Through History*. Harvard University Press, 1993

Cavalieri, Paola, and Singer, Peter, eds. *The Great Ape Project: Equality Beyond Humanity*. London: Fourth Estate, 1993

Chadwick, Douglas H. *A Beast the Color of Winter: The Mountain Goat Observed*. San Francisco: Sierra Club Books, 1983

Chadwick, Douglas H. *The Fate of the Elephant*. San Francisco: Sierra Club Books, 1992; London: Viking, 1993

Chalmers, N. R. 'Dominance as part of a relationship.' *Behavioral and Brain Sciences* 4 (1981): pp. 437–8

Clark, Bill. *High Hills and Wild Goats*. Boston (U.S.): Little, Brown, 1990

Cochrane, Robert. 'Working elephants at Rangoon', 'Some parrots I have known'. In *The Animal Story Book*, Volume IX of The Young Folks Library. Boston (U.S.): Hall & Locke, 1901

Bibliography

Colmenares, F., and Rivero, H. 'Male–male tolerance, mate sharing and social bonds among adult male brown bears living under group conditions in captivity.' *Acta Zoologica Fennica* 174 (1983): pp. 149–151.

Connor, Richard C., and Norris, Kenneth S. 'Are dolphins reciprocal altruists?' *The American Naturalist* 119, No. 3 (March 1982): pp. 358–74

Conover, Adele. 'He's just one of the bears.' *National Wildlife* (June–July 1992)

Crisler, Lois. *Captive Wild*. New York: Harper and Row, 1968

Crumley, Jim. *Waters of the Wild Swan*. London: Jonathan Cape, 1992

Dagg, Anne Innis, and Foster, J. Bristol. *The Giraffe: Its Biology, Behavior, and Ecology*. New York: Van Nostrand Reinhold, 1976

Dagognet, François. *Traité des animaux*. Paris: Librairie Philosophique J. Vrin, 1987

Darling, F. Fraser. *A Herd of Red Deer: A Study in Animal Behavior*. Oxford University Press, 1937

Darwin, Charles. *The Descent of Man; and Selections in Relation to Sex*. 1871; reprint, Princeton University Press, 1981

Darwin, Charles. *The Expression of the Emotions in Man and Animals*. 1872; reprint, University of Chicago Press, 1965; J. Friedman, 1978

Darwin, Charles. *The Correspondence of Charles Darwin. Volume 2; 1837–1843*. Cambridge University Press, 1986

Dawkins, Richard. *The Selfish Gene*. Oxford University Press, 1976; revised ed. 1989

De Grahl, Wolfgang. *The Grey Parrot*. Translated by William Charlton. Neptune City, N.Y.: T.F.H. Publications, 1987

De Rivera, Joseph. *A Structural Theory of the Emotions*. New York: International Universities Press, 1977

De Waal, Frans. *Chimpanzee Politics: Power and Sex among Apes*. London: Jonathan Cape, 1982

De Waal, Frans. *Peacemaking Among Primates*. Harvard University Press, 1989; London: Penguin Books, 1991

Dews, Peter B. 'Some observations on an operant in the octopus.' *Journal of the Experimental Analysis of Behavior* 2 (1959): pp. 57–63. *Readings in Animal Behavior*, edited by Thomas E. McGill. New York: Holt, Rinehart and Winston, 1965

Dickson, Paul, and Gould, Joseph C. *Myth-Informed: Legends, Credos, and Wrong-headed 'Facts' We All Believe*. Perigee/Putnam, 1993

Dumbacher, John P.; Beehler, Bruce M.; Spande, Thomas F.; Garaffo, H. Martin; and Daly, John W. 'Homobatrachotoxin in the genus *Pitohui*: chemical defense in birds?' *Science* 258 (30 October 1992): pp. 799–801

Durrell, Gerald. *Menagerie Manor*. New York: Avon, 1964; London: Hart-Davis, 1964

Durrell, Gerald. *My Family and Other Animals*. New York: Viking, 1957; London: Allen and Unwin, 1963

Emde, R. N., and Koening, K. L. 'Neonatal smiling and rapid eye-movement states.' *Journal of the American Academy of Child Psychiatry* 8 (1969): pp. 57–67

Emlen, S. T., and Wrege, P. H. 'Forced copulations and intra-specific parasitism: two costs of social living in the white-fronted bee-eater.' *Ethology* 71 (1986): pp. 2–29

Fagen, Robert. *Animal Play Behaviour*. Oxford University Press, 1981

Fisher, John Andrew. 'Disambiguating anthropomorphism: an interdisciplinary review.' *Perspectives in Ethology* 9 (1991)

Bibliography

French, Thomas, M. *The Integration of Behavior, Volume 1: Basic Postulates.* University of Chicago Press, 1952

Frey, William H., II, with Langseth, Muriel. *Crying: The Mystery of Tears.* Minneapolis: Harper & Row/Winston Press, 1985

Fossey, Dian. *Gorillas in the Mist.* London: Hodder and Stoughton, 1984

Fouts, Roger S.; Fouts, Deborah H.; and Van Cantfort, Thomas E. 'The infant Loulis learns signs from cross-fostered chimpanzees.' In *Teaching Sign Language to Chimpanzees,* edited by R. Allen Gardner, Beatrix T. Gardner and Thomas E. Van Cantfort. State University of New York Press, 1989

Fowles, John, with Horvat, Frank. *The Tree.* Boston (U.S.): Little, Brown, 1979

Fox, Michael W. *The Whistling Hunters: Field Studies of the Asiatic Wild Dog (Cuon alpinus).* State University of New York Press, 1984

Frank, Robert. *Passions Within Reason: The Strategic Role of the Emotions.* New York: W. W. Norton, 1988

Gallup, Gordon. 'Self-recognition in primates: a comparative approach to the bidirectional properties of consciousness.' *American Psychologist* 32 (1977): pp. 329–38

Gallup, Gordon, and Suarez, Susan D. 'Overcoming our resistance to animal research: man in comparative perspective.' In *Comparing Behavior: Studying Man Studying Animals,* edited by D. W. Rajecki. Hillsdale, N.J.: Lawrence Erlbaum Associates, 1983

Gardner, R. Allen, and Gardner, Beatrix T. 'Comparative psychology and language acquisition.' *Annals of the New York Academy of Sciences* 309 (1978): pp. 37–76

Gardner, R. Allen, and Gardner, Beatrix T. 'A cross-fostering laboratory.' In *Teaching Sign Language to Chimpanzees.* See Fouts

Gardner, Beatrix T.; Gardner, R. Allen; and Nichols, Susan G. 'The shapes and uses of signs in a cross-fostering laboratory.' In *Teaching Sign Language to Chimpanzees.* See Fouts

Gauntlett, Ian S.; Koh, T. H. H. G.; and Silverman, William A. 'Analgesia and anaesthesia in newborn babies and infants.' *Lancet* (Letters) (9 May 1987)

Gebel-Williams, Gunther, with Reinhold, Toni. *Untamed: The Autobiography of the Circus's Greatest Animal Trainer.* New York: William Morrow, 1991

Gilbert, Bil. *Chulo.* New York: Alfred A. Knopf, 1973

Godlovitch, Stanley, and Godlovitch, Rosalind, eds. *Animals, Men and Morals.* New York: Taplinger Publishing, 1972

Goodall, Jane. *The Chimpanzees of Gombe; Patterns of Behavior.* Harvard University Press, 1986

Goodall, Jane. *In the Shadow of Man.* London: Collins, 1971; revised ed., Boston (U.S.): Houghton Mifflin, 1988

Goodall, Jane. *Through a Window: My Thirty Years with the Chimpanzees of Gombe.* Boston: Houghton Mifflin, 1990; London: Weidenfeld and Nicolson, 1990

Goodall, Jane. *With Love.* Ridgefield, Connecticut: Jane Goodall Institute, 1994

Gormley, Gerard. *Orcas of the Gulf; a Natural History.* San Francisco: Sierra Club Books, 1990

Griffin, Donald. *The Question of Animal Awareness: Evolutionary Continuity of Mental Experience.* New York: Rockefeller University Press, 1976

Griffin, Donald. *Animal Thinking.* Harvard University Press, 1984

Griffin, Donald. *Animal Minds.* University of Chicago Press, 1992

Bibliography

Grzimek, Bernhard, ed. *Grzimek's Animal Encyclopedia*. New York: Van Nostrand Reinhold, 1972

Gucwa, David, and Ehmann, James. *To Whom It May Concern: An Investigation of the Art of Elephants*. New York: W. W. Norton, 1985

Hall, Nancy. 'The painful truth.' *Parenting* (June/July 1992)

Haraway, Donna. *Primate Visions: Gender, Race and Nature in the World of Modern Science*. New York: Routledge, 1989

Hargrove, Eugene C., ed. *The Animal Rights/Environmental Ethics Debate*. State University of New York Press, 1992

Harlow, Harry. 'The nature of love.' *American Psychologist* 13 (1958): pp. 673–85

Harlow, Harry. 'Love in infant monkeys.' *Scientific American* 200, No. 6 (1959): pp. 68–74

Harlow, Harry, and Suomi, Stephen J. 'Depressive behavior in young monkeys subjected to vertical chamber confinement.' *Journal of Comparative and Physiological Psychology* 80 (1972): pp. 11–18

Harre, R., and Reynolds, V., eds. *The Meaning of Primate Signals*. Cambridge University Press, 1984

Harris, Marvin. *Our Kind*. New York: Harper & Row, 1989

Hastings, Hester. *Man and Beast in French Thought of the Eighteenth Century*, Volume 27. Baltimore: The John Hopkins Press, 1936

Hearne, Vicki. *Adam's Task: Calling Animals by Name*. New York: Alfred A. Knopf, 1986

Hearne, Vicki. *Animal Happiness*. New York: HarperCollins, 1994

Helfer, Ralph. *The Beauty of the Beasts: Tales of Hollywood's Animal Stars*. Los Angeles: Jeremy P. Tarcher, 1990

Henderson, J. Y., with Taplinger, Richard. *Circus Doctor*. Boston (U.S.): Little, Brown, 1951

Hill, Craven. 'Playtime at the zoo.' *Zoo-Life* 1: pp. 24–6

Hinde, Robert A. *Animal Behavior*. New York: McGraw-Hill, 1966

Hinsie, Leland E., and Campbell, Robert J. *Psychiatric Dictionary*, 4th ed. Oxford University Press, 1970

Högstedt, Göran. 'Adaptation unto death: function of fear screams.' *The American Naturalist* 121 (1983): pp. 562–70

Holt, Patricia. 'Puppy love isn't just for people: author says dogs, like humans, can bond.' *San Francisco Chronicle* (9 December 1993)

Horgan, John. 'See Spot see blue: curb that dogma! Canines are not colorblind.' *Scientific American* 262 (January 1990): p. 20

Hornocker, Maurice G. 'Winter territoriality in mountain lions.' *Journal of Wildlife Management* 33 (July 1969): pp. 457–64

Hornstein, Harvey A. *Cruelty and Kindness: A New Look at Oppression and Altruism*. Englewood Cliffs, N.J.: Prentice-Hall, 1976

Houle, Marcy Cottrell. *Wings for my Flight: The Peregrine Falcons of Chimney Rock*. Reading, Mass.: Addison-Wesley, 1991

House, Adrian. *The Great Safari: The Lives of George and Joy Adamson*. London: HarperCollins, 1993

Humphrey, N. K. ' "Interest" and "pleasure": two determinants of a monkey's visual preferences.' *Perception* 1 (1972): pp. 395–416

Humphrey, N. K. 'The social function of intellect.' In *Growing Points in Ethology*, edited by P. P. G. Bateson and R. A. Hinde, pp. 303–17. Cambridge University Press, 1976

Humphrey, N. K. 'Nature's psychologists.' In *Consciousness and the Physical*

Bibliography

World, edited by B. D. Josephson and V. S. Ramachandran, pp. 57–80. Oxford: Pergamon Press, 1980

Hutchins, Michael, and Sullivan, Kathy. 'Dolphin delight.' *Animal Kingdom* (July/August 1989)

Huxley, Thomas H. *Method and Results: Essays*. 1893; reprint, London: Macmillan, 1901

Izard, Carroll E. *Human Emotions*. New York and London: Plenum Press, 1977

Izard, Carroll E., and Buechler, S. 'Aspects of consciousness and personality in terms of differential emotions theory.' In *Emotion: Theory, Research, and Experience, Volume I: Theories of Emotion*, edited by Robert Plutchik and Henry Kellerman, pp. 165–87. New York: Academic Press, 1980

Johnson, Dirk. 'Now the Marlboro Man loses his spurs.' *New York Times* (11 October 1993): A1, A8

Jordan, William. *Divorce Among the Gulls: an uncommon look at human nature*. San Francisco: North Point Press, 1991

Josephson, B. D., and Ramachandran, V. S., eds. *Consciousness and the Physical World*. Oxford: Pergamon Press, 1980

Karen, Robert. 'Shame.' *Atlantic Monthly* 269 (February 1992): pp. 40–70

Kavanau, J. Lee. 'Behavior of captive white-footed mice.' *Science* 155 (31 March 1967): pp. 1623–39

Kellert, Stephen R., and Berry, Joyce K. *Phase III: Knowledge, Affection and Basic Attitudes Toward Animals in American Society*. U.S. Fish and Wildlife Service, 1980

Kennedy, John S. *The New Anthropomorphism*. Cambridge University Press, 1992

Kevles, Bettyann. *Females of the Species: Sex and Survival in the Animal Kingdom*. Harvard University Press, 1986

Kitcher, Philip. *Vaulting Ambition: Sociobiology and the Quest for Human Nature*. Cambridge, Mass.: MIT Press, 1985

Kleiman, Devra G., and Malcolm, James R. 'The evolution of male parental investment in mammals.' In *Parental Care in Mammals*, edited by David J. Gubernick and Peter H. Klopfer. New York: Plenum Press, 1981

Kohn, Alfie. *The Brighter Side of Human Nature: Altruism and Empathy in Everyday Life*. New York: Basic Books, 1990

Konner, Melvin. *The Tangled Wing: Biological Constraints on the Human Spirit*. New York: Holt, Rinehart, and Winston, 1982

Kortlandt, Adriaan. 'Chimpanzees in the wild.' *Scientific American* 206 (May 1962): pp. 128–38

Krutch, Joseph Wood. *The Best of Two Worlds*. New York: William Sloane Associates, 1950

Krutch, Joseph Wood. *The Great Chain of Life*. Boston (U.S.): Houghton Mifflin, 1956

Kruuk, Hans. *The Spotted Hyena: A Study of Predation and Social Behavior*. University of Chicago Press, 1972

Kummer, Hans. *Social Organization of Hamadryas Baboons; A Field Study*. University of Chicago Press, 1968

Laidler, Keith. *The Talking Ape*. New York: Stein & Day, 1980

Lavrov, L. S. 'Evolutionary development of the genus *Castor* and taxonomy of the contemporary beavers of Eurasia.' *Acta Zoologica Fennica* 174 (1983): pp. 87–90

Lawrence, Elizabeth Atwood. *Rodeo: An Anthropologist Looks at the Wild and the Tame*. University of Texas Press, 1982

254

Bibliography

Lazell, James D., Jr., and Spitzer, Numi C. 'Apparent play behavior in an American alligator.' *Copeia* (1977): p. 188

Leighton, Donna Robbins. 'Gibbons: territoriality and monogamy.' In *Primate Societies*, edited by Barbara B. Smuts, Dorothy L. Cheney, Robert M. Seyfarth, Richard W. Wrangham, and Thomas T. Struhsaker. University of Chicago Press, 1986

Lewis, George, with Fish, Byron. *Elephant Tramp*. Boston (U.S.): Little, Brown, 1955

Lewis, Michael. *Shame: The Exposed Self*. New York: The Free Press/Macmillan, 1992

Leyhausen, Paul. *Cat Behavior: The Predatory and Social Behavior of Domestic and Wild Cats*. Translated by Barbara A. Tonkin. Garland STPM Press, 1979

Linden, Eugene. *Silent Partners: The Legacy of the Ape Language Experiments*. New York: Times Books, 1986

Lopez, Barry Holstun. *Of Wolves and Men*. New York: Scribner, 1978; London: Dent, 1979

Lorenz, Konrad. *Year of the Greylag Goose*. London: Eyre Methuen, 1975

Lutts, Ralph H. *The Nature Fakers; Wildlife, Science and Sentiment*. Golden, Colorado: Fulcrum, 1990

MacDonald, David. *Running with the Fox*. London: Unwin Hyman, 1987

Mader, Troy R. 'Wolves and hunting.' *Abundant Wildlife*, Special Wolf Issue (1992): p. 3

Magel, Charles R. *Bibliography of Animal Rights and Related Matters*. University Press of America, 1981

Magoun, A. J., and Valkenburg, P. 'Breeding behavior of free-ranging wolverines (*Gulo*).' *Acta Zoologica Fennica* 174 (1983): pp. 149–51

Mahaffy, J. P. *Descartes*. Edinburgh: Blackwood, 1901

Martin, Esmond, and Martin, Chrysse Bradley. *Run Rhino Run*. London: Chatto and Windus, 1982

Masserman, Jules H.; Wechkin, Stanley; and Terris, William. ' "Altruistic" behavior in rhesus monkeys.' *American Journal of Psychiatry* 121 (1964): pp. 584–5

Mayes, Andrew. 'The physiology of fear and anxiety.' In *Fear in Animals and Man*, edited by W. Sluckin, pp. 24–55. New York and London: Van Nostrand Reinhold, 1979

McFarland, David, ed. *The Oxford Companion to Animal Behaviour*. Oxford University Press, 1987

McNulty, Faith. *The Whooping Crane: The Bird that Defies Extinction*. New York: E. P. Dutton, 1966

'Medicine and the Media.' Editorial. *British Medical Journal* 295 (12 September 1987), pp. 659–60

Midgley, Mary. 'The concept of beastliness: philosophy, ethics and animal behavior.' *Philosophy* 48 (1973): pp. 111–35

Midgley, Mary. *Beast and Man: The Roots of Human Nature*. Ithaca, N.Y.: Cornell University Press, 1978; London: Methuen, 1979

Midgley, Mary. *Animals and Why They Matter*. University of Georgia Press, 1983. London: Penguin Books, 1983

Millay, Edna St Vincent. *Collected Lyrics*. New York: Washington Square Press, 1959

Mitchell, Robert W., and Thompson, Nicholas S. *Deception: Perspectives on Human and Nonhuman Deceit*. State University of New York Press, 1986

255

Bibliography

Moggridge, J. Traherne. *Harvesting Ants and Trap-Door Spiders: Notes and Observations on their Habits and Dwellings.* London: L. Reeve & Co., 1873

Montaigne, Michel. *The Complete Works of Montaigne.* Translated by D. M. Frame. Volume 2. Garden City, N.Y.: Anchor Books, 1960

Moore, J. Howard. *The Universal Kinship.* 1906; reprint, Sussex: Centaur Press, 1992

Monastersky, Richard. 'Boom in "cute" baby dinosaur discoveries.' *Science News* 134 (22 October 1988), p. 261

Montgomery, Sy. *Walking with the Great Apes.* Boston (U.S.): Houghton Mifflin, 1991

Morey, Geoffrey. *The Lincoln Kangaroos.* Philadelphia: Chilton Books, 1963

Morton, Eugene S., and Page, Jake. *Animal Talk: Science and the Voices of Nature.* New York: Random House, 1992

Morris, Desmond. *The Biology of Art: A Study of the Picture-Making Behaviour of the Great Apes and its Relationship to Human Art.* New York: Alfred A. Knopf, 1962; London: Methuen, 1966

Morris, Desmond. *Animal Days.* London: Jonathan Cape, 1979

Morris, Desmond, *Dogwatching.* London: Jonathan Cape, 1986

Moss, Cynthia. *Portraits in the Wild: Behavior Studies of East African Mammals.* Boston (U.S.): Houghton Mifflin, 1975

Moss, Cynthia. *Elephant Memories: Thirteen Years in the Life of an Elephant Family.* New York: William Morrow, 1988

Nathanson, Donald. *Shame and Pride: Affect, Sex, and the Birth of the Self.* New York: W. W. Norton, 1992

Nishida, Toshisada. 'Local traditions and cultural transmission.' In *Primate Societies.* See Leighton

Nollman, Jim. *Animal Dreaming: The Art and Science of Interspecies Communication.* Toronto and New York: Bantam Books, 1987

Norris, Kenneth S. *Dolphin Days: The Life and Times of the Spinner Dolphin.* New York: W. W. Norton, 1991

Ogden, Paul. *Chelsea: The Story of a Signal Dog.* Boston: Little, Brown, 1992

Orleans, R. Barbara. *In the Name of Science: Issues in Responsible Animal Experimentation.* Oxford University Press, 1992

Packer, Craig. 'Male dominance and reproductive activity in *Papio anubis*' *Animal Behavior* 27 (1979): pp. 37–45

Patenaude, Françoise. 'Care of the young in a family of wild beavers, *Castor canadensis.*' *Acta Zoologica Fennica* 174 (1983): pp. 121–2

Patterson, Francine, and Linden, Eugene. *The Education of Koko.* New York: Holt, Rinehart & Winston, 1981

Patterson, Francine. *Gorilla: Journal of the Gorilla Foundation* 15, No. 2 (June 1992)

Plotnicov, Leonard. 'Love, lust, and found in Nigeria.' Paper presented at the 1992 American Anthropological Association annual meeting, San Francisco, 2 December 1992

Pryor, Karen. *Lads Before the Wind: Adventures in Porpoise Training.* New York: Harper & Row, 1975

Pryor, Karen, and Norris, Kenneth S. *Dolphin Societies: Discoveries and Puzzles.* University of California Press, 1991.

Pryor, Karen; Haag, Richard; and O'Reilly, Joseph. 'The creative porpoise: training for novel behavior.' *Journal of the Experimental Analysis of Behavior* 12 (1969) pp. 653–61

Rajecki, D. W., ed. *Comparing Behavior: Studying Man Studying Animals.* Hillsdale, N.J.: Lawrence Erlbaum Associates, 1983

Bibliography

Rasa, Anne. *Mongoose Watch: A Family Observed.* Garden City, N.Y.: Anchor Press/Doubleday, 1986

Reed, Don C. *Notes from an Underwater Zoo.* New York: Dial Press, 1981

Regan, Tom. *The Case for Animal Rights.* University of California Press, 1983

Regan, Tom, and Singer, Peter, eds. *Animal Rights and Human Obligations.* Englewood Cliffs: Prentice Hall, 1976

Reinhold, Robert. 'At Sea World, stress tests whale and man.' *New York Times* (4 April 1988), p. A9

Roberts, Catherine. *The Scientific Conscience: Reflections on the Modern Biologist and Humanism.* New York: George Braziller, 1967

Romanes, George. *Animal Intelligence.* Kegan Paul, Trench, Trubner and Co., 1898

Rosenfield, Leonora Cohen. *From Beast-Machine to Man-Machine: Animal Soul in French Letters from Descartes to La Mettrie.* 1940; new edition, New York: Octagon Books, 1968

Rowell, Thelma. *The Social Behaviour of Monkeys.* London: Penguin Books, 1972

Rozin, Paul, and Fallon, April. 'A perspective on disgust.' *Psychological Review* 94 (1987): pp. 23–41

Rupke, Nicolaas A., ed. *Vivisection in Historical Perspective.* London: Croom Helm, 1987

Russell, Diana E. H. *The Politics of Rape: The Victim's Perspective.* New York: Stein & Day, 1977

Russell, Diana E. H. *Rape in Marriage.* New York: Macmillan, 1982.

Russell, Diana E. H. 'The incidence and prevalence of intrafamilial and extrafamilial sexual abuse of female children.' *Child Abuse and Neglect: The International Journal* 7 (1983): pp. 133–46.

Russell, Diana E. H. *The Secret Trauma: Incestuous Abuse of Women and Girls.* New York: Basic Books, 1986

Russell, Diana E. H., and Howell, Nancy. 'The prevalence of rape in the United States revisited.' *Signs: Journal of Women in Culture and Society* 8 (Summer 1983): pp. 668–95

Russell, P. A. 'Fear-evoking stimuli.' In *Fear in Animals and Man.* See Mayes

Rutter, Russell J., and Pimlott, Douglas H. *The World of the Wolf.* New York: J. B. Lippincott, 1968

Ryden, Hope. *God's Dog.* New York: Coward, McCann & Geoghegan, 1975

Ryden, Hope. *Lily Pond: Four Years with a Family of Beavers.* New York: William Morrow, 1989

Sadoff, Robert L. 'The nature of crying and weeping.' In *The World of Emotion: Clinical Studies of Affects and their Expression,* edited by Charles W. Socarides. New York: International Universities Press, 1977

St John, Patricia. *The Secret Language of Dolphins.* New York: Summit Books, 1991

Savage, E. S.; Temerlin, Jane; and Lemmon, W. B. 'The appearance of mothering behavior toward a kitten by a human-reared chimpanzee.' Paper delivered at the Fifth Congress of Primatology, Nagoya, Japan, 1974

Savage-Rumbaugh, E. Sue. *Ape Language: From Conditioned Response to Symbol.* New York: Columbia University Press, 1986

Schaller, George B. *The Serengeti Lion: A Study of Predator-Prey Relations.* University of Chicago Press, 1972

Schaller, George B. *The Last Panda.* University of Chicago Press, 1993

Schechter, Neil; Berde, Charles B.; and Yaster, Myron, eds. *Pain in Infants, Children, and Adolescents.* Baltimore: Williams and Wilkins, 1993.

257

Bibliography

Scheffer, Victor B. *Seals, Sea Lions, and Walruses: A Review of the Pinnipedia.* California: Stanford University Press, 1958

Schiller, Paul H. 'Figural preferences in the drawings of a chimpanzee.' *Journal of Comparative and Physiological Psychology* 44 (1951): pp. 101–11

Schullery, Paul. *The Bear Hunter's Century.* New York: Dodd, Mead, 1988

Seligman, Martin E. P. *Helplessness: On Depression, Development, and Death.* San Francisco: W. H. Freeman & Co., 1975

Seyfarth, Robert M., and Cheney, Dorothy L. 'Grooming, alliances, and reciprocal altruism in vervet monkeys.' *Nature* 308, No. 5 (April 1984): pp. 541–2

Sidowski, J. B. 'Psychopathological consequences of induced social helplessness during infancy.' In *Experimental Psychopathology: Recent research and theory,* edited by H. D. Kimmel. New York: Academic Press, 1971

Singer, Peter. *Animal Liberation.* London: Jonathan Cape, 1976; revised ed. 1992

Singh, Arjan. *Tiger! Tiger!* London: Jonathan Cape, 1984

Smith, J. Maynard, and Ridpath, M. G. 'Wife sharing in the Tasmanian native hen, *Tribonyx mortierii:* A case of kin selection?' *The American Naturalist* 106 (July–August 1972): pp. 447–52

Smuts, Barbara. 'Dominance: an alternative view.' *Behavioral and Brain Sciences* 4 (1981): pp. 448–9

Spiegel, Marjorie. *The Dreaded Comparison: Human and Animal Slavery.* Philadelphia: New Society Publishers, 1988

Staddon, J. E. R. 'Animal psychology: the tyranny of anthropocentrism.' In *Whither Ethology? Perspectives in Ethology,* edited by P. P. G. Bateson and Peter H. Klopfer, New York: Plenum Press, 1989

Strum, Shirley C. *Almost Human: A Journey into the World of Baboons.* New York: Random House, 1987

Symons, Donald. *The Evolution of Human Sexuality.* Oxford University Press, 1979

Teal, John J., Jr. 'Domesticating the Wild and Woolly Musk Ox.' *National Geographic* (June 1970)

Terrace, Herbert. *Nim: A Chimpanzee who Learned Sign Language.* New York: Washington Square Press, 1979

Thomas, Elizabeth Marshall. 'Reflections: the old way.' *The New Yorker* (15 October 1990)

Thomas, Elizabeth Marshall. *The Hidden Life of Dogs.* Boston (U.S.): Houghton Mifflin, 1993

Thomson, Robert. 'The concept of fear.' In *Fear in Animals and Man.* See Mayes

Tomkies, Mike. *Out of the Wild.* London: Jonathan Cape, 1985

Tomkies, Mike. *On Wing and Wild Water.* London: Jonathan Cape, 1987

Tomkies, Mike. *Last Wild Years.* London: Jonathan Cape, 1992

Trivers, Robert L. 'The evolution of reciprocal altruism.' *Quarterly Review of Biology* 46 (1971): pp. 35–57

Turner, E. S. *All Heaven in a Rage.* Sussex: Centaur Press, 1992

Tyack, Peter. 'Whistle repertoires of two bottlenosed dolphins, *Tursiops truncatus:* mimicry of signature whistles?' *Behavioral Ecology and Sociobiology* 18 (1989): pp. 251–7

Voltaire, François-Marie Arouet. *Dictionnaire Philosophique,* edited by Julien Benda and Raymond Naves. Paris: Garnier Frères, 1961

Voltaire, François-Marie Arouet. 'The beasts.' Article 6 in *Le philosophe gnorant. Les Oeuvres Complètes de Voltaire, Vol. Mélanges,* edited by Jacques van den Heuvel. Paris: Gallimard

Bibliography

Walker, Ernest P. *Mammals of the World,* 2nd ed. Baltimore: Johns Hopkins Press, 1986

Welty, Joel Carl, and Baptista, Luis. *The Life of Birds,* 4th ed. New York: Saunders College Publishing, 1988

Wierzbicka, Anna. 'Human emotions: universal or culture-specific?' *American Anthropologist* 88 (1986): pp. 584–94

Wiesner, Bertold P., and Sheard, Norah M. *Maternal Behaviour in the Rat.* Edinburgh and London: Oliver & Boyd, 1933

Wilkinson, Gerald S. 'Food sharing in vampire bats.' *Scientific American* 262 (1990): pp. 76–82

Williams, Heathcote. *Sacred Elephant.* London: Jonathan Cape, 1989

Williams, J. H. *Elephant Bill.* London: Rupert Hart-Davis, 1950

Wilsson, Lars. *My Beaver Colony.* Translated by Joan Bulman. Garden City, N.Y.: Doubleday, 1968

Wiltschko, Wolfgang; Munro, Ursula; Ford, Hugh; and Wiltschko, Roswitha. 'Red light disrupts magnetic orientation of migratory birds.' *Nature* 364 (5 August 1993): p. 525

Winslow, James T.; Hastings, Nick; Carter, C. Sue; Harbaugh, Carroll R.; and Insel, Thomas R. 'A role for central vasopressin in pair bonding in monogamous prairie voles.' *Nature* 365 (7 October 1993): pp. 545–8

Wittgenstein, Ludwig. *Philosophical Investigations,* 3rd ed. Translated by G. E. M. Anscombe. New York: Macmillan, 1968

Wu, Hannah M. H.; Holmes, Warren G.; Medina, Steven R.; and Sackett, Gene P. 'Kin preference in infant *Macaca nemestrina.*' *Nature* 285 (1980): pp. 225–7

Yerkes, Robert M., and Yerkes, Ada W. *The Great Apes: A Study of Anthropoid Life.* Yale University Press, 1929

Young, Stanley P. *The Wolves of North America: Their History, Life Habits, Economic Status, and Control. Part II: Classification of Wolves,* by Edward A. Goldman. Washington D.C.: American Wildlife Institute, 1944

INDEX

Index